POLITICAL
CAMPAIGN
COMMUNICATION

POLITICAL CAMPAIGN COMMUNICATION

Principles and Practices

BY JUDITH S. TRENT

AND

ROBERT V. FRIEDENBERG

87-1387

PRAEGER

PRAEGER SPECIAL STUDIES • PRAEGER SCIENTIFIC

Library of Congress Cataloging in Publication Data

Trent, Judith S.
  Political campaign communication.

  Includes bibliographical references and index.
  1. Electioneering. 2. Communication in politics.
I. Friedenberg, Robert. II. Title.
JF1001.T73 1983   324.7   83-2132
ISBN 0-03-062527-0
    0-03-063703-1 pb.

Published in 1983 by Praeger Publishers
CBS Educational and Professional Publishing
a Division of CBS Inc.
521 Fifth Avenue, New York, NY 10175 USA
© 1983 by Praeger Publishers

456789 052 9876543

Printed in the United States of America
on acid-free paper

This book is dedicated to the memories of our stepfather and father, Harold D. Crothers and Aaron Friedenberg. Both men died while this book was being prepared, after lending lifelong support to their children's endeavors.

Contents

Preface

To a large extent this book was born out of our frustration with not having textbooks available that we believed appropriate for classes in political campaign communication. As in the case with many of our colleagues in other colleges and universities, we used books written by scholars and practitioners in other disciplines. Many of these books are excellent, and much of the information contained in them we still believe important to the examination of political campaigns. However, what they lack is at least as important as the material they include. In few of them is there the acknowledgment that communication is the epistemological base of political campaigns. Moreover, no other book of political campaigns has been written from a speech communication perspective.

This, then, is the first book-length study of election campaigns that utilizes principles and practices of speech communication to examine elective politics. We believe that the discipline has much to offer the field of political communication, and that the body of materials produced by its practitioners not only justifies a major book-length study but adds important dimensions to the field.

If there is any one theme of this book, it is that we view political campaigns as communication phenomena and in the following pages have examined those communication principles and practices central to election campaigns. We have sought to offer all readers a realistic understanding of the strategic and tactical communication choices candidates and their managers must make as they wage the campaign.

This was a collaborative effort. We examined drafts of each chapter, shared equally in the writing of Chapter 9 and various editing chores. Chapters 1 to 4 were written primarily by Juddi, and chapters 5 to 8 were written primarily by Bob. Both share any of the successes or shortcomings of this volume.

We wish to acknowledge many people for their aid in producing this book. Particularly helpful to both authors were our students in political campaign communication classes at the University of Dayton and at Miami (Ohio) University. They made us aware of the need for such a project, and their questions and interest helped shape the topics covered. Reviewers of the first outline of the book and of the first chapter drafts offered penetrating comments that improved initial conceptions. The editorial and production staff at Praeger, particularly Ron Chambers, were helpful and pleasant. We also express appreciation to our home institutions, the University of Dayton and Miami University, for the support we received while working on the book. We particularly thank Don B. Morlan, chair of the Department of Communication Arts at the University of Dayton, for making the resources of his department available to us. Sherrie Waddell and Ginny Gauthier, who typed the manuscript, deserve our special appreciation. We also thank Emmy Friedenberg for preparing the index while under considerable time pressure.

In addition, Juddi would like to thank Gerald Sanders for providing an office at Miami during the summer so that commuting to Dayton each day was unnecessary. And most important, she would like to thank three very special people, Jimmie, Larry, and Evelyn, who were unfailingly supportive throughout the writing and editing stages and understandably anxious to have the whole project finished so that they could be joined (and beaten?) on the golf course by wife, mother, and daughter.

Moreover, Bob would like to acknowledge the tremendous aid he received from the Miami University library, particularly from librarians Becky Zartner and Louise Heidler. He also wishes to acknowledge the *Journal of the American Forensic Association* for permission to use portions of two articles he originally wrote for *JAFA*, and Doug Reed, director of the Hamilton Campus of Miami, for his encouragement, both tangible and intangible, throughout the project. Finally, he would like to acknowledge the wonderful support he received throughout the writing of this book from his mother, from his son, David, who proved to be an unending source of delightful distraction when writing became difficult, and most of all, from his wife, Emmy, for all of her support in so many ways.

Judith S. Trent
Robert V. Friedenberg

Part I

Principles of Political Campaign Communication

1

Communication and Political Campaigns: A Prologue

*I*T HAS BECOME FASHIONABLE TO CRITICIZE OUR ELECTORAL SYSTEM. CAMPAIGNS ARE TOO LONG AND TOO EXPENSIVE. CANDIDATES ARE INCOMPETENT, DISHONEST, AND SOUND ALIKE. Voters are bored with the process, distrustful of government and politicians, and frequently do not vote. Although we express these and other complaints, elections, and the political campaigns that are a part of them, are vital to us in at least three different but complementary senses.

IMPORTANCE OF POLITICAL CAMPAIGNS

Elections are important because they allow us freedom to actively participate in selecting our leaders. They are the core of democracy. Nowhere in the world are more people more freely engaged in active, responsible participation in the choice of leadership than in the United States. Whether the election will determine the occupants of two seats in city coun-

3

cil or one chair in the oval office of the White House, the political election campaign is an essential element of a democratic system. Elections provide us with the opportunity to determine how our own interests can best be served. We may, for example, try to decide which board of education candidate does not favor increasing our property taxes. We might also ask if the Republican candidate for governor sees the need to create jobs as the state's top priority or if the Democratic challenger running for Congress supports increasing money for education and public transportation. Once we feel enough questions have been answered, we must decide how actively to participate in the campaign. Will we try to ignore it? Will we work for the candidate or political party we favor? Will we vote? Any decision contributes to our self-development and expression.

Elections not only give opportunities for quiet decision making or overt participation in determining who will govern; they also provide the legitimacy with which to govern. The winners of elections receive a general acceptance of their right to power. No matter how large or small the margin of victory, the candidate who receives the necessary votes has been granted a legitimacy quite distinct from power. Any election can give the winner power. Only a democratic election will provide the sense of "rightness" or even "genuineness" necessary to govern or be governed. We may no longer "like" the president for whom we voted two years ago, but we recognize that he has a legitimate claim to the office until the next election. The president, like all other candidates we elect, can only be "overthrown" as a consequence of the next election.

Thus, in these pragmatic ways, our electoral system is important to us. No less significant, are the symbolic aspects of election campaigns. The British historian, J. H. Plumb, maintained that there are two histories: the actual series of events that once occurred and the ideal series that we affirm and hold in memory. In other words, the past is composed not only of historical "fact" but of what is "made" of history. It is, in the largest sense, the collective memory—the national myth—that

4

unites us as a people. Not only do elections provide leaders and grant them authority to govern, they also add to our memory or image of the electoral process and thus give proof that the system is a good one. The fact that we have elections, that leaders are not overthrown by revolution, that citizens freely discuss and participate in the selection process, or that the constitution "worked" during the Watergate crisis of the 1970s grants support for the belief that the "American Dream" is real and that this country really is destined to be the mighty keeper of liberty. All the fanfare and excitement of the political campaign, be it bands and parades, buttons and billboards, speeches and rallies, or television ads and debates, is important for the reinforcement provided about the rightness of what we do and the way we do it.

Now, all of this is to tell you that the subject matter of this book is worthwhile. Although aspects of our electoral system may need repair from time to time, the process and the product are worth the effort.

While the value of elections has remained constant, the manner in which they are conducted has changed enormously in recent years. As a matter of fact, the political campaign has undergone such a radical transformation that those principles and practices accepted by practitioners and theorists even 20 years ago are largely irrelevant today. Thus, before we can describe and analyze any of the dimensions of campaign communication in the chapters that follow, we must examine those changes that, to the greatest extent, comprise the essence of the new politics. There are four of them that will be discussed in the following order: 1) the decline in the influence of political parties; 2) electoral financing legislation; 3) political action committees; and 4) technological advancements.

CHANGES IN THE POLITICAL CAMPAIGN

The legendary party bosses once determined who would run for political office. In national and state politics, these people were often called kingmakers, who from the sanctity of the so-called smoke-filled rooms at nominating conventions hand-picked "their" candidate to be the party nominee. In local politics, especially in the large cities, party bosses, through a system that combined the disposition of jobs with political favors, support, and even protection, controlled the votes, the party, and thus the selection of all candidates.

Decline of Political Parties

Undoubtedly, the most significant change in presidential politics occurred when in 1976 the reform rules, adopted by the Democratic party and, to a lesser extent, the Republican party, forced changes in state laws regarding delegate selection. Under the legislation adopted before the 1976 campaign, the caucus convention procedure was wide open for participation by everyone, and any candidate who could inspire a following had a chance to win delegates. By changing the process of delegate selection, political reformers aided in reshaping the presidential nominating system. In 1968 there were only 15 primaries in which less than 40 percent of the delegates were chosen. In 1976, 77 percent of the delegates at the Democratic Convention had come from 30 primary states, reducing the strength of delegates from caucus states to 704 of the 3,008 delegates. By 1980 there were 37 primaries that determined the choices of 71 percent of the 3,330 delegates to the Democratic Convention and 75 percent of the 1,993 delegates to the Republican Convention. Finally, two years before the 1984 campaign, the Democratic party accepted a plan proposed by its Commission on Presidential Nominations to shorten the primary season by five weeks and to add 548 (or 14 percent) uncommitted members of Congress, governors, mayors, and party officials to its 3,675 delegates.* Although the proposal sought to return a little of the clout from citizen activists to elected officials, it

---

*Although Democrats shortened the primary period for the 1984 campaign, they did not attempt to reduce the number of contests.

simultaneously reaffirmed the 1976 commitment to reform, since 85 percent of the delegates to the convention would be determined in state primaries and caucuses.

The result is that the change in rules and the proliferation of primaries have weakened political parties, the traditional vehicles for building coalitions and forging consensus. In the past, candidates had to work their way up through party ranks and appeal to party bosses, but in recent years successful candidates at all levels have often ignored the party regulars, built their own organizations, and taken their campaigns directly to the people. As presidential chronicler and political journalist Theodore H. White reflected, "the old bosses are long gone and with them the old parties. In their place has grown a new breed of young professionals whose working skills in the new politics would make the old boys look like stumblebums."[1]

While for our purposes it is unnecessary to trace the fall of the political bosses from "kingmaker" to "stumblebum," it is important to realize that citizens feel little allegiance to political parties. Each year since the mid-1960s, the results of the election studies conducted by the Center for Political Studies at the University of Michigan have shown that fewer and fewer voters identify themselves as Republicans or Democrats, while more and more call themselves Independents. In 1964 approximately 24 percent of the population eligible to vote labeled themselves as Independents. By 1980 almost 40 percent claimed to be Independents. Furthermore, respect for the parties as institutions that represent the public has also decreased. The proportion of the "eligible electorate believing that political parties help a 'good deal' in making the government pay attention to what the people think, dropped from roughly 40 percent in 1964 to 29 percent in 1972 to 18 percent in 1976."[2]

Finance Reforms

The decline in party identification and influence is not the only element that has altered the nature of the election campaign. Closely related are the reforms in financing which, although initially affecting presidential candidates, have had some effect at all levels.

The Federal Election Campaign Act of 1974 and the amendment in 1976 changed much of the character of presidential campaigning, particularly in the early portion of the electoral process. The act provided for voluntary income tax checkoffs, and the money was used by the United States Treasury to provide matching grants to presidential candidates who had raised $5,000, in amounts of $250 or less, from citizens in at least 20 states. The maximum any individual could give a candidate was $1,000. But the Supreme Court ruled in 1976 that this ceiling could not prevent individuals or committees from spending unlimited amounts of money in support of a candidate so long as the effort was separate from the candidate's campaign, without any consultation or coordination. Suddenly, "running for president" became a possibility for people who were not wealthy. In fact, in the two elections immediately following the passage of the act, 22 people were serious enough as presidential contenders to have received federal matching funds.

Not only has the finance law resulted in generating more participation, it has also forced presidential hopefuls to establish themselves among small donors in a number of states. Contenders can no longer rely on the traditional "fat cats" who financed "favored" candidates in the past.

In spite of the limits imposed by legislation, campaigns continue to be very expensive. For example, in the 1980 election, candidates for Congress spent $228.8 million, which was well over the 1978 amount of $192.2 million; the 12 presidential candidates spent over $100 million during 37 primary campaigns, a sum much larger than the 1976 hopefuls had spent; and Jimmy Carter and Ronald Reagan spent $58.8 million or $8.8 million more than had been spent by Carter and Ford during the summer and fall of the 1976 campaign.

Not only do candidates continue to spend a good deal of money, they find that they can raise it themselves, even for primary campaigns. For example, during the 1982 primary campaign in California, one of the Republican candidates for the U.S. Senate, Barry Goldwater, Jr., raised $800,000 from just one letter in which his father (Arizona Senator Barry Goldwater) asked donations to his son's campaign as a "personal favor." In New Jersey, Republican senatorial contenders, Millicent Fenwick and Jeffrey Bell raised and spent a total of $2.2 million.

In Ohio a state senator who ran for the Republican gubernatorial nomination raised $350,000 during the last three weeks of the primary. Thus for many who run even for governorships and Congress, the ability to raise money has been the most important effect of the reforms. It has widened the electoral process by bypassing the political parties. Candidates run their own campaigns and frequently hire their own professionals to raise funds—often completely independent of party support or discipline. In turn, raising money has become easier because individual voters who view themselves as political independents are contributing to specific candidates and causes and not to political parties. Therefore, two factors—the decline of the influence of political parties and new campaign finance legislation—have combined to change contemporary political campaigns.

Political Action Committees

There is, however, a third and related element that has altered the way in which campaigns are waged; the political action committees (PACs) or single-issue groups.

Pressure groups have existed since the founding of the republic. Over the years, the efforts of some of these groups have brought about important changes, such as the abolitionists who helped eliminate slavery and the suffragettes who helped give women the right to vote. However, in recent years, pressure groups have become so powerful and so numerous that their efforts to influence legislation and elections have had a dramatic impact on electoral politics. Their campaigns for or against proposed legislation have often served to fragment the political system, and their efforts to affect the election of specific candidates have contributed to the declining influence of political parties.

Although by definition, the single issue or pressure groups are small, they have nonetheless become increasingly powerful. By the 1980 election, pollsters estimated that one in four voters was willing to vote against politicians for their position on a single issue, and the issues themselves affected 10 to 15 percent of the general electorate. While the issues around which the groups coalesce vary all the way from import quotas to environmental control, it is the so-called emotional or passionate issues (antiabortion, gun control, prayer in school, and sexual preference) that attract the most attention and motivate the groups to spring into action quickly if they feel that a proposed bill or even an individual legislator threatens their interests. They concentrate on the grassroots (pressuring city councils and state legislators), while simultaneously bombarding members of Congress with telephone calls, telegrams, letters, personal visits, heckling during public appearances, or letting them know that without support for *the issue*, the PAC will work to defeat them in the next election.

In 1950 there were fewer than 2,000 lobbyists in Washington. However, by the 1978 elections, pressure groups had proliferated to such an extent that there were 15,000 based just on Capitol Hill to work for the interests of over 500 corporate lobbies, 53 minority group lobbies, 34 social welfare lobbies, 33 women's lobbies, 31 lobbies for environmental interests, 21 lobbies for religious interests, 15 lobbies for the aging, 6 for population control, 12 for guns (5 for weapon manufacturing, 4 proguns, and 3 for gun control), 61 working for Japan's interests, and 10 for Israel's.[3] Although some of these groups had been around a long time, by 1980 they had formed political action committees and were much more aggressive in their attempts to influence legislation than they had been in the past. In fact, through the use of computerized mailing lists that identify supporters, many PACs have been able to raise large sums of money that is spent not only to lobby for their specific issue but to defeat legislators who do not support them and to elect others who do. The ability of the PACs to do this is directly related to the election law reforms we have already discussed. When Congress limited individual campaign donations to $1,000 per candidate per race, it permitted corporations, unions, and other groups to become involved in making direct political contributions to candidates. Although companies are still prohibited from contributing corporate funds, through their PACs they may solicit voluntary contributions from employees and stockholders and then give up to $5,000 to candidates in each of their primary and general election campaigns. Thus, for example, a congressional candidate who is oriented toward business can receive tens of thousands of dollars from dozens of corporate PACs, and a union-oriented candidate can receive thousands of dollars from union PACs.

The ability of the PACs in raising money to contribute to the campaigns of "friendly" incumbents and "promising" challengers cannot be taken lightly. It is an ability that has been proven in every election since the election law reforms. For example, during the 1980 elections, the PACs spent a record $131 million. They gave $55.2 million to congressional candidates (twice the amount contributed in 1978); $60 million to state and local candidates; and the remainder in the presidential contest, including the early primaries. The biggest spenders were the new right groups (especially North Carolina Senator Jesse Helms's National Congressional Club, which raised $7.9 million and spent $4.6 million to help elect Ronald Reagan, and the National Conservative Political Action Committee, "Nick-pack," which spent over $7 million during 1979 and 1980).[4] In the 1982 primary campaigns, PACs spent $80 million in hundreds of contests such as the reelection bid of House of Representatives minority leader, Robert Michel. According to documents on file with the Federal Election Commission, the Illinois congressman collected more than 85 percent of his campaign funds from special interest groups including the International Harvester Good Government Committee, the National Rifle Association Political Victory Fund, and the National Confectioners Association.[5] Each of these groups contributed to Michel's campaign and to the campaigns of other legislators because they believed it was in their best interests to do so.*

Just as the PACs work toward specific candidates' success, so can they work for their defeat. For example, in 1980 Nick-pack targeted five prominent liberal Democratic senators for defeat and ran an extensive media campaign against each. All five (George McGovern of South Dakota, Warren Magnuson of Washington, Frank Church of Idaho, Birch Bayh of Indiana, and John Culver of Iowa) were beaten, and Nick-pack, because of its financial involvement and the publicity generated by announcing its campaigns against the senators, received much of the credit (or blame).

Thus it would make little sense to discuss contemporary political campaigns without acknowledging the effect of the political action committees. They have become an important element because they breach party lines and make uncompromising, all-or-nothing demands on legislators and candidates. They care little for party loyalties, legislative voting records, or a candidate's overall philosophy or platform. They view every legislative roll call and every election as a major test of their cause. And perhaps, because of their zealotry, they have been highly successful in raising money. At any rate, the large-scale entrance of the single issue groups into the electoral process has contributed mightily to the changed nature of the electoral process.

---

*Although PACs do contribute a great deal of money to specific campaigns, it is important to remember that the primary source of funds remains individual citizens.

Technology

Perhaps the most obvious transformation in political campaigns has been in the area of technology. Although the additions of radio in the 1920s and television in the 1950s brought with them a number of alterations to U.S. political campaigns, as technological advancements, they were only the beginning. Today, campaigns from county to national rely on a number of devices, sophisticated enough to have hardly even been envisioned in a campaign as contemporary as John Kennedy's in 1960. In so doing, their nature as well as the people who run them have changed. For example, in statewide as well as presidential campaigns, the old electoral map on the headquarters wall showing in what districts the voters live, has been supplemented with a map of the major media markets. The new map decides how and where the candidate travels, carves new political regions around the interstate television centers, and pinpoints, with the help of the computer, the exact demographic audiences who should serve as the targets of the candidate's campaign. Specialists, not county or state party leaders, now conduct campaigns for the candidates. The specialists who understand the media map, can appreciate the intricacies of demographic target selection or the even newer zip code analysis (Potential Rating Index by Zip Market).* Today's candidates for state legislature, governor, Congress, and president pick their media consultant almost before they do anything else. In fact, as Sidney Blumenthal writes in his book, *The Permanent Campaign*, early in the contest, candidates are often viewed as successful or not successful by the person they are able to hire

---

*The system has already been used by some political organizations to direct information to specific groups among the electorate: each of the nation's 36,000 "clusters" (types of neighborhoods). The clusters are ranked according to "ZIP quality," using composite data on education, affluence, and other information as supplied by the census. The system's inventor, Jonathan Robbin, has found that neighborhoods are homogeneous groupings. Robbin maintains that ZIP clusters can take the guesswork out of politics.

to run their campaign. The bigger the name of the consultant, the more serious a contender the candidate is considered to be.

Not only have the media consultants taken over the modern political campaign, they are assisted by other specialists—in public opinion polling, in direct mail, in street and telephone canvassing, and even in ethnic analysis. As White has written, everything has changed, including the vocabulary. Anyone who has the direct ear of the candidate is now called a "strategist," the old-fashioned hatchet man out on the hustings is now styled a "surrogate,"[6] and a sudden rise in the public opinion polls conducted by the candidate's polling specialist shows "momentum."

Thus the sophisticated use of modern technology has brought significant alterations to political campaign communication. When these changes occurred is not really important. Whether they began in 1952 when Dwight Eisenhower first brought television commercial spots to presidential campaigns, in 1960 when John Kennedy became the first presidential candidate to use his own polling specialist, in 1972 when George McGovern pioneered mass direct mail fundraising, or even in 1980 when Jimmy Carter campaigned by conference phone calls to voters in Iowa and New Hampshire, the result is the same. Technology has changed the manner in which candidates run for office. A congressional contender may reject an appearance at the county fair in favor of a television interview that will be broadcast on the evening news in the major metropolitan area in the district. A candidate for the Democratic gubernatorial primary may not even publicly announce the intention to run until a direct mail specialist has raised enough money for the campaign. Presidential candidates may never set foot in a given city or state throughout the campaign but be seen by all in countless television spots as they address the public's concerns.

In short, the advances in technology as well as the advent of the single issue groups, the election law reforms, and the decline in the influence of political parties have combined to transform the nature and manner of our electoral system. Whether we like it or not, one significant result of these changes has been that we can scarcely avoid taking part in the campaign process. Those who choose not to participate directly become involved at some level even if it is only to explain to friends why they are not voting, or why they are throwing in the wastebasket personalized letters asking for contributions, refusing to respond to a candidate's telephone survey, or turning off television to avoid political programs and advertisements. "We must actively choose not to be active; hence we are participating symbolically even if not actually" because the political campaign is ubiquitous.[7] Somebody is always seeking elective office and the "somebodies" are no longer strangers but your neighbor, the clerk in the store, or the mother of your best friend. The modern campaign knows no season. It seems that as one ends, another begins. Candidates start running for office months and even years in advance of the primary election.* Thus campaigns are now an unavoidable part of our environment, forcing us to become consumers of political communication.

COMMUNICATION AND POLITICAL CAMPAIGNS

The major argument of this book is that political election campaigns are campaigns of communication. Certainly, numerous forms or combinations of economic, sociological, psychological, and historical factors are crucial to or reflective of the electoral process. However, the core of each campaign is

---

*Even the political parties are beginning to "run" early. In 1982 the Democratic party met in a miniconvention in Philadelphia to express their unity and opposition to the current administration by writing a 50,000-word position statement on foreign and defense policy, the economy, individual rights, energy, and federalism. The miniconvention was held two years in advance of the presidential nominating convention.

communication. This is not to argue that a variety of economic and situational needs, power relationships, and a whole host of additional elements and demands do not affect the campaign process or outcome, but rather to say that all of these other factors become important in the electoral system principally through the offices of communication. It is communication that occupies the area between the goals or aspirations of the candidate and the behavior of the electorate, just as it serves as the bridge between the dreams or hopes of the voter and the actions of the candidate. It is through communication that a political campaign begins. Individuals verbally announce their intention to run or posters/billboards announce nonverbally that election time has begun. During the campaign, candidates and their staffs debate, appear on television, prepare and present messages for media commercials, take part in parades and rallies, wear funny hats, submit to media interviews, write letters and position papers, and speak at all forms of public gatherings. They kiss babies, shake hands at factory gates and supermarkets, prepare and distribute literature, wear campaign buttons, and establish phone banks to solicit money, workers, and votes. In addition, countless hours are spent during the campaign trying to raise enough money to buy radio and television time or computerized lists of voters. All of this effort is for the single purpose of communicating with the electorate, the media, and each other. And when the time comes, it is through communication that the campaign draws to a close. Candidates verbally concede defeat or extol victory, and the posters/billboards are taken down announcing nonverbally that one campaign is over, even as another begins.

Hence, communication is the means by which the campaign begins, proceeds, and concludes. It is, as we suggested, the epistemological base. Without it, there is no political campaign. It is, therefore, not enough to approach the study of political campaign communication by analyzing the demographic characteristics or the attitudes of the electorate, although the information provided by such work is significant for our overall understanding of the phenomenon. It is also not enough to examine political campaign communication by studying only psychological construct theory or even the relationship and effect of the mass media on the campaign, in spite of the fact that each explains much about the contemporary electoral process. What is needed is a study that provides a communication perspective of a communication event or series of events—the political election campaign. Although you will find references to the works of political scientists, historians, and psychologists, as well as political journalists, we have drawn primarily on the work generated by scholars in communication.

In exploring such theoretical concerns as agenda setting, uses and gratifications, targeting, gatekeeping, information diffusion, positioning and repositioning, functionalism, legitimizing, or even in analyzing the pragmatic details of planning, organizing, and presenting speeches, debates, or fund raising appeals, we have been guided by one question: what is it that we ought to study as political campaign communication? Our answers are contained in the subject areas we examine in the following chapters.

ORGANIZATION AND PREVIEW OF CHAPTERS

This book has two sections. Chapters 2 through 4 analyze important principles and theoretical concerns of political campaign communication, while chapters 5 through 8 examine the crucial practices of contemporary political campaign communication. Although this distinction is designed to help you better understand the phenomenon, in the real world of political campaigns, principles and practices blend. As you read the section on principles, keep in mind that in political campaigns, principles often generate practices and practices often generate principles. For example, in Chapter 2 when we discuss the principles involved in an individual's surfacing as a viable candidate, principles cannot be meaningfully presented without examining the practices of many individuals who have surfaced. In turn, those practices have subsequently generated many of the principles. Similarly, in Chapter 5 when we discuss the practice of political speechwriters, we cannot readily examine them without developing some of the principles that speechwriters utilize. Thus, artificial as the distinction is, it does provide us with a pedagogically useful organizational framework from which to view political campaign communication.

Following this introductory chapter, the next three chapters focus on principles of political campaign communication. Political communication is a broad term. It has been used to describe the communication involved in winning elections, governing a nation, reporting on governmental activity, gathering and determining public opinion, lobbying, and socializing people into a nation. We have deliberately chosen to narrow the term and focus not on political communication, but rather on political *campaign* communication. We do not deny the validity of studying other forms of political communication. However, in a democratic society, to govern one must first win an election. To report governmental activity, there must first be an elected government about which to report. To lobby, there must first be elected officials to be persuaded. To gather and determine public opinion about candidates and their progress, there must first be a campaign. And to socialize people so that they accept cultural norms, elected officials must first help set the norms. In other words, we believe that political campaign communication is the root of all other forms of political communication. It is undoubtedly for this reason that political campaign communication has been the focus of far more scholarly and popular journalistic inquiry than any other form of political communication. In addition, the number of elaborately planned and professionally implemented campaigns is growing each election year. Thus it is particularly appropriate to limit our examination of political communication to political campaigns.

Chapter 2 examines the four stages of a political campaign, discussing the many pragmatic and symbolic functions provided by communicative acts to the electorate, the candidates, and the media.

Chapter 3 analyzes the communicative strategies and styles that incumbents and challengers have used in U.S. elections from 1789 to the present. In addition, the emerging campaign style of women is examined.

Chapter 4 presents an examination of the means or channels used in contemporary political campaigns. Theoretical approaches used to study the effect of the mass media on political campaigns are discussed.

At the conclusion of these three chapters, many of the principles associated with political campaign communication will have been explored. We hope that by the end of Part I, our readers will have an appreciation of the theoretical basis of campaign communication from the vantage point of a consumer, but we also hope that campaign communication principles will be understood from the vantage point of a user, one actively involved in campaigning for public office. We are aware that readers majoring in such fields as speech communication, mass communication, and public relations anticipate being involved in political campaigns professionally. Many other readers may also participate in campaigns, if not professionally, at least as highly interested citizens concerned with their communities. We believe that Part I can provide a valuable understanding of the principles of campaign communication from any vantage point that readers choose to follow in the future. Part II focuses on practices of political campaign communication. In this section, we will discuss four of the most common communication events in contemporary political campaigns. Chapter 5 examines public speaking in campaigns. It explains how political candidates decide where and when to speak, how they develop speeches, and how they utilize speechwriters and surrogate speakers.

Chapter 6 also focuses on public speaking in political campaigns. But whereas Chapter 5 concentrates on the normal day-to-day public speaking that characterizes campaigns, Chapter 6 examines forms of speeches that occur in most campaigns, are unique unto themselves, and are not day-to-day occurrences. For example, portions of the chapter deal with announcement speeches, press conferences, speeches of apologia, and acceptance speeches, among others. Each of these forms takes place in virtually every campaign. The purposes and strategies involved in each genre are presented.

Chapter 7 deals with political debates. Debates are often the most anticipated and most publicized communication activity engaged in by candidates. The chapter presents a history of political debating and then discusses the factors that motivate candidates to accept or reject the opportunity to debate, the strategies that are used, and the effect of political debates.

Chapter 8 concludes the section on practices by examining interpersonal communication in political campaigns. Three interpersonal communication situations, typical of all campaigns, are analyzed in light of current interpersonal communication theory.

We find the study of political campaign communication to be fascinating and believe that some of our enthusiasm for the subject is apparent in the following pages. We hope readers come away from this book not only better informed, but also with renewed respect and interest in a political system that, although abused and attacked in recent years, does not depend on coercion or force but derives its strength from the fact that it relies on human communication, largely as manifested in political campaigns, as a major means of decision making.

NOTES

1. Theodore H. White, "The Search for President," *Boston Globe*, February 24, 1980, p. A1.

2. Arthur H. Miller, "Partisanship Reinstated?," *British Journal of Political Science* 8 (1978): 133.

3. "Single-Issue Politics," *Newsweek*, November 6, 1978, p. 49.

4. "PACs Pack Clout in Right Turn," *Chicago Tribune*, February 21, 1982, p. A16; Adam Clymer, "Conservative Political Committee Evokes Both Fear and Adoration," *New York Times*, May 30, 1981, p. A1.

5. Jill MacNeice, "Special-interest Groups Boost Michel's Coffers," *Chicago Tribune*, May 10, 1982, p. A5.

6. White, "Search for President," p. A1.

7. Bruce E. Gronbeck, "The Functions of Presidential Campaigning," *Communication Monographs* 45 (1978): 271.

2

Communicative Functions of Political Campaigns

ONE OF THE WAYS TO EXAMINE POLITICAL CAMPAIGNS IS TO ANALYZE THEIR COMMUNICATIVE FUNCTIONS, THAT IS, TO INVESTIGATE WHAT FUNCTIONS THE VARIOUS forms or acts of campaign communication provide to the electorate and to the candidates themselves.[1] Many of these functions are instrumental or pragmatic in that they make specific tangible contributions. Others are consummatory or symbolic in nature; they fulfill ritualistic expectations or requirements. Both are discussed in this chapter.

The modern political campaign passes through relatively discrete stages, which can be categorized as preprimary, primary, convention, and general election. This chapter is organized and divided analogous to the campaign itself; the different functions are discussed in terms of these four specific stages. It is important to remember that each stage, although discrete, has a direct relationship to and bearing on all that follow. In other words, the functions of each stage affect the entire campaign.

FIRST POLITICAL
STAGE: SURFACING

Although the first or preprimary stage has been called the "winnowing period,"[2] we have labeled it "surfacing" because this term more completely conceptualizes those communication activities that occur. Surfacing was originally labeled and defined as "the series of predictable and specifically timed rhetorical transactions which serve consummatory and instrumental functions during the pre-primary phase of the campaign."[3]

It would be difficult to set an exact time limit on the first stage because it can vary from candidate to candidate and election to election. Political hopefuls must assess their visibility and credibility as well as determine their financial backing and organizational strength. Predictable rhetorical activities (the verbal and nonverbal communication acts)* during the surfacing stage include building a political organization in each city, district, state, or region (depending on the geographic scope encompassed by the office being sought), speaking to many different kinds of public gatherings in an attempt to capture attention (media attention for state and national campaigns), conducting public opinion polls to assess visibility or to determine potential issues for which stands will later have to be devised, putting together an organizational structure and campaign blueprint, and raising money. These activities take time whether an individual is running for mayor or for president. As one woman who was elected to a seat on her city council told us, "I didn't just start campaigning. I started planning in January for the November election. And this involved an organized plan—contracting for billboards, purchasing material for signs, mapping out financing, and finding volunteers for sign lettering and door-to-door canvassing."[4] A gubernatorial contender, who announced his candidacy 13

---

*Forms of communication used in campaigns are virtually limitless. For a list of the most common verbal and nonverbal acts, see Chapter 1.

24

months before the 1982 Democratic primary in Ohio, justified his early start by saying that his campaign could not be tied to traditional timetables because he had to let people know who he was and what his ideas were so that voters would know that alternatives existed to the "same old names."

If surfacing takes months for city council and gubernatorial candidates, it appears to take even longer for presidential contenders. For example, during the 1976 campaign, presidential hopefuls Jimmy Carter and Morris Udall surfaced 15 months before the first state primary. In the 1980 campaign, Phillip Crane announced he was a candidate for president 19 months before the New Hampshire primary. In October 1981, almost two and a half years before the first primary of the 1984 presidential campaign, former Vice-President Walter Mondale established a national action committee (a common device necessary to begin raising money in a sufficient number of states so that eventually the candidate can qualify for federal matching funds) and announced on "Meet the Press" that he was considering running for president. Although it is impossible to place a definite time structure on the first stage, we have listed some of the important rhetorical activities the period demands. Thus surfacing begins with candidates' initial efforts to create an interest and image of themselves as candidates and extends through a variety of public rhetorical transactions prior to the first primary election.

But not only do we know what is typically demanded of the candidate during the first stage, we also have some idea of the characteristic functions served by the communication acts of the surfacing period. Although these can vary with the level of office sought (just as the time period does), we have observed seven functions that appear to be important in all political campaigns.

The first function is to provide an indication of a candidate's fitness for office—the "caliber" of the individual. During the campaign, especially the earliest portions when public images of potential candidates are beginning to be formed, the electorate draws inferences from campaign actions about how a particular contender would behave as mayor, or governor, or even president.

The electorate does not want elected officials who are viewed as dishonest, dull, unjust, immoral, corrupt, incompetent, or who are even the brunt of jokes such as television host Johnny Carson's labeling of Senator S. I. Hayakawa as "sleeping Sam" and the "Sominex kid." In other words, U.S. voters have some preconceptions about people who run for public office. Generally, successful candidates will be perceived as trustworthy, intelligent or competent enough to do the job, compassionate, articulate, poised, honorable, and perhaps male.* The higher the office, the more judgmental voters become. For example, voters expect those candidates who run for or serve as our chief executive to be of "presidential timber"— to possess special qualities not always found in the same degree in all people. And although there is not a one-to-one relationship between the two, campaign actions are taken as symbolic of actions as president. We do not want presidents who hit their heads on helicopter doors, fall down steps, mispronounce words, or who are attacked by "killer rabbits." These are behaviors that cause a candidate to be characterized as "clumsy," "dumb," or "loser" as Gerald Ford and Jimmy Carter were labeled during the surfacing period of the 1976 and 1980 campaigns. As a matter of fact, perhaps conditioned by the negative perceptions of Ford and Carter's actions, voters' assessment of many of the 1980 and 1984 presidential hopefuls were sometimes harsh. For example, former Texas Governor John Connally, a 1980 contender, was perceived as having charisma because of his tough-guy, macho image, but he was also viewed as arrogant and too tough to be president.

---

*While more women than ever before are now running for and being elected to office, relatively few are even nominated for important state or federal offices. Certainly one reason for this is that the image of women and the image of political leaders do not mesh. For a discussion of the image and style of political women, see Chapter 3.

26

He may have frightened voters with his hardline, two-fisted public speaking style, for as one person commented after hearing him, "he'd sure make a good dictator. I don't know that we need a dictator now, but he'd sure make a good one."[5] A 1984 hopeful, Senator John Glenn, was frequently termed as "too boring" to be president.

Potential presidents are not supposed to frighten or bore people, but neither should reference to them produce laughter. This was the problem with the general perception of California Governor Edmund (Jerry) Brown, who during the 1980 presidential campaign was nicknamed "Governor Moonbeam" and was the object of countless one-liners depicting his visionary themes ("protect the earth," "serve the people," and "explore the universe"). Although Brown may have been a prophet of a new era of "holistic politics," real or successful presidential contenders are not the brunt of such jokes as "do you realize that Jerry Brown is the only governor whose parents are trying to deprogram him?"* Whatever the ultimate judgment, certainly one function of the pre-primary period is to provide an indication of a candidate's fitness for office.

A second communication function of the surfacing stage is that it initiates the ritualistic activities important to our political system. In his book, *The Symbolic Uses of Politics*, social scientist Murray Edelman discusses the idea of U.S. political campaigns as traditional, rule-governed rituals and then discusses rituals as a kind of motor activity that involves its participants symbolically in a common enterprise.[6] While each of the stages of the campaign demands certain rituals, none is more clearly defined than the activities surrounding the pre-primary announcement speech. (Although the announcement

---

*Certainly Jerry Brown's political problems were not helped by Johnny Carson's comments about him on the "Tonight" show. Carson's jokes about Brown began when he became governor of California, continued throughout Brown's 1980 presidential campaign, and resurfaced as Brown announced his 1982 senatorial ambitions.

speech itself will be discussed in Chapter 6, here we will consider its ritualistic aspects).

When candidates decide to enter the political arena formally, there are certain protocols that must be performed because they are expected. For example, a press conference is called, the candidate is surrounded by family and friends while announcing the decision to run for office, and then embarks immediately on a campaign swing through the district, state, or nation. The candidate may only be announcing a campaign for the mayor's office, but there are expectations concerning how it is done. However, to capture the full flavor of the announcement ritual, it might be best to consider the presidential politics of 1980.

The ritual began on August 1, 1978, when Phillip Crane, a relatively obscure congressman from Illinois, surrounded by his wife and eight children, said that he was proud to be the first officially announced candidate for the Republican nomination. Robert Dole, the senator from Kansas who had been Gerald Ford's running mate in 1976, went home to Russell, Kansas, to announce his intentions. The town honored him by declaring the day "Bob Dole Day." Children were given the morning off from school, businesses were closed until noon, bands played, and the senator stood on the steps of city hall and promised that during his campaign "he would neither attack opponents in the Republican Party nor the incumbent President." However, the campaign's most extravagant production belonged to the former governor of California, Ronald Reagan.

When Ronald Reagan announced his candidacy in 1979, it was his third such campaign kickoff. Thus he went to far more trouble and expense than his colleagues had done. He taped a speech, put together a makeshift network of local television stations to carry it, and used ads in newspapers that read: "See Ronald Reagan make news tonight—it's history in the making; a special announcement of importance to all Americans." The speech itself was delivered live at a fund-raising dinner in New

York, and the following day the speech was broadcast on local radio stations throughout the country. Clearly, one communicative function of the surfacing stage is that it initiates the ritual vital to U.S. politics.

Thus far in discussing the preprimary period, we have been focusing on what has been termed "consummatory functions of campaigning." These functions are essentially symbolic in nature—functions that seem to be rooted more deeply in the heart or soul rather than in the mind of the electorate. In other words, as communication scholar Bruce Gronbeck has written, "campaigning creates second-level or metapolitical images, personae, myths, associations, and social-psychological reactions which may even be detached or at least distinct from particular candidates, issues, and offices."[7]

Thus communication during the first stage plays two symbolic but important roles: it provides an indication of a candidate's fitness for office and initiates the ritual we have come to expect in political campaigns. However, there are five additional contributions provided by the communication acts and symbols during the surfacing period. These functions are related to the pragmatic aspects of the campaign and have thus been labeled "instrumental." The first of these functions is that the electorate begins to have some knowledge about a candidate's goals and potential programs.

It is during the surfacing period that the electorate begins to learn something about a candidate's goals or initial stands on issues. In an attempt to determine if and with whom their campaign has any appeal, candidates must speak at countless neighborhood coffees, potluck dinners, and service club meetings. During these appearances, they often have to answer questions about why they are running for office as well as state their positions on specific issues important to those attending the gathering. Answers may at first be sketchy, but as the frequency of the speaking occasions and the perceived receptivity of the audiences increases, so does the candidate's confidence. Statements about political goals and aspirations as well as positions on issues become refined. What was in the beginning somewhat tentative, now becomes more definite as the candidate proceeds to formulate statements of philosophy apparently acceptable to most potential constituents. For example, when Congresswoman Elizabeth Holtzman decided to enter the 1980 New York senatorial race, she began scheduling a number of appearances throughout the state months before the primary. Countless efforts were made to not only expand her visibility from one congressional district to the whole state, but also to let the electorate know what her positions were on issues wider than those facing her current constituents.

During the eight years in which Holtzman had been a member of the House of Representatives, she had demonstrated an ability to work for the fairly narrow concerns of her Kings County New York constituents. But with the decision to move from the House to the Senate, the congresswoman had to establish her understanding of and commitment to problems and issues facing a larger and more diverse audience. The surfacing period provided Holtzman the opportunity to not only determine what the issues were but to formulate positions that could be and were used during the second or primary stage of her campaign for the United States Senate.

Closely related is the second instrumental function—voter expectation regarding a candidate's administrative and personal style begin to be established. For example, candidates who have well-organized and -disciplined staffs provide some knowledge about the kind of administration they might have if they are elected. Even in a campaign for a seat on the local school board, those candidates who right from the beginning appear to be operating from a precise plan or blueprint with regard to where and when they will canvass the district, or distribute literature, or speak at neighborhood coffees provide voters with information regarding the level of organization and efficiency it might be reasonable to expect if and when they are elected to the school board.

The personal style of a candidate is also revealed during the early days of a campaign. Perhaps one of the most interesting examples occurred during the preprimary period of the 1980 presidential campaign. Before Edward Kennedy began his pursuit of the presidency, he, like his brothers before him, had been perceived as an excellent speaker, a master of the art of campaigning and campaign rhetoric. Thus the expectations of the public were high—so high that it is unlikely that any candidate could have lived up to the dimensions of the Kennedy mystique. But in the first few ventures away from Washington and Boston, the senator fell far short. He read his speeches (he always had, but no one ever seemed to have noticed before), mispronounced words, seldom looked up from manuscripts to establish eye contact with his audience, stumbled frequently using vocal pauses of qualifiers such as "uh" or "ah," appeared confused in answers to questions on material and issues he should have known, rambled, and appeared unable to speak without constant reliance on manuscripts and especially prepared charts. Deficiencies were exaggerated because of high expectations, but the point is that the surfacing period is important for its revelations of a candidate's personal and administrative style.

The third instrumental function of surfacing is that it aids in determining what the dominant theme or issues of the campaign will be. The early candidates set the rhetorical agenda for the campaign. As they crisscross the country, state, congressional district, or even the city, they begin to come to grips with the issues on people's minds, begin to address themselves to those issues, and as we noted earlier, begin to formulate "solutions" to problems that seem to be compatible with popular perception. In national or statewide elections, the media repeat a candidate's statements and thus aid in translating the problems and positions into national or state issues. In local campaigns, candidates often determine the problems by word of mouth rather than the media. A friend of ours who ran for a seat on city council had a fairly direct method for determining the issues on voters' minds. Instead of polling, which he could not afford, or public appearances before various groups, which he wished to avoid until the announcement of candidacy, he simply began attending weekly meetings of the city council nine months before the election. In this way, he had some guidance in selecting issues for his campaign because he was able to learn on a firsthand basis which issues were important or controversial enough to be discussed in council meetings. Thus the surfacing stage is important because the rhetorical agenda begins to be established. If these early concerns are widespread enough, they can become the dominant issues in succeeding stages of the campaign. And those candidates who surface early help determine what will be the agenda.

The first stage is also important because it begins the process of selecting front runners or separating the serious contenders from the not so serious. Becoming a serious candidate during the surfacing period involves obtaining visibility. In even small races, much less in state or national contests, obtaining visibility requires persuading the media that one is a viable enough candidate to deserve attention.

Almost from the beginning, at least in state and national contests, the media strongly influence who will be considered a major candidate. Visibility during the surfacing period is often the initial reaction of the media to a candidate's past or present self. This has been illustrated a number of times when people who have achieved national recognition in the nonpolitical arena have decided to run for public office and the media have, in a relatively short period of time, turned them into serious candidates. Consider the cases of Senator John Glenn (one of the first U.S. astronauts), Governor J. Y. Brown (the Kentucky Fried Chicken "King" with a famous wife), Senator John Warner (a former secretary of the navy who married actress Elizabeth Taylor), or even the former governor of California, Ronald Reagan (a movie actor and television host). This was also demonstrated during the surfacing period of the 1980 presidential campaign when Gerald Ford, Ronald Reagan, and John Connally, because of previous roles, were selected by the media as serious presidential contenders and thus accorded early and extensive coverage. To a lesser extent, this was also a factor affecting Governor Jerry Brown and Senator Edward Kennedy. However, in 1980 neither the past nor current positions of Brown and Kennedy were as important in generating visibility as was the fact that each was challenging his party's incumbent. Intraparty challenges such as theirs in 1980, Ronald Reagan's in 1976, and Eugene McCarthy's in 1968 normally attract media attention.

Who candidates are and their current position also aid in determining initial visibility. For example, as governor of Ohio, James Rhodes was given considerable media attention throughout 1981 as he "semipublicly" considered running for the Senate seat of Howard Metzenbaum. Howard Baker was considered a leading contender during the early stage of the 1980 presidential campaign because of his position in the U.S. Senate—just as Walter Mondale and Edward Kennedy were initially during the 1984 surfacing period. Similarly, George Bush, John Anderson, Phillip Crane, and Benjamin Fernandez were not thought of as serious candidates by the media because they did not have current or powerful positions in government.

Quite apart from persuading the media that one is a front runner based on roles and present positions, a candidate may also emerge from the surfacing period as a possible leading contender by successful grassroots organizing and fund raising. Acquiring sufficient money to generate the momentum necessary to do well in the primary stage has always been and continues to be important for local, state, and congressional candidates. But with the advent of the campaign-financing laws, motivating enough support to raise the money to qualify for federal matching funds has become crucial to presidential contenders.

Becoming a front runner because of early grassroots organizing and successful fund raising helps explain the initial successes of presidential contenders such as George McGovern in 1972, Jimmy Carter in 1976, and George Bush in 1980. Not one of them had been considered a serious candidate by the media prior to the first competition. Each used the surfacing period to gather the strength necessary to do well in the first contest and thus forced the media to acknowledge them as serious presidential candidates.

The final communicative function of the surfacing stage is that the media and the candidate get to know each other. While this function is often not vital for local campaigns, it can be important in congressional and state races, and it is absolutely crucial in presidential campaigns. It is in these contests where we can most completely understand the significance of the function to the entire campaign.

At each stage of the campaign, the relationships between candidates and the media who cover them are vital not only to the candidate but to the individual media representative. The candidate needs the visibility that only the media can provide and the media need information that only access to the candidate or immediate campaign staff can provide. It is not, especially in the preprimary period, the adversary relationship as is commonly pictured. As one analyst who studied the media-press relations of the 1976 Carter campaign summarized:

> A symbiosis of the goals of journalists and those who manage campaigns provides for a good deal of mutually beneficial interaction. On the one hand, news reporting organizations certainly define the presidential race as a story which must be covered . . . and are willing to expend considerable resources in news gathering. . . . Presidential candidate organizations, on the other hand, seek to use the news reporting process as a relatively inexpensive means of communicating with voters and political activists. Campaigns, therefore, are happy to facilitate journalists in the conduct of their work.[8]

Relationships can be established during the surfacing stage because there are few media representatives assigned to cover a specific candidate and because the candidate has a skeleton traveling staff—perhaps only the campaign director and candidate. Contact is informal; candidates and staff are accessible. It is a time for finding out details and learning enough about each other to know who can be counted on when or if the candidate's campaign begins to gather momentum. Conditions change from the first stage to the second, and it is the surfacing period that allows media and candidate to get to know each other. The importance of the relationship is first that it provides the opportunity for local media/candidate interaction, which is not always available after candidates find they can get national exposure, and second it gives both candidate and national media representatives a contact to be used later. In other words, the reporter soon discovers who on the staff will have the "real" story or lead and the candidate's people know not only who they can trust but which reporter has the best chance of getting stories in print or on the air. It is a reciprocal relationship and a significant function of surfacing.

These, then, are the necessary functions served by communicative acts during the first political stage. The period is crucial because of the functions it provides. Candidates who announce late and thus do not participate in surfacing activities or those who fail to use the period wisely have little success and frequently do not even advance to the second stage.*

SECOND POLITICAL STAGE: PRIMARIES

Primary elections are, at any level, "America's most original contribution to the art of democracy."[9] Under the primary system, voters who make up the political party determine who the party's candidates will be. Although the system varies from

---

*In 1976 Frank Church and Jerry Brown did not even enter the race until the primary stage. After a few successes in individual primaries, they were out of the contest, having lost to the two major "surfacers" of 1976, Jimmy Carter and Morris Udall. In 1980 Howard Baker refused to leave his duties in the Senate until the primary stage had begun. Once again, it was too late.

state to state, generally, primaries provide for a full-fledged intraparty election with the purpose of choosing a single candidate from each party to run in the general election. The direct primary elections, unlike the presidential primary, normally have a degree of finality in that the winning candidate is automatically placed on the November ballot. But in instances where there are a number of candidates competing for the same office, it is often necessary to have a second or run-off primary because one candidate usually does not capture a majority of votes in the first election. In the case of the presidential primary, even after all of the state elections have been held, the party nominees still have not been chosen. The national nominating convention (the third political stage) officially selects the candidate. Thus in presidential campaigns, primary elections are only one phase of the nominating process, not the final act or choice.

There are almost as many variations of primaries as there are states. For example, Wisconsin for many years had what was known as the most "pure" of the open primaries because voters could vote in any primary (it was not necessary to be preregistered and vote as a Republican or as a Democrat and vote only in that party's primary) and have their vote remain secret. Registration took place on primary day and crossover voting was the norm.* Connecticut, on the other extreme, has only recently even held primary elections. For many years, the state allowed party leaders to choose its statewide candidates without fighting it out in primary elections. In fact, 1976 was the first year that both Republican and Democratic parties held a primary, and 1980 was the first year that a full-fledged presidential preference primary was held.

Not only are there different forms of state primaries, some states do not even hold direct primaries but operate under the caucus system to determine nominees. To further complicate

---

*In March 1981, the Supreme Court denied the constitutionality of the Wisconsin primary system.

the process, the political parties within one state may vary in terms of their selection procedure. For example, in 1980 in Michigan, while the Republicans stayed with the direct primary, the Democrats switched to a caucus system after they were unsuccessful in their efforts to get the legislature to change the state's law to prevent or inhibit crossover voting. But the caucus system chosen by the Michigan Democrats was the most restrictive in the nation. Participants were required to register by February 26 (the day of the New Hampshire primary) and had to pay fees to take part. Iowa is undoubtedly the best known caucus because since 1976 it has been the first real presidential testing ground. In 1980 the Iowa caucus began the night of January 21 in living rooms, schools, church basements, and firehouses. Democrats and Republicans gathered by precinct to elect delegates to county conventions, who in turn, chose delegates to state conventions and finally to the national conventions. The whole process took until June. Maine has essentially the same system, but timing has given the Iowa caucuses inordinate importance. In spite of the fact that local and state nominees are not selected at the precinct level and although proportionately fewer national nominating convention delegates for either party come from Iowa, the candidates who win the precinct caucuses receive enormous publicity boosts from the national media.

Many professional politicians and party leaders hate the primary stage of a campaign because a genuine primary is a fight within the family of the party—a fight that can turn nasty as different factions within the family compete with each other to secure a place on the November ballot for their candidate. In addition, primaries can exhaust candidates, leaving them physically and emotionally drained just before the most important battle. Charges and countercharges of candidates and their staffs often provide the opposition party with ammunition they can use during the general election campaign. Moreover, the presidential primaries of 1980 brought another problem when the unit rule forced changes in strategy and thus made the presidential primary system even more detested by party leaders than it had been. Under the new rules, there could be no winner-take-all victory anywhere. Every state and every congressional district was forced to divide its delegates in proportion to the votes the candidates had won, and then candidates would "own" the delegate chosen in their name. In practical terms, it meant that no state was worth a candidate's full attention, and yet no state could really be ignored. Each candidate had to campaign everywhere in each primary because even in losing the state, the candidate could still get a substantial share of the delegates (as was the case with Carter in New York and Reagan in Pennsylvania).

Finally, primaries use a lot of money—funds not only from contributors who might have been generous for the later campaign, but money that can be a drain on state and national resources in terms of matching funds. For example, because of the large number of people who ran in the 1982 New Jersey gubernatorial primary, the state had to spend over $13 million in matching funds. In Ohio contenders for the 1982 gubernatorial primary spent as much as $2 million each for the Democratic primary. And the 1980 presidential primaries were the most expensive in history. Contenders spent over $100 million, while network television spent over $300 million just to cover the four-month string of the Tuesday night "political dramas." One reason inordinate amounts are spent on this stage of presidential campaigns is that there are so many primaries and they last for so long. In 1980 the primary season began on January 21 and did not conclude until June 3 when eight states, including California, Ohio, and New Jersey, voted. The drawn out schedule also gave disproportionate influence to smaller states such as Iowa and New Hampshire with early caucuses and primaries, while larger states such as California and Ohio found that the race was over before they had a turn.* For example, in spite of the fact that 12 presidential candidates had

---

*The 1984 primary calendar was shortened, as we have discussed in Chapter 1.

entered the 1980 primaries, Ronald Reagan and Jimmy Carter were assured of victory by March, before the primaries where large numbers of delegates could be awarded.

Yet, for all of the problems with this second political stage, there are five functions that the communication acts and symbols of the period provide. While we do not want to suggest that primaries (particularly the presidential primary system) need no revision, we do believe these five functions are important to the entire political campaign process. The first relates directly to the candidates and the final four to the electorate.

For candidates, the primary season is a source of feedback from the voters about their campaigns, the organization they have put together, the competence of staffs, fund-raising efforts, physical stamina—in other words, their strengths and weaknesses as campaigners. During the surfacing period, the candidates' only measures of how they are doing are the comments of the media and, in some cases, the results of polls. But the primaries provide direct feedback from the voters and thus a chance for repositioning in terms of stands on issues, themes, images, and overall campaign strategies. Obviously, for those candidates who have only one primary in which to compete (most local, state, and congressional contenders), the feedback is either of no use (except as it may account for defeat), or it is used to plan for the general stage. For example, feedback from the first campaign of candidates such as John Glenn of Ohio, Lee Dreyfus of Wisconsin, and S. I. Hayakawa of California allowed them to reposition their public images from astronaut or academician to senator or governor. For presidential candidates, the early contests are direct sources of feedback that can be used immediately as preparations are made for campaigning in subsequent states. There are times, of course, when repositioning does not work, as was the case in 1976 when Morris Udall attempted to reposition his image from "liberal" during the early primaries to "progressive" during the later competitions. But there are other times when it has. One of the most dramatic was the repositioning of

39

Ronald Reagan's image and campaign strategy during the 1980 primaries.

As conceived originally by then campaign manager, John Sears, Ronald Reagan's 1980 quest for the presidency was to be a regal campaign, one in which Reagan would slowly but surely win the delegates necessary to assure the nomination. The front-runner campaign conceptualized by Sears would be characterized by an "above-the-battle" posture in which Reagan would campaign leisurely in each state by making only one or two appearances in any one day, not appear on forums or debates with his Republican rivals, honor his own already famous "eleventh commandment" (thou shall not speak ill of other Republicans), and be assisted with a well-planned and -financed media campaign.

The strategy was tested in Iowa, the birthplace of Reagan and the center of his so-called rural heartland. A week before the caucuses, Iowa newspapers talked about Reagan's failure to campaign in the state or to even appear with each of the other Republican candidates in the nationally televised forum sponsored by the *Des Moines Register*. Reagan's absence was noted throughout Iowa at countless fund-raising dinners, or as they are termed by politicans and the press, "cattle shows," where each of his Republican opponents made appearances and speeches. In fact, at some of these party functions, there were not even any signs of a Reagan campaign in the state—no campaign buttons, no posters, no candidate. By the time of the caucus, Reagan had spent only 41 hours in the state, had avoided discussing the issues, and had made only one televised speech. It had been, as one newspaper headline proclaimed, a campaign that was "Invisible to Many." In defending this strategy, Sears said that "as a front-runner, Reagan could set the pace for the campaign, decide whether to give an event like the forum the prominence of his presence, and that the job of the other candidates was to make Reagan turn around and confront them."[10]

In contrast, one Republican, George Bush, had spent a full 59 days campaigning in Iowa and had thoroughly extended his campaign organization throughout Iowa months in advance of the caucus. On January 21, it was clear that the effort had paid off when Bush upset front-runner Reagan and finished first among the Republican candidates.

Although we do not know Reagan's immediate private reaction to his Iowa upset, we do know that he must have accepted the caucus result as instructive feedback about his campaign strategy or image. By the following week, a "new" Reagan was campaigning in New Hampshire. This Reagan was talking about issues, riding a press bus, speaking at rallies throughout the state, appearing at all multicandidate Republican gatherings, participating in (in fact, pursuing vigorously) all opportunities to debate his Republican rivals, and using an expanded media campaign to present his view to New Englanders. Perhaps the clearest indication that Reagan had used feedback from Iowa Republicans to reposition his campaign strategy and thus his image came on election day in New Hampshire when he fired his press secretary, his operations director, and his manager, John Sears.

Important also are the functions provided to the electorate. Just as the primary campaign is valuable in giving candidates the feedback necessary for repositioning, so too can it offer voters the information necessary for cognitive adjustment or readjustment.

Images are rather easily acquired by voters during primaries. As candidates crisscross the city or the state, speaking at all types of political receptions, coffees, rallies, or fund-raising events, voters have the opportunity to see and hear potential mayors, governors, or presidents. They can witness for themselves the candidate's habitual patterns of thinking and acting. They need no longer rely solely on earlier, perhaps inaccurate, accounts of a candidate's style or position on issues. A candidate for mayor does look and sound capable of coping with the city's striking sanitation and transportation workers. The Republican candidate for governor does have a plan for enticing major industry into the state. The nonincumbent candidate for city council is unable to answer a simple question about zoning ordinances. And the presidential candidate uses so many "ahs," "umhs," and "huhs" that it is impossible to understand responses to questions.

In other words, as the candidates seek all possible arenas of political talk during the primary stage of the campaign, voters can see on a firsthand basis just how candidates handle themselves verbally and nonverbally. The information they receive aids in determining or readjusting their opinions. As a matter of fact, political scientist Thomas Patterson has found that these early impressions gained during the primary stage tend to remain throughout the campaign.[11] From speeches and answers to audience questions, voters begin to have some information regarding the candidate's beliefs, attitudes, and value orientations. If Jerry Brown can only talk about protecting the earth and exploring the universe, how will he ever get the U.S. hostages home from Iran? If Edward Kennedy can only talk about spending more money on comprehensive health care insurance for everyone, how will he ever understand that most citizens are sick of federal government welfare programs? If George Bush is so proficient and experienced in so many different government and political roles, why is it that he has never held any one job longer than two years? Answers to these questions and countless others provide information about the candidates that allows voters to create what one communication theorist, Samuel L. Becker, has called a "mosaic model of communication," learning bits of information and then arranging those "bits" into a new or reinforced cognitive pattern.[12]

The third function of the primary period is that it involves many citizens in the democratic process. Involvement in the political process can take a number of different forms. For example, a person can engage in *overt political action* by participating in such activities as raising money for candidates, preparing placards, canvassing door to door for a party or for a candidate, attending a rally or a neighborhood coffee, distributing literature, licking envelopes, or voting. While there are, of course, many other activities possible for those engaging in overt political action, involvement can also be at the *social interaction level*. By this we mean simply that politics gives people a variety of topics or issues for discussion at work, parties, or anyplace where people interact with one another. Involvement may be no more than talking with a friend about whether or not a particular candidate believes in reinstating the draft or using nuclear power as a source of energy, but social interaction is one form of involvement in the political process. A third form of involvement is *parasocial interaction*. This is interaction not with other people but interaction with the messages provided by radio, television, newspapers, brochures, and so on. In other words, it is arguing or agreeing with a political ad when it comes on your television set or a candidate's speech that you read in his literature or in the evening newspaper. Finally, involvement can be a matter of *self-reflection*—examination of your ideas or perceptions on economic or social priorities in light of the position or platform of a given candidate.[13]

Although the other political stages of the campaign do encourage forms of overt political action, social or parasocial interaction, and self-reflection, it is increasingly becoming the primary period where involvement is most intense because the sheer number of candidates and the attention given to the primaries by the media demand it. In his book on the role of the mass media in the 1976 presidential campaign, Patterson argues that one of the changes in contemporary campaigns is that public interest now peaks more quickly. In the election of 1940, for example, interest in the campaign did not peak until the general election stage, whereas interest in the 1976 campaign rose sharply in the early primaries. Patterson also found that interest in the campaign decreased during the later primaries, and so the overall interest of voters was no greater than it had been in 1940; it just peaked earlier.[14]

In 1980 the public was once again interested in the primary stage of the presidential campaign, and once again, its interest peaked early and declined. The 1980 general election turnout (only 53.95 percent of the country's eligible voters cast ballots) was the lowest in 32 years, but the early primaries set voting records. In Iowa, for example, more than 200,000 people took part in the process of selecting a president. This figure was up from 61,000 in 1976 and more than double the previous high of 88,000 set in 1968, when a desire to protest the Vietnam War drew thousands of supporters of former Senator Eugene McCarthy to attend caucus meetings. In New Hampshire, some 261,000 people, or 52 percent of the state's registered voters, cast ballots. This too was a record turnout. In Massachusetts, nearly 1.3 million people voted, which was up from 950,000 in 1976, nearly double the number who voted in 1972, and triple the 1968 total. And when Vermont held its first primary in 60 years in 1976, about 72,000 people cast ballots. In 1980 the Vermont secretary of state's office reported that 101,405 people voted.

Why are citizens becoming involved in the primary stage of the campaign? Although there are no certain answers, participation has undoubtedly been strengthened for three important reasons. First, with the increased number of primaries, the public is growing more accustomed to them and the major changes they have contributed to the process of selecting a president over the last decade. People have discovered that presidential primaries are exciting, almost like a carnival, as 10 or 12 presidential hopefuls, each with family, large contingents of secret service, and hundreds of national media representatives, descend on a state for three or four weeks during the winter or spring every fourth year. Even states that had never had or rarely had presidential primaries joined the swelling list by 1980. Perhaps one reason for the excitement generated by the primaries is the direct personal contact with a potential president. Primary campaigning allows the candidate to meet individual voters. It is unlike the general election when the candidate is remote, isolated, and appears to be existing only for the national media. The primaries, like the surfacing stage, are a time for interpersonal communication as candidates and citizens interact at dozens of small group gatherings throughout an individual state.

A second reason for increased involvement may be that a larger number of presidential candidates are actively campaigning and spending extraordinary sums of money in the primary states. For example, in Iowa the major candidates in 1980 spent record amounts on television and radio advertising, with many media budgets running to six figures. Each commercial for a candidate was also an advertisement, in a sense, for the caucuses themselves. The increased publicity given the caucuses may have led a lot of Iowans to attend them out of curiosity. In Massachusetts, television spending in 1980 was even higher. Many commercials aimed at New Hampshire voters were aired on Boston television, and candidates had to pay for large audiences, often including more Massachusetts residents than New Hampshire citizens.

Another explanation for the high levels of involvement in the second stage of the campaign is media coverage. The national media have also discovered the glamor, the excitement, the "gamelike" stakes of the presidential primary. Accordingly, each of the television network's evening news programs devotes substantial amounts of time to covering the candidates in Iowa, New Hampshire, Florida, or wherever the primary or caucus happens to be that week. In addition to regular news features, the primaries are highlighted by special programs such as the Tuesday night telecasts of primary election returns and interview programs such as "Meet the Press." The media create "winners" and "losers" even though the "winner" may have won by only a few percentage points or maybe did not even win at all but did so much better than was expected or came so close to the "front runner" that he is declared by the television commentators to have "won" the election. As Patterson argues, the media treat primary elections much as they do the general election—there must be a winner. Each primary is only incidentally treated as part of a larger nominating system.

There is, however, a fourth and closely related function of the primary period. As candidates campaign, regardless of what level of office is sought, they often make promises about what they will do if elected. Some promise little, others promise everything from lower taxes to increased morality, but few actually deliver once they take office. We believe that one of the important communication functions of primary campaigning is related to these promises made by candidates during the heat of the campaign. As we have already observed, one characteristic of primary campaigns is that they are normally more personalized than the general election stage. That is, voters have more of an opportunity for direct interaction with candidates. Campaigning is personally oriented as candidates attend countless events at which the relatively small number of people present familiarize them with the problems important primarily to their specific neighborhood, city, or state. The voters try to elicit promises of help and assistance from the candidates if they are elected. Once the promise is given, we believe that there is more likelihood of promises being kept after the election because of the physical proximity in which they were articulated and the fact that they are given to a specific individual or small groups of individuals, not an amorphous large audience or an impersonal camera.

Finally, we suggest that there is a fifth function performed by the primary stage of the campaign. The voters have a chance to determine the "real" front runners or leading contenders for the nomination. Throughout the surfacing period, the media label candidates as "possible winner," or "dark horse," or "a favorite," or even "front runner." With the primary, voters have the opportunity to go over and above the media and actually select the nominees or at least give true meaning to the term "front runner." While we would not deny the influence the media have extended over the years in the self-fulfilling prophecy of their labels, there has still been a considerable number of instances when the voters, not the media, have determined the serious candidates. Consider the 1976 presidential campaign in which the media, overanxious perhaps because the surfacing period had been so long, had a whole string of candidates they labeled front runners at one time or another. The list included senators Henry Jackson and Birch Bayh but never the former governor of Georgia, Jimmy Carter. The voters from Iowa and New Hampshire determined that Jimmy Carter was a front runner. The 1980 campaign was pretty much the same as the media labeled candidates such as John Connally and Senator Howard Baker serious enough contenders to defeat front runner Ronald Reagan. As it worked out, of course, the only Republican candidate who ever defeated Reagan in a primary was George Bush. The media had not even considered Bush a serious candidate until the voters from Iowa determined his front runner status. The reverse, of course, was true in the case of Senator Edward Kennedy. Prior to the first vote, the media gave the impression that Kennedy had already defeated President Carter. The voters, however, in Iowa and New Hampshire believed that the president was the Democratic front runner and removed Kennedy from his preprimary position.

These then are the communication functions of the primary stage of the campaign. They are significant because the second stage is vital to our political system. The primary campaigns represent the people in that the process of determining who the candidates will be is taken from the hands of the political parties and the media and given to the voters. The communication functions are crucial to the process.

THIRD POLITICAL STAGE:
NOMINATING CONVENTIONS

Although a majority of citizens regularly tell pollsters that they would prefer some other method for nominating presidential candidates, the national party conventions remain as they have since their inception: the bodies that make official, presidential, and vice-presidential nominations for the Republican and Democratic parties.* However, just as the first two political stages of the modern campaign have changed, so has the third. Where instrumental or pragmatic communicative functions were once the primary reason for holding party conventions, now the symbolic or ritualistic functions are, in most instances, the chief purpose. In other words, the convention stage is an important and distinct period in the four-step process because of the symbolic functions it provides.

From the time that the anti-Masons held the first national nominating convention in Baltimore in 1832 until the Democratic convention in 1972, nominating conventions could be viewed as deliberate bodies—assemblies faced with difficult and important decisions to make in a few days. In addition to participating in the "required" political rituals of the day, delegates made decisions that often determined the success or failure of their political party during the coming election. In other words, the conventions served important pragmatic or instrumental functions in that the presidential and vice-presidential nominees were selected, the platforms were determined, and even the tone or "battle posture" for the general election campaigns were established. In short, the convention met to make party decisions. For many years, decisions were made and the conventions were controlled by bosses and special interests. Some of those conventions nominated candidates of top quality such as Abraham Lincoln and Woodrow Wilson, and other

---

*In many states and localities, parties also hold nominating conventions. However, since their structure, functions, and organization vary so much, it would serve little purpose to discuss them.

conventions tapped candidates of dubious quality such as Franklin Pierce and Warren Harding. Whatever the caliber of the candidates nominated or the platform written, it is important to remember that the nominating conventions actually made party decisions; in other words, they served instrumental functions.

However, beginning in 1952 and strengthened by action taken for the 1972 Democratic Convention, at least three significant changes have occurred, thus shifting the communicative functions of conventions from instrumental to symbolic. While they have been discussed earlier, their impact on the third stage of the campaign has been so enormous that they should be understood with regard to the nominating conventions.

The first change was the introduction of television to the campaign. Although television did not bring the sights and sounds of a presidential contest to millions of people until the 1952 campaign, nonprint media had been involved in the nominating conventions for many years. In 1912 movies and phonograph records captured Woodrow Wilson's acceptance speech; in 1924 the acceptance speech of presidential nominee John Davis was broadcast over a network of 15 radio stations; and by 1928 the influence of the medium was so pervasive that the time and date of Alfred Smith's acceptance speech were determined by the network of the 104 radio stations that were to broadcast the speech.[15] However, when television was first used during the 1952 primary campaigns, the public apparently became more interested in the election battle than it had been in the past. Turnout jumped from less than 5 million primary voters in 1948 to almost 13 million in 1952. The new medium brought a different dimension first to the primaries and then to the conventions by dramatizing suspense, conflict, and excitement, as well as projecting a visual image of the candidates that had never before been possible. Television gave the public a sense of involvement in the conventions, and as many delegates and reporters covering the convention soon discovered, the television viewer could see more and know more of what was going on than the persons could who were on the floor of the convention hall.[16]

During the 1952 campaign, there were 108 television stations on the air, and as one study of the election showed, the impact of the new medium was significant:

> The public went out of its way to watch the campaign on television. Only about 40 percent of the homes in the U.S. have television sets, but some 53 percent of the population saw TV programs on the campaign—a reflection of "television visiting." On the other hand, the campaign news and other material in newspapers, magazines and on the radio did not reach all of their respective audiences: more than 80 percent of the population take daily newspapers and have radios and more than 60 percent regularly read magazines, but in each case the number following the campaign in these media was smaller than the total audience. . . . In the nation as a whole, television, though available to only a minority of the people, led the other media in the number of persons who rated it most informative.[17]

As important as was television's influence in 1952, it can be seen as just a mere shadow of what it was to become in all stages of subsequent campaigns, including the nominating conventions. In fact, by 1976 when electorate interest in that year's presidential contest was studied, it was discovered that television coverage of the conventions boosted voter interest and attention to the campaign, especially among those who were not strong political partisans.[18] Perhaps in response to electorate interest, coverage of the 1980 conventions was increased to the point that media representatives outnumbered delegates by four and five to one at the Republican and Democratic conventions. As a matter of fact, according to the *New York Times*, the Democratic convention included 3,381 delegates and 11,500 reporters, editors, cameramen, and broadcasters. And although the public appeared as bored with the

1980 conventions as it had been interested in those of 1976 (network ratings showed a sharp drop in the number of people watching the 1980 conventions as compared with four years earlier), the presence of the networks has nonetheless had a profound effect on modern nominating conventions. One reason is that the presence of the networks has restructured convention programming so that the party's "important" events occur during "prime time." To make certain that this happens, the convention chair often ignores the activities of the delegates on the convention floor and rushes through any official party business to make certain that those events planned to give the party the most favorable image (for example, ecumenical prayers, civic greetings, performances by show business personalities, keynote and acceptance speeches, and controlled and planned "spontaneous" demonstrations for candidates) will be seen during the hours in which most people watch television. Whether this strategy fails (as, for example, it did in 1972 when George McGovern's acceptance speech began hours after most people had gone to bed or in 1980 when Congressman Morris Udall's keynote address started as the delegates were leaving Madison Square Garden for the night) or is successful, the convention proceedings become ritual with little or no pragmatic value.

Another effect of the presence of the networks has been that convention participants have become almost more aware of media presence, particularly television cameras, than of convention business and thus alter their behavior and interaction. As one critic of the 1980 Democratic Convention wrote:

> The omni-present camera eye contributed to the funny hat, placard, banner and button syndromes. . . . At times, the television camera introduced an almost schizophrenic atmosphere as speakers addressed themselves to an unlistening, often chaotic arena audience, while really hoping that their individual performance would coincide with network coverage.[19]

The last and undoubtedly most significant effect of the networks has been that television covers only those events it decides are important, thereby altering the shape, structure, and activities of the convention. There were times during the 1980 conventions for example, when the networks conducted interviews with relatives of the candidates while prominent convention participants were debating platform positions. In fact, there was so much "gatekeeping" by the networks covering the Democratic Convention that one scholar estimated that television viewers saw less than half of the proceedings during those times when the networks were on the air. CBS, for example, made decisions about what to show or not to show viewers based on whether Walter Cronkite judged the event to be very exciting. A film shown to convention delegates regarding the construction of the party platform was not shown to the television audience by any of the networks. CBS covered the last few minutes of a speech by Senator Patrick Moynihan, but ABC decided not to cover it at all. Thus we believe communication analyst Gary Gumpert was correct when he wrote that television has helped to render the nominating conventions little more than "a series of arranged and controlled visual and auditory images."[20]

The second factor that has had a profound influence in changing the nature of the third political stage has been the reliance on primaries as the vehicle for selecting delegates to the national party conventions. As we discussed in the first chapter, the proliferation of primaries has contributed to the decline of the political parties, but now we want to emphasize that it has also changed the role of the national nominating convention from decision maker to "legitimizer." Perhaps this statement is explained best by taking a brief glance at the history of the presidential primary.

The presidential primary is a "uniquely American institution born, after decades of agitation, in the early twentieth century."[21] In the post–Civil War era, the party organizations in many states and cities came under the control of often corrupt political machines dominated or allied with public utilities, railroads, and others who manipulated the convention system to suit their ends. In an effort to reform the system, the Populists and later the Progressives advocated the substitution of direct primary elections for party-nominating conventions. By 1917 all but four states had adopted the direct primary method of nomination for some or all offices filled by statewide election. However, the extension of primary elections from the local, state, and congressional levels to presidential politics was much more difficult.

In 1904 Florida held the first primary election for the choice of delegates to a national party convention, and by 1916 presidential primaries were held in 22 states amid speculation that within a few years the national convention would be only an ornament for making official those decisions already arrived at by the electorate. Calculations such as these, however, were a few years premature because two decades after the first presidential primary had taken place, the movement came to a halt with the number of states stabilized at around 15. Turnout remained low, and there was little popular interest in them until the 1952 campaign when the entrance of television into the primary elections renewed voter enthusiasm and then again in 1956 when Senator Estes Kefauver became the first candidate to use the New Hampshire primary as a way to call attention to his campaign. Although the outcomes did not determine the parties' ultimate choices, they generated more interest than they had at anytime since 1912.

Twenty years later, in 1972, a major incentive for the adoption of presidential primaries was provided when the Democratic Party's Commission on Party Structure and Delegate Selection to the Democratic National Committee, popularly known as the McGovern-Fraser Commission, sought to stop some of the injustices apparent to many liberals at the 1968 convention. The commission prepared 18 guidelines intended to insure that the state Democratic parties' procedures for selecting delegates to the 1972 convention were open, fair, and timely. At least two other commissions followed McGovern-Fraser in the intervening years, and the guidelines have become so complex (to make certain that there is enough representation of minorities and women) that the state parties have found that they can best comply with them, and not disturb traditional ways of conducting other party business, by adopting a presidential primary law. Thus the number of presidential primaries has proliferated. As primaries grew, so did the number of delegates pledged to a specific candidate, and since 1972 everyone has known before the conventions begin who the candidates will be (except in 1976 at the Republican Convention when Ford and Reagan fought down to the wire). The conventions no longer determine the candidates. Voters in those states holding presidential primaries have decided who will be nominated. The convention meets to legitimize the earlier selection.

The third factor that has influenced the changing nature of the convention stage has been the emergence of the campaign specialists who, with the consent of the candidates for whom they work, determine important aspects of the convention that were once the domain of delegates and party leaders. The consultants have planned the candidate's strategies through the first two stages for the precise purpose of winning the nomination. With the nomination secured before the convention even begins, the specialists now turn to "putting on the best show" possible for the television-viewing audience. The party platform is negotiated in advance of the convention, with the staff of the candidate certain to be the nominee controlling the deliberations. If a spirited debate concerning a specific issue would enhance the "television show" or if, in the spirit of compromise, it becomes important to give the losing candidate and his supporters the chance to "air" a minority position, portions of the party's platform will be discussed during the convention itself. However, even when this has happened, as in the case of the "debate" on the MX missile at the 1980 Democratic Convention, the vast majority of the delegates paid no attention to the debaters. In fact, as one communication analyst who attended the convention noted:

Signs against the MX popped up and down in the Garden: "X-rated Missiles Aren't Sexy," "NIX the MX," "MX-Missile Madness," "No MX—Nobody Wins World War III," "MX Says Have a Nice Doomsday," "Mighty Expensive," "MX Makes US the Target." Delegates wandered around talking to friends. There were many empty seats. The clear impression was of a ceremonial occasion rather than a deliberative one. . . . The debates served the symbolic function, though, of letting off steam for those who really did care.[22]

In other words, all real decisions regarding the convention are made by the candidate, based on the advice of consultants. The candidate, not the party leaders, determines the platform, the issues to be debated, the songs to be played, the identity of those who will speak from the podium during prime time, the name of the keynote speaker or speakers, and the content and length of the "spontaneous" demonstration. As one delegate to the 1980 Democratic Convention said, "We've turned over absolute control of the nominating process to the presidential candidates, and worse, to their staffs."[23]

Thus, because of the influence generated by television coverage, presidential primaries, and campaign specialists, the overall function of the national nominating convention to the campaign has been altered. Gone is the once powerful role of decision maker. In its place is a new function, no less important in a sense, but quite different in its style. The primary significance of the modern nominating convention is symbolic—ritualistic—and as such, it serves four important communication functions.

The first function, and one of the most significant, is that convention rituals provide an opportunity for the legitimation and reaffirmation of the "rightness" of the American way or dream. The various communication acts and symbols of conventions (keynote speeches, nomination speeches, debates, demonstrations, state-by-state roll call balloting, official "greetings" from past party heroes, patriotic music, buttons, hats, placards, as well as nomination acceptance speeches) serve to renew our faith that U.S. citizens share not only a glorious tradition but a grand and proud future. In a sense, each convention can be viewed as a huge political rally where the candidate shares the spotlight with the democratic system that made his success possible. When, for example, the presidential and vice-presidential nominees make their triumphant entrance to the speaker's platform the last night of the convention, their appearance reinforces the belief that citizens are bound together in a noble tradition. There have been instances when nominees have acknowledged the reciprocity of the relationship during the nomination acceptance speech. For example, in 1960 Richard Nixon said: "I can only say tonight that I believe in the American Dream because I have seen it come true in my own life." As one writer has pointed out, eight years later, Nixon expanded his autobiographical account in his 1968 acceptance speech when he recalled how as a child he had listened to the nighttime passing of trains and dreamed of faraway places. He reminisced that he had risen in the world, helped by his self-sacrificing father, his Quaker mother, a teacher, a football coach, a minister, and a loyal wife. Finally Nixon, referring to himself, said: "And tonight he stands before you, nominated for President of the United States of America. You can see why I believe so deeply in the American dream."[24]

Certainly, conventions function to legitimize the selection of the candidates, the platform, and the unity of the party and its leaders. But in the largest sense, the communication rituals celebrate what is good about our system and thus ourselves. Convention sessions, for example, open and close with prayers (we are a spiritual and Godly people). During the convention, former heroes are acknowledged (we have a sense of our roots), and countless speakers evoke selected elements of the "American Dream" (we believe that the United States is destined to become a mighty empire of liberty where everyone can share in the prosperity of society). On the final night, the selected candidates articulate their visions of a grand and more noble country (we value the traditions of reform and progress), while national songs provide periodic emotional climaxes (we have pride in and deep-seated feelings about our country).[25] The convention rituals are, in short, a kind of emotional/spiritual/ patriotic catharsis in which we can, if necessary, lament current shortcomings within the party or the country while remaining proud of and faithful to our legacy.

In writing about conventions as legitimation rituals, one communication scholar found that typically the ritual has three steps: it begins with a statement and demonstration of theme (traditionally the responsibility of keynote speakers); progresses to a clustering or gathering of stereotypical character types who are given convention time for speeches or "greetings" to the delegates (the hero or heroine, the also-rans or those who fought the good fight but lost in a noble cause and are now vindicated through history, and leaders representing the right and left and all divergent interest groups within the party); and culminates in the anointing of the nominee who symbolizes and enacts the convention's theme. However, not only are there identifiable steps or phases in the convention ritual, a variety of ritualistic forms are possible. For example, the 1976 Democratic Convention explored the theme of conflict—the "dramatic tensions and release generated by an uncertain contest for leadership roles."[26]

Not only do the communicative acts of the convention serve to reaffirm our general commitment to the electoral process, there is a second and closely related function. The convention provides legitimation for the party's nominees. When the struggle for nomination is long and intense (as it has been for presidential nominees since 1972) or when the selection has gone to a relative newcomer (as it did when the Democrats nominated Jimmy Carter in 1976), the ritual of the convention confirms or legitimizes the candidate as the party's nominee as a possible governor, senator, or even president of the United States. A person may have won primary after primary, but not until the convention delegates affirm selection through their votes at the convention can the candidate be-

POLITICAL CAMPAIGN COMMUNICATION

come the nominee. With the act of confirmation comes added prestige and respect. The person is no longer just a candidate, but the nominee of a political party.

The third function provided by the convention stage is that the party has a chance to show its unity. Whether the cohesion is more apparent than real, the convention is the time when wounds from the primary campaigns can be addressed and healed. Perhaps the importance of a unified party to the success of the approaching campaign can be understood by examining instances when the convention ritual has failed to produce cohesiveness. In 1964 the Republican Convention that nominated Barry Goldwater appeared to repudiate Republicans whose political philosophies were more liberal than those of the conservatives who dominated the convention. The governor of New York, Nelson Rockefeller, who had been a contender for the nomination, was booed and not given the opportunity to finish a speech. When Goldwater concluded his nomination acceptance speech with an endorsement of extremism, many liberals walked out of the convention. The Republican party remained divided throughout the campaign, and Goldwater lost the election by one of the largest margins in the history of presidential politics. Similarly, in 1968 and again in 1972, the Democratic National Convention failed to unify and come together to support either Hubert Humphrey or George McGovern. Humphrey was tormented throughout the 1968 general election campaign by those in the Democratic party who felt his nomination was a betrayal of party principle and a disfranchisement for liberals. McGovern, on the other hand, was never able to unify the traditional or "old-line" party leaders with his more youthful and/or liberal insurgents. In each case, the Democrats remained divided throughout the convention and general election campaign and lost in November.

Thus, even when tension below the surface is strained, the political parties strive for the appearance of unity during their conventions. At the 1976 Democratic Convention, for example, one communication analyst recalled that following Jimmy Carter's acceptance speech, party chairman Robert Strauss gathered all the party's candidates and factions on the speaker's platform as Martin Luther King, Sr. delivered the benediction to the convention:

> King stunned the noisy delegates and galleries into silence, asking that they "cease walking, talking" and that "not a word be uttered unless that word is to God." In a rousing sermon that brought forth shouts of "Amen" from the audience, the father of Martin Luther King, Jr. cried: "Surely the Lord sent Jimmy Carter to come out and bring America back where she belongs. . . . As I close in prayer, let me tell you we must close ranks now. If there is any misunderstanding anywhere, if you haven't got a forgiving heart, get down on your knees. It is time for prayer." As Daddy King concluded, the delegates joined hands, linked arms, and slowly began to sing "We Shall Overcome Someday." The television cameras focused on the faces of the delegates, who wept and swayed as they achieved a cathartic moment of emotional release and affirmation.[27]

In a similar though less emotional manner, the Republicans in 1976 and the Democrats in 1980 attempted to evoke images of unity in the closing moments of their conventions. Although the 1976 Republican Convention began with conflict as Gerald Ford and Ronald Reagan battled for the nomination, the victorious Ford called on a surprised Reagan to join him at the speaker's podium after he had delivered his acceptance speech. And in 1980 Carter supporters spent much of the convention trying to ensure that the defeated Edward Kennedy would join the president and other party faithfuls on the dais following Carter's address. In each instance, intraparty tensions were not erased because all factions of the party appeared together at the podium. However, the symbolic act of party leaders closing ranks around their nominees preserved the image of unity.

The fourth communication function served by nominating conventions is that they provide the public introduction of the candidate's rhetorical agenda for the general election campaign. Whether Republican or Democrat, the acceptance speeches of the nominees have frequently signaled the issues on which they plan to campaign (typically through the introduction of a specific slogan) and/or have announced an overall campaign style/plan they intend to follow (sometimes accomplished via a direct challenge to the opposition).

Franklin Roosevelt initiated the process of the nominee speaking to the delegates in person when in 1932 he flew to the Democratic Convention in Chicago. During his acceptance speech, he introduced the phrase the "New Deal," which became the slogan for his campaign and subsequent administration. In 1948 Harry Truman not only announced that the central issue in his campaign would be the "do-nothing Congress," but he also explained that he was going to keep Congress in session during the summer to try and get some legislation from them. In 1960 Richard Nixon announced his intention to take the campaign to all 50 states, while John Kennedy introduced the "New Frontier" as the slogan/theme for those issues important to his campaign. Finally, in 1976 while accepting the Republican nomination, President Gerald Ford announced his intention to debate, virtually challenging his opponent to a face-to-face confrontation when he said: "This year the issues are on our side. I'm ready—I'm eager to go before the American People and debate the real issues face-to-face with Jimmy Carter."[28]

These, then, are the communication functions served by the third political stage of the campaign. As we have pointed out throughout our discussion of this stage, because the nominating convention serves only ritualistic functions, it is no less critical to the overall campaign than are the other stages. In fact, as we suggested earlier, a campaign that fails to get the most out of the ritual demanded during the nominating convention will proceed to the fourth stage with a potentially fatal handicap.

FOURTH POLITICAL STAGE:
THE GENERAL ELECTION

"Electing time"[29] means speeches, parades, debates, bumper stickers, media commercials, bandplaying, doorbell ringing, posters, billboards, polling, and direct mail fund raising. As we have discussed throughout this chapter, these acts and symbols are no longer reserved exclusively for the last stage, although they remain a significant and expected part. It is almost as if all has been in readiness—a type of dress rehearsal for this final and most important scene. Certainly, candidates may have been appearing and speaking at all manner of gatherings for many months. Thirty- and sixty-second television spots may have been interfering with television viewing since the primaries. Citizens may have even voted for their candidate in a primary or watched a part of one of the conventions on television. However, once the final stage begins, the campaign communication is at once more intense, less interpersonal but more direct, and certainly more important because the candidate who emerges will be the new mayor, governor, legislator, or president. It is precisely because of the importance of the general election stage that we must discuss briefly three communicative functions, which although not unique to it, are nonetheless reflective of it.

The first function is cognitive. The electorate voluntarily seeks or involuntarily learns of information about some feature of the election and/or the candidates. News regarding the campaign is so widespread during the fourth stage that additional or restructured information may be gained from something as simple as talking with a friend, watching the evening news, or reading a newspaper or magazine. Because so much information permeates the environment during the general election, the majority of the electorate possess at least minimal knowledge about the election.

In recent years, people have been acquiring political knowledge from yet another source, the public opinion polls of the media. While syndicated polls during election years have

61

POLITICAL CAMPAIGN COMMUNICATION

been a regular feature of the press since the inception of modern public opinion polling in 1936, by the 1970s news organizations began to serve as their own polling agencies. News-gatherine organizations were not simply printing or broadcasting the findings of others, they were creating news on their own initiative with their own polls—often extending opinion soundings down to the local level. The impact of this development is reflected in the results of a 1979 study by the National Research Council, which showed that in two parallel surveys conducted during the heat of the 1976 campaign, only 16 percent of those interviewed failed to recall hearing something "in the news or in talking with friends" about "polls showing how candidates for office are doing."[30] By the time of the general election stage of the 1980 campaign, virtually every major news organization was conducting some poll each week, thus providing a constant stream of information regarding the election. Perhaps the most dramatic evidence of the importance of polls as a source of information was the continued candidacy of John Anderson during the fourth stage of the 1980 presidential campaign. As one writer suggested:

> The primaries produced two presidential candidates, whose victories were ultimately certified by party conventions. They were joined by a maverick independent whose candidacy was buoyed up by the uncertainty or disappointment felt by an appreciable segment of voters over the choices confronting them. Rep. John Anderson, it was claimed during the primaries, was a serious candidate because he had demonstrated significant appeal to voters. But how had he done so? Not by his unimpressive vote totals in the few Republican primaries that he entered. Rather, it was the polls that initially documented his appeal to the satisfaction of leading media political correspondents, who confirmed his status in their reporting. And it was also the polls that were chosen by the League of Women Voters to play a prime gatekeeping role in deciding that he could appear in the fall TV debates. Thus, unlike other "serious" independent candidates for the presidency in this century,

who had established their claims by prior vote-getting, in 1980 an independent had his candidacy assessed as significant primarily by the results of opinion polls generated by or channeled through the mass media and widely accepted as accurate by strategic elements of the political system.[31]

Not only do communicative acts serve as cognitions during the general election stage of the campaign, there is a second function. The general election assigns legitimacy, the idea that the campaign process itself provides further proof that the system works.

In discussing the ritualistic functions of the nominating conventions, we discovered the importance of legitimation in affirming the candidate as the party's choice and the electoral system as superior. Legitimation is also an important function of the general election. As people stand in line to greet a candidate, put up posters for "their" candidate for city council, attend a rally, watch the presidential candidates debate, discuss with a friend the merits of one of the mayoral candidates, vote, or engage in any of the participatory activities typical of the final stage of the campaign, they symbolically reinforce the values for which the activities stand.[32] Thus campaigning becomes a self-justifying activity that perpetuates two primal U.S. myths, according to Bruce Gronbeck:

Acquiescence—providing a paradigmatic, "fail-safe" rationale for choosing leaders and fostering programs with particularly "American" bents, making it difficult for anyone to object to the process (for if you do, the system's ideological web reaches out, telling you to seek the desired change by participating—running for office, pressuring the parties, voicing your opinions in public forums); and, Quiescence—reasserting the values associated with campaigning and its outcomes (free-and-open decision-making, public accountability, habitual and even mandatory modes of campaigning, the two-party system), in order to remind a citizenry that it is "happy" and "content" with its electoral

63

system; emphasizing the mores and ceremonial rituals associated with elections which make the country "devil-proof," invincible to attacks from within or without.[33]

Finally, the fourth stage of the political campaign contributes to fulfilling our expectations regarding campaign rituals. We expect candidates to address themselves to society's problems; we expect debates, rallies, door-to-door volunteers, bumper stickers, buttons, continuous election specials and advertisements over radio and television, polls, and all manner of drama, excitement, and even pageantry. In other words, we have any number of expectations regarding political campaigns. While the previous stages also function to fulfill our "demands," the directness, intensity, and finality of the fourth stage emphasize our pleasure or displeasure with the way in which a particular election has or has not met our pragmatic or ritualistic expectations. If during the general election stage the candidates fail to address those issues of paramount importance to us, fail to debate each other, or even fail to provide for us any of the excitement or drama we normally expect, we may feel cheated. It is, in short, the climax of a political season—a time for decision and participation. It is electing time.

CONCLUSIONS

With the changes in election campaigns in recent years, there have been countless proposals to modify or alter each of the four political stages. While many of the suggestions might well prove beneficial, we hope that you can now better appreciate that our system is far from purposeless. The various verbal and nonverbal acts of communication provide a full range of instrumental and consummatory functions for the candidate and the electorate in each political stage. While some of the functions are perhaps more significant than others, taken together, they are justification enough for the routines and rituals that in this country comprise the political election campaign.

NOTES

1. Bruce E. Gronbeck, "The Functions of Presidential Campaigning," *Communication Monographs* 45 (November 1978): 268–80.

2. Donald R. Matthews, "Winnowing: The New Media and the 1976 Presidential Nominations," in *Race for the Presidency*, ed. James David Barber (Englewood Cliffs, N.J.: Prentice-Hall, 1978), pp. 55–78.

3. Judith S. Trent, "Presidential Surfacing: The Ritualistic And Crucial First Act," *Communication Monographs* 45 (November 1978): 282.

4. The commentary is taken from an unpublished 1979 survey of all women officeholders in Ohio. Partial results of the survey were presented by Judith S. Trent at the 1979 convention in St. Louis of the Central States Speech Association.

5. This statement is attributed to a Conoco distributor from McAllen, Texas, who heard Connally speak in Dallas. See Tony Fuller, "Connally's Bitter End," *Newsweek*, March 24, 1980, p. 37.

6. Murray Edelman, *The Symbolic Uses of Politics* (Urbana: University of Illinois Press, 1964).

7. Gronbeck, "Presidential Campaigning," p. 271.

8. F. Christopher Arterton, "The Media Politics of Presidential Campaigns: A Study of the Carter Nomination Drive," in *Race for the Presidency*, ed. James David Barber (Englewood Cliffs, N.J.: Prentice-Hall, 1978), p. 26.

9. William R. Keech and Donald R. Matthews, *The Party's Choice* (Washington, D.C.: Brookings Institution, 1976), p. 91.

10. Adam Clymer, "Reagan's Fortunes in Iowa Caucuses Appear to Hang on His Organization," *New York Times*, January 13, 1980, p. A13.

11. In studying the effects of the media on the 1976 presidential campaign, Patterson found that even in the final stages of the campaign intense partisanship and overtly partisan media communication did not override early impressions. In fact, in 80 percent of the cases analyzed by Patterson, he found that any single impression of a candidate held during the general election was related more closely to earlier impressions of the candidate than to partisanship. Those people who thought favorably of a candidate's background, personality, leadership, or positions before the conventions also thought favorably about the candidate in these areas after the conventions, regardless of partisan leanings. See Thomas E. Patterson, *The Mass Media Election* (New York: Praeger, 1980), pp. 133–52.

12. Samuel L. Becker, "Rhetorical Studies for the Contemporary World," in *The Prospect of Rhetoric: Report of the National Developmental Project*, eds. Lloyd F. Bitzer and Edwin Black (Englewood Cliffs, N.J.: Prentice-Hall, 1971), pp. 21–43.

13. Bruce Gronbeck talks about five classes of consummatory effects in "The Functions of Presidential Campaigning," p. 272. See also Jay G. Blumer

and Elihu Katz, eds., *The Uses of Mass Communication* (Beverly Hills: Sage, 1974). For further discussion of the uses and gratifications perspective, see Jay G. Blumler, "The Role of Theory In Uses And Gratifications Studies," *Communication Research* 6 (January 1979): 9–36.

14. Patterson, *Mass Media Election*, pp. 67–75.

15. David B. Valley, "Significant Characteristics Of Democratic Presidential Nomination Acceptance Speeches," *Central States Speech Journal* 25 (Spring 1974): 56–62.

16. Samuel L. Becker and Elmer W. Lower, "Broadcasting in Presidential Campaigns," in *The Great Debates*, ed. Sidney Kraus (Bloomington: Indiana University Press, 1962), pp. 25–55.

17. Ibid., p. 45

18. Patterson, *Mass Media Election*, pp. 71–75.

19. Gary Gumpert, "The Critic In Search Of A Convention Or Diogenes In Madison Square Garden," *Exetasis* 6 (October 1980): 5.

20. Ibid.

21. Keech and Matthews, *Party's Choice*, p. 92.

22. Kathleen Edgerton Kendall, "Fission And Fusion: Primaries And The Convention," paper presented at the Central States Speech Association, Chicago, 1981.

23. "Changing Times May Make Old-Style Conventions Obsolete," *Cincinnati Enquirer*, August 14, 1980, p. C3.

24. Kurt W. Ritter, "American Political Rhetoric and the Jeremiad Tradition: Presidential Nomination Acceptance Addresses, 1960–1976," *Central States Speech Journal* 31 (Fall 1980): 153–71.

25. Ibid., esp. pp. 165–70.

26. Thomas B. Farrell, "Political Conventions as Legitimation Ritual," *Communication Monographs* 45 (November 1978): 293–305.

27. Ritter, "American Political Rhetoric," p. 170.

28. When Gerald Ford issued his challenge to Carter, he was trailing badly in the polls and needed something to give a boost to his campaign. As Bitzer and Rueter point out, Ford chose a prime moment at the convention to announce his intention to debate. In his speech accepting the nomination, Ford was aggressive and confident and when he challenged Carter to a debate, the convention audience gave sustained applause. See Lloyd Bitzer and Theodore Rueter, *Carter vs. Ford: The Counterfeit Debates of 1976* (Madison: University of Wisconsin Press, 1980).

29. This phrase is borrowed from Edwin Black, "Electing Time," *Quarterly Journal of Speech* 58 (April 1973): 125–29.

30. Albert E. Gollin, "Exploring the Liaison between Polling and the Press," *Public Opinion Quarterly* 44 (Winter 1980): 451.

31. Ibid., 445–46.

32. Gronbeck, "Presidential Campaigning," p. 272.

33. Ibid., p. 273.

3

Communicative Styles and Strategies of Political Campaigns

O NE OF THE CENTRAL IMPERATIVES OF PO-
LITICAL CAMPAIGN COMMUNICATION IS
THE WHOLE NOTION OF THE MANNER IN
WHICH INCUMBENTS SEEK REELECTION
and their challengers seek to replace them, in other words, the
style and strategies used by candidates as they campaign.
Campaign styles have undergone significant changes over the
years. There have been, for example, elections when candidates campaigned by staying home and saying nothing. There
have been others when the contenders "swung around the circle" on anything from trains to jets to river boats in an effort to
draw attention to themselves and to be seen and heard by as
many voters as possible. And we can each recall instances of
campaigns that have been waged primarily by means of the
mass media. In short, there has been no one way in which local,
state, or national contenders have gone about the task of getting our vote. Strategies have been as varied and sometimes
outrageous as those who have used them. Perhaps because of
this there has been relatively little systematic investigation or
analysis of the communicative strategies and styles that have

69

been, and continue to be, used by all manner of incumbents and challengers.

Thus the subject of this chapter is the exploration of campaign styles. While it may be that readers are more interested in contemporary examples, the present is better understood when viewed from the perspective of the past. For this reason, examples from nineteenth and early twentieth century campaigns have been incorporated, thereby providing a more complete catalogue of the communication strategies important to all who have sought and those who will seek elective office.

In addition, there will be a brief section devoted to an examination of the campaign styles of women. While there is, of course, some overlap between those strategies employed by political men and women, there are enough differences so that the manner in which women campaign merits specific analysis.

Finally, understanding of the material in this chapter will be enhanced by an examination of three preliminary considerations that are important to the way in which candidates campaign. A consideration of the term "style" is first. Second is a discussion of political image and its role in developing campaign styles. Third is an exploration of the relationship of technological advancements and styles of campaigning.

PRELIMINARY CONSIDERATIONS

Style

For many years, style has been studied by scholars who are interested in the customs and rules governing the use of language, including the choice of words (figures of speech) and the way the words are arranged (syntactical patterns) in oral and written communication. Although controversy over its meaning occurred historically because some believed style was divorced from content and only a frill or ornamentation,* the conception of style as the particular manner in which people express themselves by means of language has been generally accepted. In other words, style traditionally has been the province of those concerned with the correctness, beauty, or even workability of language—the investigation or analysis of the words and arrangements a speaker or writer chooses in preparing a message. Thus one of the elements to be considered in the analysis of campaign style is the language that political candidates use as they campaign.

More recently, however, communication theorists have argued that style should not be limited to the study of language but ought to be considered a quality pervading all elements of an individual's communication. Considered in this way, style would include each of the nonverbal aspects of communication, including physical behavior, sound of the voice, body shape and movement, appearance, clothing, and choice of settings, that operate as symbols to create the meanings we infer from the transaction.† Thus, in election campaigns, style can be seen as a blend of what candidates say in speeches, news conferences, interviews, advertisements, brochures, and so on, as well as their nonverbal political acts or behavior, such as kissing babies, wearing funny hats, shaking hands at rallies, waving at crowds from the motorcade, as well as their facial expressions and gestures while answering a question. It is

---

*Roman and medieval writers used the word *elocutio* for style, which we associate with eloquence or elocution (aspects of delivery). In this sense, the classical teachers of rhetoric and their orators became concerned with "levels" of style ("grand," "middle," and "plain") and how they could be maneuvered with very little regard for the ideas contained in their utterances.

†In written messages, a number of symbols (in addition to language) create meaning, such as the quality, texture, size, and color of the paper and whether it is handwritten or typed for one particular person or printed and prepared for distribution to many.

71

what Bruce Gronbeck terms a question of "leadership style"—a combination of habitual modes of thought and action upon which individuals perceive or judge a candidate.[1]

What does any of this have to do with our analysis of campaign styles and strategies? In this chapter, style is a manner of campaigning that can be recognized by the characteristics defining it and giving it form. We have termed these characteristics "communication strategies" and the styles "incumbency" and "challenger." Certainly, in describing each of the styles we have been concerned with the traditional dimension of language; but as you have seen in the first two chapters, we believe strongly that political campaign communication is much more than just "talk." Thus as the styles are explored, it will become obvious that many of the characteristics deal with nonverbal political behaviors as well as verbal.

Image and Campaign Style

Imagery plays an important role in the consideration of style. All candidates, whether they campaign using the strategies of incumbency or those of the challenger, must do and say whatever it is that will enhance voter perception of them. They are concerned, in other words, about their image.

Although widespread awareness regarding the significance of image creation to the political campaign did not occur until the early 1970s,* it had been used for years. The first major image campaign took place in the presidential campaign of 1840 when the Whigs, after searching for a candidate they thought could defeat Martin Van Buren, found no one. So they invented a national hero, gave him a slogan, said he was a

---

*The so-called new politics (a blend of computer technology, Madison Avenue marketing and advertising skills, and a heavy reliance on television) was pushed into popular consciousness with the publication of such books as *The Selling of the President 1968* and *The Political Image Merchants: Strategies for the Seventies.*

champion of the ordinary citizen as well as a giant of the frontier, and elected a president.[2]

When William Henry Harrison was "discovered" by the Whigs, he was 67 years old, a long retired army officer, and had spent four uneventful years as a senator from Ohio. While military and legislative experience must be considered reasonable credentials for a presidential challenger, Harrison's career had been distinctly undistinguished. The Whigs, however, billed Harrison as a legendary Indian fighter and maintained that he was known widely and fondly as "Old Tippecanoe." The fact that Harrison's "glories" on the battlefield had been limited to one day, 30 years earlier, when he had repulsed a Shawnee attack on a place in the Wabash River called Tippecanoe, did not stop his campaign managers from creating the image of a military hero. The Whig campaign ignored all issues, except those relating to the personality of their candidates, and gave image creation and "hype" a permanent place in presidential politics. When Democrats suggested that the aging Harrison might be content to spend his declining days in a log cabin "studying moral philosophy"—provided he had a barrel of hard cider at his side—the Whigs cleverly turned the attack into a reinforcement of Harrison's contrived image as a "common man."[3] From then on, every Whig rally sported cider barrels and miniature log cabins, and songs were written and sung celebrating Harrison's humble tastes (the idea being that if logs and liquor were good enough for the people, they were also good enough for the president). Lyrics from one of the campaign songs best describe the image created by the Whigs:

No ruffled shirt, no silken hose,
No airs does Tip display;
But like the 'pith of worth' he goes
In homespun 'hodding gray.'
Let Van from his coolers of silver drink wine
And lounge on his cushioned setee,
Our man on a buckeye bench can recline
Content with hard cider is he![4]

Image campaigns did not end with the elevation of "Old Tippecanoe" to the presidency. Instead, the place of imagery became entrenched in elective politics, especially in the area of campaign style where specific strategies must be created and utilized to keep alive the perception of an incumbent or a challenger. The importance of imagery is evidenced each time we see yet another television commercial of a candidate surrounded by family, talking earnestly with a senior citizen, or walking through a peanut field. Whether or not the candidate really does have a loving and supportive family or knows and cares about the problems of individual older people is, at least in this regard, immaterial. What is important is the image projected—the attributes the public believes to exist. As Kenneth E. Boulding wrote in his classic book, *The Image*, each of us possesses a store of subjective knowledge about the world, a collection of ideas we believe to be true. This knowledge constitutes our image.[5]

Thus candidate images consist of all of the subjective impressions voters have. The impressions can be of any type; that is, they can be thoughts about a candidate's issue positions, political philosophy, family or background, personality and leadership, or even campaign style.[6] Moreover, scholars have found that these impressions are then compared in the voter's mind not only to those of competing candidates but to the overall vision of an "ideal" candidate. In other words, for any election, voters acquire a mental picture of an ideal candidate and use it as a gauge in evaluating the acceptability of the actual candidate.[7] Voters might ask themselves if the candidate campaigns as an incumbent should or if the challenger fulfills expectations. Viewed from this perspective, the reason for two common campaign activities becomes clear. First, one of the most crucial tasks facing candidates, especially during the surfacing stage, is to determine just what attributes voters believe are ideal for the office sought. Second, campaign activities in later stages are designed to attempt to illustrate that the candidate possess these qualities.

Although for many years scholars have consistently found that public perceptions of a candidate's image act as a significant factor in voting behavior[8] (far more important, for example, than party identification), we are not yet able to delineate precisely what qualities constitute the ideal candidate in the public mind. One reason for this failure is that voters' priorities can change from election to election. For example, experience in federal government and national politics was traditionally considered an important quality for a presidential candidate to possess. Yet, in 1976 in the wake of the Watergate scandals, being perceived as an experienced politician, one who knew the "ins" and "outs" of Washington, was a distinct disadvantage. Similarly, while truthfulness and morality have long been viewed as desirable qualities for any candidate, a legislator who was awaiting trial for his participation in Abscam was reelected. In short, public standards regarding ideal characteristics change. While it may be premature to project those attributes that will determine "idealness" throughout the remainder of the 1980s, one national study has already revealed that religious belief is a more powerful factor in U.S. life than whether someone is liberal or conservative, male or female, or young or old, and that honesty is the most important quality a national leader can possess.[9] Now, if these results are accurate, does it mean that candidates who wish to be perceived as ideal during the remainder of this decade will have to convince voters of their religious fervor, professional integrity, personal honesty, and circumspect private lives? Will they be forced to prove they possess these qualities more than candidates have had to do in the past?

Whatever the years will ultimately bring in terms of public standards for ideal candidates, the identification of attributes is, for now, somewhat unclear. Certainly, much of the literature in the field of political communication has indicated the existence of three overall dimensions or major determinants of a voter's image of the ideal candidate. These dimensions, called source valence criteria, are composed of approximately three equal determinants. The first is credibility, in such qualities as high ability, good character, and energy. The second is interpersonal attraction, which can be thought of as a candidate's social and physical attractiveness, and the third is homophyly, the similarities in personality, social class, educational background, or beliefs voters believe they share with the candidate.[10] However, there has been some fairly persuasive evidence to suggest that these dimensions may, in fact, be overemphasized as they relate to the total image of a political candidate simply because it is difficult to make distinctions among them.[11] It has also been argued that the credibility dimension is far more important to the voter than is any perceived similarity with the candidate.[12] Obviously, further research is needed before we can say with any degree of certainty what qualities an ideal candidate must possess. One thing though is clear. The creation and maintenance of image, long a part of political campaigns, plays a dominant role because voters have a whole series of impressions regarding those who seek elective office that they compare with a personal vision of an ideal candidate. And although other factors are important to the consideration of campaign style, it may well be that the extent to which a candidate is able to live up to these idealized conceptions is the extent to which success can be achieved on election day.

Technology and Campaign Style

During the earliest period of our electoral system, the style of political campaigning was, at least in part, defined by the limits of our transportation system. This is one of the reasons that there were no national political campaigns as we think of them today. While it is true that in 1789 and again in 1792 George Washington had no opposition, it would have been difficult for him to have conducted a national campaign even had it been necessary for him to do so. Travel was difficult, uncomfortable, and time consuming. Even in 1800, when the

Jeffersonian Republicans launched the first activity that could be called a presidential campaign, it was not a national or even a regional effort. The rallies, parades, and leaflets were not nationally planned but the work of individual county and state political committees. The national road system, begun in Maryland in 1808, was the chief east-west artery, and it did not reach even the Ohio border until 1817. Commercial water travel started in 1807, but it took many days just to go from Pittsburgh to New York City. Therefore, the presidential election of 1824 was the first one in which any real mass campaigning took place. Friends of the three candidates (John Quincy Adams, Henry Clay, and Andrew Jackson) traveled within their own and neighboring states to campaign for the presidential contenders.

Although the Baltimore and Ohio Railroad began in 1829, it was 1853 before the tracks reached the Mississippi River and 1869 before the transcontinental railroad system was completed in Ogden, Utah. By 1854, although the transportation system had improved, it still took 30 hours to travel from Indianapolis to Cleveland by rail and 24 hours from Chicago to St. Louis. Thus it is small wonder that 1840 was the first time a political party conducted a national campaign by sending speakers to 26 states or that 1860 was the first time a presidential candidate traveled throughout the north campaigning for his own election. Moreover, it was not until 1896, after railroads serviced most of the nation and automobile production had begun, that a presidential challenger, William Jennings Bryan, was able to "whirl" through 21 states, give 600 speeches, and be seen by 5 million people.

Developments in the transportation network continued to affect the style of political campaigning. For example, the beginning of air travel in the 1920s allowed Franklin Roosevelt to fly to Chicago to accept the Democratic presidential nomination in 1932 just as the initiation of commercial jet service in 1959 afforded Richard Nixon and John Kennedy the opportunity to conduct "jet-stop" campaigns in 1960.

However, by the middle of the nineteenth century, a second factor had become important to the development of campaign style. With the invention of the telegraph in 1835, a communication network was able to transcend those of transportation because messages were able to move at the speed of electrical impulses rather than the speed of humans, horses, boats, or trains.[13] Moreover, the emergence of the telephone in 1876, wireless telegraph and the motion picture camera in 1895, commercial radio in 1920, and motion pictures with sound in 1927 allowed the public to "bypass the written word and extend communication senses and capabilities directly."[14] Communication scholar Frederick Williams has written "speech and images could now span distances, be preserved in time, and be multiplied almost infinitely."[15]

Even the first advances in the communication network began to influence political campaigning. For example, one of the primary issues of the 1848 presidential campaign was the almost two-year war with Mexico. The Whigs selected one of the war's heroes, General Zachary Taylor, as their candidate. The principal reason the war could become important to the campaign was that the initiation of commercial telegraph service in 1844 and the subsequent founding of the Associated Press Wire Service had provided far more rapid news than the country had ever known. Citizens were aware of specific battles and vigorously applauded each victory over the Mexicans. In other words, the telegraph was able to inject the war into the campaign with a realism not known before.

By the campaign of 1884, telegraph had so unified the nation's communication system that even one election eve gaffe could be telegraphed across the country and influence election returns.*

---

*The day before the election, a Republican clergyman denounced the Democratic candidate, Grover Cleveland, by saying that his party was the party of "Rum, Romanism, and Rebellion." Republican candidate James G. Blaine failed to disavow the statement and therefore lost the support of Irish Catholic voters. A thousand more votes in New York, a stronghold of Irish Catholics, would have elected him.

Although each early communication development had some influence on political campaigning, certainly the most dramatic were the changes brought about by radio. Beginning in 1921, when President Warren Harding first used the new medium to talk with the public, the radio became the nation's most important means of political communication. It remained so until the widespread use of television in 1952.[16] Radio had a direct effect on campaign style because it made the personal appearances of candidates less necessary by providing an option. For the first time, candidates (even unknown ones) could become public personalities without campaigning around the country. In 1924 William McAdoo, a contender for the Democratic presidential nomination, hoped to establish a radio station powerful enough to reach all parts of the country so that he would not have to travel around the nation making speeches.[17] Although McAdoo never put his plan into action, losing the nomination to John W. Davis, subsequent candidates did. In 1928 Republican contender Herbert Hoover undertook only a few public appearances. Rather, he made seven radio speeches the focal point of his campaign. In 1936, 1940, and 1944, incumbent Franklin Roosevelt used radio extensively so that he could reach the entire nation without traveling.[18]

Thus the early achievements in electronic media had a profound effect on the manner of political campaigning. As technological advancements, however, they were only the beginning. The real "revolution" in communications technologies has been more recent and is, according to Williams, still accelerating.[19] Although there have been many innovations, those that have had some direct effect on campaign style include: the beginning of scheduled television broadcasts in 1941; the first electronic computer in 1942; the beginning of color television in 1951; the introduction of portable video recorders in 1968; the widespread use of microelectronic chips in 1970; the perfected development of fiber optic signal transmission in 1975; and the popularity of home computers in 1980.[20]

In the largest sense, television, as radio had done earlier, increased the number of campaign strategies available because candidates no longer had to be dependent on extensive national speaking tours to become well known to the public. A few nationwide television speeches, a series of well-executed and well-placed advertising spots, an appearance on one of the news/issues programs such as "Meet the Press," campaign coverage on the evening network news broadcasts, and perhaps a guest shot on one of the popular talk shows guaranteed public awareness. In addition, television, unlike radio, enhanced campaign swings by showing parts of them in evening news broadcasts. Although the candidate might go to one state or region of the country to campaign in person, millions of people across the country participated in the rally or parade by watching the pageantry from their own living rooms. Not only did a television campaign provide candidates with more exposure, it also allowed for more flexibility in the management of physical and financial resources. Perhaps the essence of the mass media strategy is explained best in a memorandum written by H. R. Haldeman (and interpreted by Theodore White), in which he outlined the plan for Richard Nixon's 1968 presidential campaign:

> Americans no longer gather in the streets to hear candidates; they gather at their television sets or where media assemble their attention. A candidate cannot storm the nation; at most he can see and let his voice be heard by no more than a million or two people in a Presidential year (the reach of the individual campaigner doesn't add up to diddly-squat in votes). One minute or thirty seconds on the evening news shows of Messrs. Cronkite or Huntley/Brinkley will reach more people than ten months of barnstorming. One important favorable Washington column is worth more than two dozen press releases or position papers. News magazines like *Time* or *Newsweek*, picture magazines like *Life* and *Look* are media giants worth a hundred outdoor rallies. Therefore the candidate must not waste

time storming the country, personally pleading for votes—
no matter what he does, he can appear in newsprint or on
television only once a day. The inner strength and vitality of
the candidate must not be wasted; if you do more than one
thing a day, you make a mistake. If you test a man's physical
strength too far, you push him beyond the realm of good
judgment; both candidate and the following press must be
given time to stop, rest, reflect and write. The importance of
old-style-outdoor campaigning now lies less in what the
candidate tells the people than in what he learns from them
with the important secondary value that outdoor exertions
do provide the vital raw stuff for television cameras.[21]*

Although 1968 was not the first time televison had been
used extensively in a campaign, it was the first time that a presidential candidate had planned his entire candidacy around
the medium. Richard Nixon not only used technology to help
him win an election, he added an important dimension to campaign style—one that has extended far beyond his tenure as a
political candidate.

In a similar fashion, the computer has made a profound
impact on the manner of political campaigning. Its speed in information processing and its ability to interact intellectually
with us and to automate many of our methods of information
analysis have provided the candidate with an invaluable resource in such traditional tasks as identifying and communicating with specific publics or raising funds. Direct mail,
instant voting prediction and analysis, and accurate and rapid
public opinion research are all part of the new politics facilita-
ted by the computer.

---

*Part of the reason for Haldeman's concern in conserving a candidate's
physical energy was that during the 1960 campaign Nixon had made a pledge
(which he kept) to campaign personally in each of the 50 states. Thus, for
most of the fall, Nixon was physically exhausted and even ill as he barnstormed the nation (via jet).

But just as important as the past are the possibilities for the future. Such communication technologies as the computer, cable television service, and push-button telephones may completely change the nature of campaigns in the next decades by allowing voters to interact with the candidate from their own living room. In other words, instead of a candidate simply stating a position on an issue to a mass audience during a television speech, debate, or interview, the candidate could ask a question or invite comments. Large numbers of viewers could press buttons on their television sets or on their phones and respond immediately to the candidate. This rapid and somewhat personal interaction might allow candidates the opportunity for repositioning their ideas and might also encourage voters to modify or change their beliefs regarding the candidate.[22]

Obviously, the effect on campaign style would be enormous. Incumbents and challengers alike could have the benefits of person-to-person campaigning without ever leaving the television studio. In addition, the determination of public opinion on a given issue would no longer be subject to the intervention of a third party (such as pollsters or the press). Mass media campaigning would, in effect, become true two-way communication.

Thus far, interactive television has been used primarily for commercial functions. Yet, as we have suggested, there is potential for so much more. Even now, one government agency has experimented with the Qube two-way cable system in Columbus, Ohio to determine public opinion on political issues and events. And many newspapers are using cable to deliver news, especially to carry updates on stories that are still breaking, thereby providing additional information in an instant instead of hours.

The computer is not the only technology that has altered the nature of campaigns. During the 1982 elections, microwave transmission and cable television allowed Ronald Reagan to make a 10-state campaign swing, appearing at rallies for 14 Republican congressional candidates, without ever leaving the

White House. In addition, the potential for satellite campaigning is unlimited. Microwave transmissions can be received by broadcast outlets or by the 4,780 cable systems in the United States. Cable is attractive to candidates because it is cheaper than network time, it is more selective in the geographic range it covers (there is no spillage or waste), and political programs or spot advertisements can be written and targeted for a specific city, congressional district, or even a particular group of citizens. In short, microwave transmission and cable television have the potential for creating almost personalized networks for candidates.

Although it is impossible to know just what impact new technologies will ultimately have on political campaigns, as we have seen before, innovations in transportation and communication networks have an infinite capacity to alter the strategies that candidates use to seek political office. As such, they are an important consideration in any examination of campaign style.

STYLES AND STRATEGIES
OF CAMPAIGNS

Essentially, campaign styles are sets of communication strategies employed at times by all candidates, whether they run for president, mayor, governor, or legislator. Moreover, those who hold office may campaign in the manner of those who do not just as those who challenge may adopt strategies of incumbency. In other words, those candidates who are incumbents are not restricted to a specific set of incumbency strategies any more than challengers are confined to a particular set of challenger strategies. In fact, candidates frequently combine styles so that there are times during the course of one contest where an individual contender may do and say all of those things normally associated with incumbency campaigning and at other times may appear to be campaigning as a challenger.

This combination may well be a result of the seasonless electoral process discussed in the first and second chapters.

As candidates extend the length of the campaign, no one style is likely to remain appropriate for the duration. New events, as well as changes in conditions, force modification in the manner of pursuit. While in February an attack on the incumbent's economic policy might be appropriate, by August the situation may be different enough to make attack an inappropriate strategy. As such, it would be misleading to try to analyze style by only examining the practice of one candidate or one campaign. Styles (incumbency and challenger) are a product of whatever candidates and their staffs believe is needed at a particular time within the context of their particular campaign. Therefore, the best way to understand them is to determine the composition of each, that is, to catalog their strategies.

Incumbency Style

Incumbency campaigning in the United States is almost as old as incumbents,* and its various strategies have been used by almost all who have sought election to any level of government.

Given its longevity and frequent use, one might assume it would have been defined long ago and its characteristics carefully delineated. While that is not the case, incumbency has been considered a "symbolic resource"[23] and the "Rose Garden Strategy."[24] Although each idea is useful in attempting to understand what it is that candidates do and say when they appear to be "running as an incumbent," each is nonetheless incomplete. Incumbency campaigning is a blend of both symbolic and pragmatic communication strategies designed to make any candidate appear as both good enough for the of-

---

*George Washington, the first presidential incumbent, was unopposed in the election of 1792.

fice sought and possessing the office (an assumed incumbency stance). This is not an easy task. We know that image creation and maintenance take significant amounts of skill, time, and money. But developing a credible incumbency style is well worth the effort. The results of countless elections indicate that incumbents tend to win. For example, during the twentieth century, only four presidents have lost their reelection bids, and congressional incumbents, especially those in the House of Representatives, almost always defeat their challengers (in some elections, they have won as many as 97 percent of their contests). Given this kind of success, it is not surprising that political scientist, R. F. Fenno, has suggested that incumbency is "a resource to be employed, an opportunity to be exploited."[25]

With this understanding, we now consider the specific strategies that candidates employ when they seek the advantages of incumbency. The first 4 are symbolic in nature and the remaining 11 are pragmatic or instrumental.

In exploring the symbolic characteristics of incumbency campaigning, we are, in essence, discussing presidential candidates because there is no other elective office for which the public has the same kind of feelings.* In one sense, the presidency can be thought of as a focus of impressions and beliefs that exist in our minds—a kind of "collage of images, hopes, habits, and intentions shared by the nation who legitimizes the office and reacts to its occupants."[26] Viewed from a related perspective, when we speak of the presidency, we are dealing with the myth of the office, the image we have possessed since childhood of the one institution that stands for truth, honor, justice, and integrity. We have a conception of an individual and an office that in ennobling each other, ennoble us. Perhaps Theodore White described it best when he wrote:

---

*Obviously, there are symbolic aspects to incumbency campaigning at lower levels. However, it is the presidential election that provides the richest example.

> Somewhere in American life there is at least one man who stands for law, the President. That faith surmounts all daily cynicism, all evidence or suspicion of wrong-doing by lesser leaders, all corruptions, all vulgarities, all the ugly compromises of daily striving and ambition. That faith holds that all men are created equal before the law and protected by it; and that no matter how the faith may be betrayed elsewhere, at one particular point—the Presidency—justice will be done beyond prejudice, beyond rancor, beyond the possibilities of a fix.[27]

People may debate the character, quality, and personality of the men who have filled the office, and public opinion polls may indicate dissatisfaction with the performance of an incumbent, but the presidency is, for most citizens, an idealized institution, headed by a single visible individual through whom it is possible to grasp a "cognitive handle" or an understanding of "political goings on."[28]

In this context, then, the identity of a particular president is irrelevant; the concern is the office itself and the symbolic role it can play in a campaign.

Symbolic Trappings of the Office

The first strategy is the use of symbolic trappings to transmit the absolute strength and importance of the office. The presidency stands for power, and therefore incumbents take on the persona of the powerful. They are surrounded by large numbers of carefully trained and "important looking" bodyguards who appear to anticipate their every move; their song (played when they enter or leave a public ceremony) is "Hail to the Chief"; incumbents are addressed by title, never by name; when they travel a whole contingent of secret service, media reporters, technicians, and lesser governmental officials accompany them in a caravan of planes and limousines; their home, although the property of "the people," is heavily guarded and off limits to all who have no official business to conduct with them or their staff; incumbents can be in instant communication with the leader of any other country of the world; they serve as commander in chief of all armed services; incumbents can command nationwide media time; and they are always close to a small black bag, the contents of which provide them the capability to blow up the world.

Thus, it is little wonder that those who have campaigned against a president have objected to the continual and conscious use of devices that remind voters that they are seeing and hearing "the president," as opposed to "just another politician." For example, when Jimmy Carter was challenging Gerald Ford in 1976, he strongly denounced the incumbent's use of such trappings as the presidential seal on the speaker's stand and the use of the title, Mr. President, during their televised debates. One of the reasons for his concern was his awareness that the symbols of the office convey power and voters connect the image with the incumbent.

Legitimacy of the Office

The second strategy involves not so much what incumbents do, that is, the use of specific tangible symbols to remind voters of their power, but an intangible tool that only they possess and about which their challengers cannot even object. The presidency stands for legitimacy, and therefore the person who holds the office is perceived as the natural and logical leader. In other words, no matter who the incumbent may be (or regardless of the incumbent's current rating in the public opinion polls), the president is accorded a kind of sociopolitical legitimacy—a public trust. As one theorist has argued, we place our faith and trust in the hands of our leaders because they project an image that seduces us into participating in the comforting illusion that through rigid adherence to the constituted ideals of the society they can guide us through whatever possible troubles the future might present.[29] Moreover, their position provides automatic legitimacy during a campaign, in that they, unlike any of their opponents, are, from the beginning, considered legitimate candidates for the job.

Competency and the Office

The third strategy is also an intangible tool that comes with the office. The presidency stands for competency and therefore the person who holds the office can easily convey that impression. To trust in the president's competence is to accept the incumbent as a symbol "that problems can be solved without a basic restructuring of social institutions and without the threat a radical reordering poses both to the contented and to the anxious."[30] In other words, when we attribute a sense of competency to the president, it provides us with reassurance that all can be right. We want to believe that the person who is president is capable (after all, we elected the president in the first place).

As a matter of fact, our feelings about the office itself are so strong that whatever a specific president has done with regard to individual issues, a large number of people will always be supportive. For example, each year since World War II, every president has been ranked by U.S. citizens as one of the ten most admired persons in the world.[31] Perhaps a reason for this is, as Murray Edelman suggests, that "public issues fade from attention after a period in the limelight even when they are not 'solved' because they cannot remain dramatic and exciting for long and the media then have economic and psychological reasons to softpedal them."[32]

For whatever reasons or in whatever manner goodwill is retained, our point is simply that any president possesses a sense of competency that none of their rivals can share. It is, of course, a distinct advantage of the office.

Charisma and the Office

The final symbolic strategy, like the first three, is dependent on the ability of the office to transfer its persona to the incumbent. However, this one is not an intangible resource in that it has had deliberate use since presidents began barnstorming the country for their own elections. The presidency stands for excitement, a kind of patriotic glamor, and therefore the person who holds the office takes on these characteristics. In no other way is the mystique of the presidency more visible than it is during a presidential campaign visit almost anywhere in the country. When the president comes to town (advance and security personnel have already been there for at least a week), roads are blocked, airports are closed, children are dismissed from school, bands play, television cameras and reporters are everywhere, hundreds or thousands of people converge along the streets or at the airport to greet the president; the very sight of the magnificent Air Force I produces a sense of awe, and for a while, we are participants in a warm and patriotic festival. It matters little whether or not we plan to vote for the incumbent; regardless of how dull and unimaginative the president may have been before living in the White House, once there, the office itself envelops the president in its aura or charisma.

Although campaign tours were not undertaken by incumbents (at least during the election period) until Herbert Hoover paved the way, their symbolic power has not been lost on any of the presidents who have succeeded him. The reasons for their trips have been as varied as have been their modes of transportation. For example, in 1948 Harry Truman whistle-stopped his way across 32,000 miles to blame what he termed the "do-nothing, good-for-nothing 80th Congress" for the nation's problems; in 1956 Dwight Eisenhower, in spite of two international crises, felt he had to undertake an extensive tour through the southern states to blunt his opponent's charges that he was too old and too sick to be president; in 1964 Lyndon Johnson barnstormed his way across the country, in part, because he felt a psychological need to be "out with the people" and experience their warmth and acceptance of him; and in 1976 Jimmy Carter boarded the Delta Queen and traveled the

Ohio and Mississippi rivers, campaigning at each stop, in an almost frantic effort to restore his popularity with voters. For the most part, other incumbents have used campaign trips for the same reasons. They have known that the glamor and excitement, the drama and pageantry of a presidential visit will, even if just for a short time, transfer the charisma of the office to them. As such, the trips are well worth the effort.

In turning to the pragmatic strategies of incumbency, it is important to note that they are more universal than are their symbolic counterparts because they can be and have been employed by candidates who are neither presidents or, in some cases, even incumbents. Certainly, there are those strategies which depend on the legitimate power that holding an office provides, but others have been used by candidates who only borrow the mantle or style of the incumbent.

Strategies that are examined in this section are:

1) creating pseudoevents to attract and control media attention
2) making appointments to state and federal jobs as well as appointments to state and national party committees
3) creating special city, state, or national task forces to investigate areas of public concern
4) appropriating federal funds/grants
5) consulting or negotiating with world leaders
6) manipulating the economy or other important domestic issues
7) endorsements by party and other important leaders
8) emphasizing accomplishments
9) creating and maintaining an "above the political trenches" posture
10) depending on surrogates for the campaign trail
11) interpreting and intensifying a foreign policy problem so that it becomes an international crisis.

Creating pseudoevents.   As the use of public relations experts and publicists has increased in political campaigns, so too has the frequency of hyped or manufactured news. Essentially, pseudoevents are defined as occurrences that differ from "real" events in that they are planned, planted, or incited for the primary purpose of being reported or reproduced.[33]

While all candidates use pseudoevents to try to capture media attention, incumbents have more success because they are in a better position to create them. For example, a governor or state senator may be featured on the evening television and radio news throughout the state because of an announced "major" initiative in attracting a specific corporation to the state and thus creating new jobs. A member of Congress may receive headlines from appointment to a special committee or commission created by the president. Moreover, incumbents have many opportunities for participation in ceremonious occasions—events that are sure to bring the local media. The ceremonies can be as different as the groundbreaking for a new government building to the announcement that a special day has been set aside to honor the city's firefighters. But each can be hyped up enough to guarantee publicity for the candidate. However, not only do incumbents have more opportunities to attract the attention of the media, they are better equipped to control the kind of coverage they receive. Perhaps the best example of what we mean is the mayor of Chicago.

During her years as mayor, Jane Byrne has learned to control Chicago media. She is seen on television virtually every evening; most of the time it is as the leading participant in a special occasion or ceremony (Chicago is a big city, and therefore many events can be made important enough to make the mayor's attendance seem appropriate). But equally important, the pillar of her media policy has become a news conference held at least twice a week in a room in City Hall especially equipped to make her telegenic. Reporters may not question her on any issue other than the announced subject of the meeting, cameras may not show her smoking, and technicians are not allowed to use their own lights. In between conferences, she is normally unavailable for one-to-one interviews and will not talk with reporters who cover her participation in special events.[34]

In short, incumbents such as Jane Byrne, have at their disposal the ability to create pseudoevents that not only guarantee media exposure but allow some measure of control over the coverage.

Making appointments to jobs and committees. One of the most common yet powerful incumbency strategies revolves around the ability to appoint personal or political friends—or potential friends—to local, state, and federal jobs or to give them key positions on party committees. Although patronage has been condemned by reformers in both political parties, it continues largely because it is so advantageous to everyone concerned. First, it allows candidates (and is not limited to incumbents in that all contenders can hold out the "promise" of appointment) to reward those who have helped them in the past. Second, it creates potential friends or at least puts people in a position of gratitude, and third, and undoubtedly most significant, it places supporters in key positions that may well be important in later stages of the campaign or even in subsequent elections. As such, few candidates, from county commissioner to governor to president, have failed to use this strategy.

Creating special task forces. Modern candidates understand the need to not only determine which issues are of concern to the voters in their city, district, or state but to speak to those concerns. One way to do this is to announce the formation of a special task force whose purpose is to investigate the issue/ problem and make recommendations to the candidate regarding steps or actions to be taken in the future. The strategy is employed by incumbents as well as those who are not incumbents because the act of forming the task force is all that is really required to create the illusion that the candidate is concerned about the problem.

The primary advantage of the strategy is that the candidate is perceived as a person who understands and cares about those issues important to a particular constituency. However, a second benefit is that the candidate is in the position to post-pone taking a stand on a controversial issue—one that might create as many enemies as supporters. Thus every election year seems to bring a plethora of specially created task forces composed of concerned community/state/national citizens who investigate topics as varied as mental health facilities and taxes for a new sewer system.

Appropriating funds/grants. Absolutely no incumbency strat-egy is less subtle or more powerful than appropriating special grants to "cooperative" (politically supportive) public officials for their cities and states. It is reserved only for incumbents (in that the strategy does not include promises for the future) and is viewed best at the presidential level, although it is certainly done at state and local levels as well.

Although every modern president (going back at least as far as Franklin Roosevelt) has had a prodigious amount of dis-cretionary money to distribute in the form of federal grants, by the election of 1980, the amount totaled $80 billion. Like his predecessors, Jimmy Carter was determined to use it to aid him in the primaries—especially the early contests when the campaign of Edward Kennedy was still viewed as a threat. The money was employed to reward those public officials who an-nounced their preference for the president, to gain a public en-dorsement where there had not been one, or to punish those who denied or withdrew support. For example, prior to the Illi-nois primary, Jane Byrne was told by the White House that U.S. Air Force facilities at O'Hare Field would be relocated to allow Chicago to expand its major airport. However, after the mayor announced her support of Senator Kennedy over the president, the secretary of transportation said that the cabinet had "lost confidence in Mayor Byrne, and would look for op-portunities to deny transportation funds to Chicago and its mayor."[35]

Thus, the Carter White House went into the 1980 cam-paign determined to "grease" their way through the primaries.

Florida (in advance of the Democratic straw primary) received a $1.1 billion loan guarantee to an electric cooperative, $29.9 billion in grants for public housing in various counties, and $31 million for housing projects for the elderly throughout the state. Prior to its primary, New Hampshire received funds for such projects as a four-lane highway from Manchester to Portsmouth and a special commuter train from Concord to Boston.[36]

Is the appropriation of funds a successful incumbency strategy? While it is impossible to claim the effect of any one element in a phenomenon as complex as a primary election, the president soundly defeated Kennedy in New Hampshire and virtually annihilated him in the Florida and Illinois primaries.

Consultation with world leaders. While at first glance consultations with world leaders may appear to be a strategy possible for only presidential incumbents, the fact is that this strategy is employed by any number of governors and members of Congress as they attempt to build their credentials for reelection. Governors extend invitations to athletic teams or artists and may even negotiate with foreign business corporations and governments about the prospect of building a major factory in the state. Members of Congress take frequent junkets overseas in the effort to illustrate their power and importance to voters in their districts or states.

In addition to its use by incumbents, the strategy is employed by challengers who must also build credentials and convey a sense of their individual importance. Moreover, its use may be even more crucial for them because they do not possess the real authority or power of the incumbent. Thus a meeting with foreign governmental leaders grants at least a sense of legitimacy because it illustrates acknowledgment and a kind of acceptance into an important and official group of leaders.

While significant to congressional and gubernatorial candidates, a trip to Europe—especially the Soviet Union, China, or the Middle East—is virtually a prerequisite for potential presidential contenders, particularly those whose previous experiences have not included "official" foreign travel and consultation with government officials. At the very least, it allows them to work their trips into their discourse with such phrases as, "in my meeting with the prime minister, I was told that. . . ." But even more important, the strategy provides those candidates who have absolutely no foreign policy experience the appearance of seeming to be a part of or involved in international affairs. As such, it is a useful strategy of the incumbency style.

Manipulation of important domestic issues. As a number of these strategies illustrate, incumbents have considerable power, which is, of course, one of the reasons they are difficult to defeat and challengers are so eager to assume their campaign style. However, the manipulation or management of important issues is one strategy that can be assumed only by the incumbent.

For example, throughout the years, the economy has been a primary area of presidential management. One way this has been done is timing economic benefits to specific groups within the electorate to ensure their vote in the election. Political scientist Frank Kessler has pointed to the following social security incident during the 1972 presidential campaign as a case in point:

> Checks went out in October 1972, one month before the elections, with the following memo enclosed and personally approved by President Nixon to each of the 24.7 million Social Security recipients: "Your social security payment has been increased by 20% starting with this month's check by a new statute enacted by Congress and signed into law by President Richard Nixon on July 1, 1972. The President also signed into a law a provision which will allow your social security benefits to increase automatically as the cost of living goes up."[37]

In using this strategy, presidents have not limited themselves to economic manipulation; other issues have been managed. For example, as Ronald Reagan's administration prepared for the 1982 congressional election, the president's Council on Environmental Quality prepared a report documenting improved air quality in 20 to 40 cities across the country. The report was prepared in the hope that it could refute environmentalists' charges by showing that although the administration had reduced the influence and number of personnel in the Environmental Protection Agency, air quality had not been adversely affected.

Thus the manipulation or management of important domestic issues is yet another strategy of incumbency.

Endorsements by other leaders.   Although not as important as they once were,* endorsements are an attempt to identify and link the candidate with already established, highly respected, and generally acknowledged leaders. The idea is that endorsement by respected leaders signifies that the candidate is already part of their group and should therefore also be thought of as a leader; in other words, credibility by association. Obviously, this perception can be crucial for a nonincumbent who wishes to adopt the incumbency style. It is, of course, equally significant for the incumbent because continued acceptance by other governmental or political leaders is one way of advancing the perception of a successful first term of office. Similarly, candidates hope they receive no endorsements from individuals or groups who are not perceived positively by large segments of society because negative association is also possible. For example, during the 1960 presidential campaign, Richard Nixon was endorsed by the president of the Teamsters

---

*Before changes were made in the delegate selection process for the national nominating conventions, presidential hopefuls were dependent on endorsements from party leaders. Once the system for selecting delegates changed, that is, presidential primaries became dominant, endorsements were no longer necessary to secure the nomination (see chapters 1 and 2).

Union, Jimmy Hoffa. Because Hoffa was already thought of as a "racketeer" or worse by many citizens it was an endorsement that Nixon tried to ignore. When reporters questioned John Kennedy about his reaction to Hoffa's endorsement of Nixon rather than himself, Kennedy responded humorously that he guessed he was just lucky, which of course reinforces our point.

Emphasizing accomplishments. One of those strategies forming the core of the incumbency style is emphasizing accomplishments. Candidates must be able to demonstrate tangible accomplishments either in their first term of office if they are incumbents or in some related aspect of public service if they only assume the style. This is, of course, the reason that incumbents go to great lengths to list for voters all that they have done while in office. Thus the strategy is simple as long as the deeds exist. The difficulty occurs when there have been few accomplishments or when major problems have arisen that overshadow positive contributions (taxes are higher than they were before the incumbent took office, inflation is worse, unemployment has not been reduced). When this happens, the strategy becomes more complex in that the incumbent must either deny that the current problems are important ones (normally an impossible task for even the most persuasive) or blame them on someone else—even on uncontrollable forces. Blaming someone, scapegoating, is the path normally chosen. Examples are as numerous as candidates. State legislators blame the governor, governors blame the federal government (especially Congress), presidents blame Congress, and surprisingly enough, members of Congress often blame other Congress members.

The practice of casting blame elsewhere is certainly not a new variation of the accomplishment strategy. However, its most interesting use is by members of Congress, especially the House.

Popular conceptions of Congress are not high. For example, in 1976 one public opinion poll revealed that citizens believed that Congress ranked low in ethics (of ten groups scaled, only corporation executives and labor leaders ranked lower), and in 1978 the results of another survey indicated that only 10 percent of the public had "a great deal of confidence" in the institution.[38] However, despite these feelings, congressional incumbents win most of their elections. One of the reasons for this paradox is that when individual representatives seek re-election, they disassociate themselves or even "run against" the institution of which they are a member. They talk about their accomplishments rather than those of Congress, and as two political communication scholars have noted, they play up the negative "myths" (Congress is a kind of shadowy process in which sinister figures operate) while projecting themselves as hardworking and honest people who work against evil.[39] In this way, then, even when genuine accomplishments may be few, scapegoating makes the strategy possible.

Above the political trenches image.   Another strategy that is at the center of incumbency style is the technique in which candidates try to create the image that they are somehow removed from politics. Essentially, the strategy is composed of any combination of the following three tactics (each designed to create the impression that the contender is a statesman rather than a politician):

1) the appearance of being aloof from the hurly-burly of political battle—that the office has sought them and thus they run because of a sense of love of country and duty
2) failure to publicly acknowledge the existence of any opponent—candidates may have opponents, but statesmen do not
3) sustained political science (the absolute refraining from any personal campaign trips or confrontations with opponents, including not answering any charges or attacks or discussion of partisan issues).[40]

While portions of the strategy are used by contemporary candidates, it has been around for a long time. As a matter of fact, its progenitor was George Washington. He did not have to create a nonpolitical or statesman image because he was not a politician. He had been reluctant to become president and, once there, never campaigned for reelection. In spite of this, for candidates who were to follow (at least presidential candidates), he bequeathed a legacy of "being above politics," in a sense, conveying the attitude that being political would somehow "dirty" the office. Thus, for many years, the public picked presidents without ever seeing or hearing what their ideas or policies were—at least during the time in which they were candidates. With only two exceptions,* no major party candidates, even after formal nomination, personally solicited votes. They were not expected to (even after transportation networks improved) because the prevailing attitude was that the office must seek the person; that is, the appearance of modest reluctance—of being above politics— had to be maintained. Stephen Douglas was the first to break the taboo in 1860 when he shocked people with speaking tours on behalf of his own candidacy. Although other Democratic candidates followed his example, none were successful until Woodrow Wilson was elected in 1912. Republicans remembered Washington's example longer and eschewed mass campaigning until the 1932 campaign when an incumbent was faced with a problem of such magnitude that he felt he had to travel the country explaining why he should not be blamed for the Great Depression.

Thus this strategy has a long history, and its use, in combination with the next two strategies, continues to play a central role in the development and maintenance of incumbency style.

Use of surrogates on the campaign trail. This strategy is closely related to the last one in that it is possible for candidates to assume an above-politics posture because others are

---

*William Henry Harrison in 1840 and General Winfield Scott in 1852 made, at the insistence of their managers, some speeches that were described as nonpolitical.

overtly campaigning for them while they stay home being non-political. While the strategy is employed by a wide spectrum of candidates, it is the sophisticated use by recent presidential incumbents that allows us to see most clearly the technique at work. For example, in 1972 Richard Nixon depended on the campaign tours of over 49 surrogates (including members of his family, cabinet officers, and other high-level government officials) while he stayed in the White House during most of the fall campaign against George McGovern. As a matter of fact, Nixon was so intent on creating the illusion of a hard-working, nonpolitical statesman that not only did he rarely take a political trip or make a speech in his own behalf, but when asked once by a reporter about his campaign, he cut off questioning with the remark, "let the political people talk on that."[41]

The use of surrogates did not end with Richard Nixon's election. As a matter of fact, it became more pronounced, especially when the media dubbed it the "Rose Garden" strategy during the stay-at-home period of Gerald Ford's campaign in 1976. What they meant was that for weeks on end, as part of a specifically designed plan, Ford did not leave the White House to campaign for his reelection. Members of his family, his cabinet, and hundreds of Republican party faithful were out on the hustings for him as he stayed close to the White House and acted "presidential." In addition, as part of the plan, the media were alerted several times each day to witness pseudoevents (the president's welcome to visiting dignitaries or his signature on legislation), most of which occurred in the area adjacent to the Oval Office, the Rose Garden (thus the name). But what is most interesting about surrogates and rose gardens is that the strategy is a direct descendant of the "Front Porch" campaigns used by Republicans many years earlier.

In 1888 the grandson of "Old Tippecanoe," Benjamin Harrison, was the Republican candidate for president. The party believed it had lost the 1884 election because of the mistakes their candidate made. Therefore, it was decided that

Harrison would campaign from his home in Indianapolis against the Democratic incumbent, giving rehearsed and dignified speeches to delegations of visitors who were invited to hear him speak while other party leaders toured the country on his behalf. In other words, the challenger would not only appear presidential, he would have little opportunity to err. Thus, when Harrison won, the Front Porch or Rose Garden strategy was born.

As is the case with most campaign strategies, success means repetition. So in 1896 Republicans went back to the porch with a new candidate and increased zest for a campaign style that was in stark contrast to the "swing around the circle" effort of the Democrats.

Although William McKinley never left his porch in Canton, Ohio, he nonetheless was part of a far more vigorous campaign to return the White House to the Republicans than had been conducted for Harrison. Hundreds of visiting delegations were invited to visit his home and hear him speak. He gave as many as 12 carefully prepared speeches a day (each on a single issue specifically directed to the interests of the delegation), and copies were supplied to all major papers. Thus, while remaining at home, McKinley received daily nationwide press coverage—more in fact than did his opponent. In addition, 1,400 surrogates were sent out from party campaign headquarters to speak for him all across the country. With all this effort, McKinley defeated William Jennings Bryan.

In part because of their victories the first two times, Republicans returned to the porch for the 1920 election. While the Democratic candidate toured the country, the Republican managers sat Warren G. Harding on the front porch in Marion, Ohio (where day after day he delivered quiet and dignified platitudes about common sense and clean living) and then supplemented the porch performances with touring surrogates. Once again, the strategy worked as Democratic contender James Cox lost in the worst defeat a presidential candidate had known.

With this kind of success, it should now be easy to understand why front porches (currently called rose gardens) and surrogates have remained popular with modern presidential candidates.

Interpreting or intensifying foreign policy problems into international crises. Although variations of the strategy of interpreting or intensifying foreign policy problems into international crises are employed by incumbents at all levels, it is most completely studied as it has been used by presidents. Its purpose is simple: to create enough of a crisis situation so that voters (either because of patriotism or not wanting to change leaders at the time of an emergency) will be motivated to rally around the president. There have been many instances when the technique has been successful. In 1916 and again in 1940, presidents Woodrow Wilson and Franklin Roosevelt campaigned with the specter of war in Europe in the minds of the electorate. In 1964 when U.S. ships in the Gulf of Tonkin were fired upon, President Lyndon Johnson interrupted his "campaigning" to go on television where he pledged that the United States would take rigorous defensive measures. In 1975 when the U.S. merchant ship, the Mayaguez, was captured by Cambodian forces, President Gerald Ford (who was about to make official his bid for reelection) used the situation to build his leadership or command credentials by ordering marines to bomb Cambodia until the Mayaguez crew was released. However, one of the most adept uses of the strategy occurred in the surfacing and primary stages of the 1980 campaign when President Jimmy Carter (who had two genuine foreign policy problems with the seizure of the U.S. embassy in Iran and the Soviet advances into Afghanistan) combined the use of surrogates, a nonpolitical image, and international crises to promote his renomination campaign.

Prior to the Iowa caucus and continuing through the Maine and New Hampshire primaries, Carter pledged that he would not personally campaign until the hostages in Tehran

102

were released. Later, when the Soviets marched into Afghanistan, the president reinforced his earlier vow when he announced that because "this is the most serious crisis since the last World War," he would be unable to leave the White House to campaign in person for reelection. In addition, when other candidates (notably Senator Edward Kennedy and Governor Edmund Brown) questioned the administration's handling of the "crisis," the president completed the strategy by suggesting that attacks on his policy were "damaging to our country and to the establishment of our principles and the maintenance of them, and the achievements of our goals to keep the peace and to get our hostages released."[42]

Until the very last round of the primaries, the president stuck to his pledge. He emerged only rarely from the White House or Camp David and left most comments on politics to his surrogates. Carter's use of incumbency strategies was eminently successful. While giving the appearance that he was too busy trying to solve the international crises to campaign for reelection, he was defeating his opponents in the Democratic primary elections.

These then are the strategies that comprise the incumbency style. There are, as we have seen, a large number of them—each somewhat different from, although often dependent on, the others and each potentially effective in the hands of candidates who understand and appreciate their power. Perhaps what is most startling about them is the extent to which they work. Normally, it takes enormous amounts of money, organization, and skill to defeat even somewhat inept incumbents. They have at their command not only the strategies we have examined, but whatever privileges the office itself provides—including public awareness (visibility) and the opportunity to perform various popular and noncontroversial services for constituents. These strategies have repeatedly enabled incumbents to overwhelmingly win reelections and win by larger margins than victorious nonincumbents. As we have said before, given all of the benefits, it is no wonder that candidates who are not incumbents often assume elements of the style.

But under what conditions can incumbents lose? In other words, are there burdens of the style as well as benefits? It seems to us that there are at least four major disadvantages of incumbency campaigning. First, and maybe most important, incumbents must run (at least in part) on their record. While they may cast blame elsewhere or minimize the scope or significance of problem areas within their administration, an effective challenger can make certain that the record of the incumbent (and shortcomings can be found in virtually all records) forms the core of the campaign rhetoric. The incumbent can be kept in a position of having to defend, justify, explain—answering rather than charging, defending rather than attacking. Being forced to run on one's record can be a severe handicap particularly in the hands of a skilled challenger.

The second and related burden faced by many incumbents is simply that the public may blame them for all problems—whether or not they were at fault. Incumbents are in the public eye and if the city sanitation workers refuse to pick up the garbage for a week or if the public transportation system is shut down because of weather, an accident, or striking employees, they are held accountable. At the very least, the question of competency or job effectiveness is raised in the public mind, waiting perhaps for the skilled challenger to capitalize on it.

The third disadvantage, although quite different from the first two, can be equally troublesome. The challenger is free to campaign, but incumbents must at least give the appearance of doing the job for which they have been elected. As campaign seasons become longer, this becomes more difficult. Incumbents often find it unnerving to go about the day-to-day task of administering a city, state, or nation while their opponents spend countless hours out on the hustings—garnering media attention with attacks against them and their policies.* If they

---

*This has been emphasized in recent presidential campaigns when the leading challengers have been unemployed and could devote all of their time to being candidates.

respond by indulging in overt campaigning, they are criticized for not doing their job. If they ignore it, they may well be accused of having no defense and being afraid to go out and face voters. In other words, it is a real damned if you do and damned if you don't situation.

Finally, because incumbents are at the center of media/public attention (far more than are their opponents), expectations are great regarding their "front runner" status. If those expectations are not met, the incumbent is in trouble. Nowhere has this been more thoroughly illustrated than in presidential primary campaigns. Even when incumbents win, if they fail to meet some preconceived percentage set by the media or even by their own staffs, they have, at least in terms of media publicity, lost.

Thus there are some burdens. Even the incumbency style does not guarantee election. With this in mind, we will now contrast the strategies of the incumbent style with those of the challenger, knowing that in each there are burdens as well as benefits.

Challenger Style

Challenger campaigning is not easy because the style demands a two-step process, the implementation of which requires not only a good deal of deliberate planning but equal portions of skill and even luck. The style can be defined as a series of communication strategies designed to persuade voters that change is needed and that the challenger is the best person to bring about the change. While the kind of change can vary all the way from shifts in a whole economic system to personality characteristics desired in the officeholder, challengers must convince the electorate that some kind of alteration is necessary if they stand any chance for success. However, the second part of the process is equally important; the voters must also be persuaded that the challenger is the candidate most likely to produce more desirable conditions or policies. Therefore, the complexity of the style is increased be-

105

cause not only must those who challenge call for change, they must simultaneously demonstrate their own capability in bringing about that change. As if all of this was not difficult enough, it is entirely possible that the success of the challenger may ultimately depend on the skill of the incumbent—whether or not the incumbent makes a major mistake in campaign strategy or becomes a victim of prevailing conditions. Thus it is no understatement to maintain that the task facing most challengers is formidable.

In spite of the potential hazards or burdens, advocating change—the challenger campaign style—is not new. As a matter of fact, it probably got its start in the presidential campaign of 1800 when Jeffersonians distributed leaflets that asked: "Is it not time for a change?" Whenever it began, it has been used by many candidates who have sought elective office. Moreover, elements of the style have even been employed by incumbents such as Harry Truman and Gerald Ford who felt it would be more beneficial to their candidacies to call for a change in Congress rather than only try to explain the present problems.

The strategies examined in this section include:

1) attacking the record of opponents
2) taking the offensive position on issues
3) calling for a change
4) emphasizing optimism for the future
5) speaking to traditional values rather than calling for value changes
6) appearing to represent the philosophical center of the political party
7) delegating personal or harsh attacks in an effort to control demagogic rhetoric.

Attacking the record. Just as running on the record of their accomplishments is a central strategy of incumbency, so too is attacking that same record a prime characteristic of the challenger style. As a matter of fact, the ability to criticize freely (and often in exaggerated terms) may well be one of the most important benefits the challenger possesses.[43]

When there is no incumbent, candidates attack the record of the current administration (if they do not represent the same political party) or even an opponent's record in a previous position. Whatever becomes the focus of criticism, the object is to attack—to create doubt in voters' minds regarding the incumbent's/opponent's ability—to stimulate public awareness of any problems that exist, or to foster a sense of dissatisfaction and even unhappiness with the state of affairs generally.

In addition, a few challengers extend the attack strategy to demand publicly an investigation of some aspect of the incumbent's record or administration. This was the case, for example, during the 1982 gubernatorial campaign in Connecticut. The Republican challenger demanded that the Democratic governor's transportation department be investigated because he said that nearly all companies who won contracts from the department were big contributors to the Democratic party.* Whether or not investigations such as these ever take place is almost unimportant. The tactic is to call attention to some alleged problem or instance of wrongdoing within the incumbent's administration and thus imply, at least indirectly, that the incumbent has some serious difficulties and therefore does not deserve another term.

Interestingly, attack is so much a part of challenger style, that it frequently occurs even when the predominant public perception of the incumbent is that a credible job has been done. In this instance, the challenger may minimize the importance of the accomplishments, credit them to someone or something else (often another branch or level of government that happens to be controlled by their own party), never mention the accomplishments, or point out that in the years ahead ac-

---

*To some extent, the governor and his party were vulnerable on the issue in that the former commissioner of the department had, some months earlier, been arrested and charged with taking kickbacks.

complishments will be viewed as problems. However various challengers go about it, their ability to attack existing records or policies is a crucial tool and integral to the overall style.

Taking the offensive position on issues. Essentially, the strategy involves nothing more than taking the offensive position on issues important to the campaign—probing, questioning, challenging, attacking but never presenting concrete solutions for problems. It is the incumbent who has to defend unworkable solutions to insolvable problems; the challenger can limit rhetoric to developing problems, keeping the incumbent in a position where all actions have to be defended.[44] In a sense, it is part of a challenger's expected role—to criticize, attack, point out needs—generally guiding voters to begin thinking that the incumbent has been ineffective. Challengers are not expected to solve problems (they have had no chance as officeholders to do so). This is, of course, a major advantage (one of the relatively few), and those who abandon it often lose the election. As a matter of fact, the more detailed that challengers become in offering solutions, the more material they provide to be attacked themselves. In other words, when they drop the offensive, they have essentially traded places with incumbents, thus compounding their difficulties because unlike incumbents they lack the tools to solve problems. Thus the strategy is simply to talk about what is wrong without suggesting any precise ways in which conditions can be righted.

History is replete with examples of successful challengers who used this strategy and won. In 1932 Franklin Roosevelt never divulged the contents of his "New Deal"; in 1952 Dwight Eisenhower never suggested how he would deal with the Korean conflict except to promise that he would personally go there and look it over; in 1960 John Kennedy never shared the details of the "New Frontier"; in 1968 Richard Nixon only said he had a plan regarding the war in Vietnam but never provided any clues regarding it; in 1976 Jimmy Carter seldom offered solutions more substantive than his love and admiration for the people; and in 1980 Ronald Reagan never explained just how his supply-side economics would do all he claimed for it in terms of solving the nation's problems. In retrospect, it is unlikely that most of these challengers even knew how they might solve all of the problems they discussed once they were elected. Whether they did or not, solutions were not offered, and the candidates managed to keep their offensive position on the issues while forcing their opponents to defend, justify, and offer plans.

Conversely, in 1964 and again in 1972, two challengers never seemed to understand the essential nature of the strategy. Barry Goldwater and George McGovern thought they had to present specific proposals on topics as varied as welfare and the way to fight wars. As the details of their plans became known, they were subjected to intensive analysis, debated, refuted by opponents and media, and finally rejected as absurd. Goldwater and McGovern not only lost their credibility as serious presidential candidates, they lost an important advantage. Taking and keeping the right to attack without proposing solutions is a major challenger strategy that only the foolish abandon.

Calling for a change. From the beginning of each campaign season, it becomes clear that many candidates announce that they are "willing" to run for office because they believe that a change is necessary. Whether it involves specific programs and policies, philosophical assumptions regarding the nature of government, or even modification in administrative style, calling for a change has become the dominant characteristic of those who challenge.

There are various ways in which the strategy has been employed. For example, John Kennedy talked about the need to "get the country moving again"—a stylistic and substantive change from a passive attitude to aggressive, take-charge action. Jimmy Carter urged a moralistic change—a return to honest, decent, and compassionate government. Ronald

Reagan argued for economic as well as philosophical change, while Edward Kennedy gave, as his only reason for an intra-party challenge, the need for a change in the manner and style of presidential leadership. Perhaps one of the most specific uses of the strategy was exemplified by Senator John Glenn, who in the early months of the surfacing stage of the 1984 presidential campaign, called for a change of direction in budgeting for basic research and technological development as well as a dramatic overhaul of the social security system.

Thus regardless of how it is employed, the essence of challenger style must revolve around seeking change. If a change from existing conditions, incumbents, or administrations is unnecessary, then so too are challengers.

Emphasizing optimism for the future. While most candidates, regardless of the level of office sought, traditionally spend some time during the campaign talking about their vision or their optimism for the future, the strategy is particularly important for those who would challenge the status quo. After all, if existing conditions are so bad, can they ever be better? Thus the task of the challenger is not only to attack but to hold out the promise of a better tomorrow—a day when wrongs will be righted, when justice will prevail, and when health, wealth, and happiness will be more than just vague illusions. In other words, challengers must assume a "rhetoric of optimism" as opposed to a "rhetoric of despair."[45]

This is not to suggest that candidates who employ the strategy dismiss the nation's needs from their discourse; rather, it is a question of emphasis. For example, in 1932 Franklin Roosevelt obviously acknowledged the problems created by the severe economic depression, but the central focus of his campaign was hope for the future. John Kennedy talked about problems, but his emphasis was on the country's potential to get moving again, and Ronald Reagan pledged that he would lead a crusade to make the United States great again. In short, a part of the challenger style is reliance on the positive—

emphasizing hope and faith in the future, an optimism that the nation's tomorrows will, in fact, be better days.

Speaking to traditional values. Even though the overall challenger style is dominated by a call for redirection or change, it does not mean a redefinition of values. In fact, it is just the opposite. Successful challengers must reinforce majority values instead of attempting to forge new ones. In other words, they must have some understanding of the way in which people view themselves and their society—some understanding of the current tenets of the American Dream.

While this strategy has been understood by challengers such as Richard Nixon, Jimmy Carter, and Ronald Reagan, it may be more interesting to explain it by the example of one who did not. In 1972 before suffering the worst defeat in the history of presidential politics, Democratic challenger George McGovern seemed to have little comprehension of what most citizens wanted. He talked about massive or radical changes in welfare and tax reform, military spending and inflation, school busing, amnesty for those who had left the country rather than participate in the Vietnam War, and the need for more civil rights legislation. What McGovern failed to understand was that most citizens "were tired of social reforms, tired of the 'good-cause' people; that the majority preferred to live their own lives privately, unplagued by moralities, or war, or riots, or violence."[46] Middle-class citizens viewed McGovern as a candidate of an elitist upper class whose values they did not understand except to know that they angered and frightened them. Through his failure to speak to the dreams or visions of the electorate, McGovern abandoned an important strategy of the challenger style.

Appearing to represent the philosophical center. Throughout our political history, successful challengers have been ideological representatives from the mainstream of the major parties, or they have tried to appear as though they were. While some

111

may have been, on one or two issues, a bit to the right or left of the majority of the party, they have not been representatives of the outer or fringe groups. In most campaigns, the fringe groups eventually have compromised and supported their party's candidate, even though that candidate may have been more conservative or liberal than they would have preferred. Even in the presidential campaign in 1980, Ronald Reagan, who had long been the champion of the ultraconservatives within the GOP, attempted to position himself closer to the ideological Republican middle once he had secured the nomination.

The only two major exceptions in contemporary presidential politics have been Barry Goldwater and George McGovern, each of whom, as the candidate of fringe groups, did not try to reposition himself in the center of his respective party. Instead, each attempted to reform the ideological majority around the ideological minority. In so doing, they failed to employ a traditional challenger strategy.

Delegating personal or harsh attacks. Although attack remains a central imperative of the challenger style, successful candidates (particularly in statewide or national races) do not themselves indulge in demagogic rhetoric. While smear tactics and political hatchet work have been a part of elective politics for years, wise challengers have left harsh or vitriolic language to running mates, surrogate speakers, or to their campaign ads and printed materials. The reason for delegating this kind of attack is, at least in part, related to the symbolic nature of the campaign itself. As we have mentioned earlier, campaigns are a symbolic representation of what or how candidates might behave if elected—a kind of vignette from which voters are able to transfer campaign performance into performance as officeholders. Thus the challenger who likens the incumbent to Hitler, asserts that the president behaves like a reformed drunk, or argues that the incumbent is ignorant of foreign policy, as did George McGovern in 1972 and Edward Kennedy in 1980, is unwise.

Demagogy is never viewed as an asset and normally back-fires for the challenger who employs it. Perhaps the comment of one New Hampshire voter after witnessing a Kennedy attack on President Carter illustrates our point: "Carter right now is running as the President of the United States. He's got opposition from big business, other countries, and rabble-rousers like Ted Kennedy. I'm going to back the President of the United States."[47]

These then are the strategies that comprise the challenger style. While there are fewer of them than there are incumbency strategies, they can also be powerful when used correctly. However, those who employ them, just as those who employ their counterparts, must understand the importance of image creation and maintenance. For example, it does little good if a candidate attacks the record of the incumbent but does so using demagogic language or leaves no outlet for the promise of a better tomorrow. In a similar manner, those who fail to understand the necessity of appearing to represent the values of the majority of the electorate as they call for a change in the course or direction of present policies will have little success. In short, challenger campaigning is difficult primarily because being a challenger is not nearly as advantageous as being an incumbent. Challengers win but not as often. Challengers have some advantages over incumbents but not very many. In the final analysis, challengers may be only as successful as incumbents are incompetent to employ the symbolic and pragmatic strategies their office provides.

Campaign Style and Political Women

Perhaps the observation of one political woman is our best entry into the paradoxical area of campaign style and women. As a former New Jersey assemblywoman said: "The biggest asset for a woman candidate is being a woman, and the biggest liability is not being a man."[48] This comment strikes at the heart of the major issue facing most women who are candi-

113

dates for elective office because gender is still a variable that significantly influences the manner in which campaigning is accomplished.

To some extent, whether or not a candidate happens to be a woman may seem to be a concern of the past because the number of females in elective office has increased a great deal in a relatively short time. For example, prior to 1970 there were no female governors (elected in their own right), no women mayors of major cities, no women serving as lieutenant governors, and less than 350 women in state legislatures. Women were numerous only at the lowest levels of politics— organizing or attending party events, getting out the vote, putting up posters, arranging coffees for neighbors to meet male candidates, doing the telephoning, collecting money, and organizing other women to volunteer their time to campaign door-to-door for male candidates. However, by 1979 there were 6 women serving as lieutenant governors, 2 governors, 1 senator, 735 mayors (including five mayors of big cities), 770 in state legislatures, and 16 members of the House of Representatives. Following the 1980 elections, there were 16,136 women serving in elected offices or 10,371 more than there had been just five years earlier.

Thus there has been an important increase in the number of women who have not only sought but have been successful in overcoming enough of the obstacles to win elective office.* What these figures do not reveal, however, is that even with the advances, the ratio of women to men remains small at all levels of elected governmental positions. In addition, the rate of change is slow for the most competitive offices at the federal level. For example, women seldom receive a nomination for the U.S. Senate or House races where seats are actually open

---

*As a number of studies have illustrated, the obstacles of political women include little party support, lack of professional positions that prepare them for political leadership, public suspicion regarding their family life, little access to the financial elite in a community, and personal appearance and demeanor.

(the incumbent is retiring or new districts have been created) or where the party has a numerical advantage. Finally, even when women receive the nomination of their party, they still face a more difficult race than their male counterparts because their gender creates unique problems in campaign style.

In examining the manner in which candidates campaign for elective office, two major styles have been identified along with the strategies that define them and give them form. While these styles do characterize the campaigning of men, they do not work as well for women, largely because their employment would violate still dominant public norms and expectations regarding appropriate behavior. In other words, some of the basic strategies of the incumbency and challenger styles cannot be used successfully in the campaigns of most women.

In spite of the increased number of women who run for office each election year, most candidates and therefore most incumbents are still men. Thus the overwhelming majority of women have run and continue to run "in the unenviable position of challengers."[49] Not only are they challengers, they are office seekers for the first time, which means that like all beginning candidates they must face the hurdles of finding supporters, attracting resources, and building a campaign organization for the first time.[50] The problem is that, unlike male candidates, each of these tasks is more difficult since three important challenger strategies frequently cannot be employed because to do so might well create problems with their public image. For example, one of the core strategies of the challenger is attack. In fact, attacking the record of the incumbent is one of the few real advantages the challenger possesses. Yet women who initiate aggressive and forceful attacks may be viewed as unfeminine, shrill, vicious, nagging, or (as one candidate put it) a "superbitch"[51] and therefore be dismissed as abnormal. The traditional view of women as deferential, soft, and feminine continues to dominate public attitudes. Thus the use of vigorous attacks conflicts with accepted stereotypes of the ideal or typical woman.

A second problem for women as challengers relates to taking the offensive position on issues important in the campaign. Ordinarily successful challengers will push opponents (especially the incumbent) to offer solutions but carefully avoid doing so themselves. However, women (largely because some suspicion remains that they have little competence in public affairs and do not really understand complex issues) must make it clear that they are competent and knowledgeable. To avoid offering solutions to problems may well reinforce the old "dumb female" stereotype. But when women offer detailed solutions to evidence knowledge and familiarity with issues, they lose the offensive position crucial to challengers.

The final strategy women are limited in employing is speaking to traditional values. The strategy is restricted largely because their candidacy itself is inconsistent with conventionally held values and stereotypes regarding women.

Even though increased employment outside the home in the last 15 years may have weakened the traditional role of women, in a great many families it remains true that the wife is expected to maintain the household and raise the children. Her role is one of nurturing, not of leading. This is why the female candidate who has a family frequently goes to great lengths to exhibit or talk about how much they support her political efforts—trying to show that in spite of her candidacy she has not ignored tradition. Like the other problems, this one also poses a real dilemma. If she emphasizes that her values and personal orientation are conventional (not really so different from those whose votes she seeks), she could well lose the support of what might have been a natural constituency. Feminists may work against her just as they might any other candidate whom they feel does not represent their interests. There is evidence suggesting that women do vote for and support women,[52] but she loses this vote if she employs to any significant extent the traditional challenger strategy.

The problems of political women are not confined to those who employ the strategies of the challenger. Even on the rela-

116

tively rare occasions when the woman is the incumbent, she is still unable to use at least two important incumbency strategies because, once again, they may create risks for her candidacy. For example, one of the hallmarks of the incumbency style is running on one's record—talking about accomplishments. The skillful incumbent does not get sidetracked into answering all of the charges and attacks of the challenger but instead makes accomplishments the focus of rhetoric. However, when women try to employ this strategy, it seldom works because even though they are incumbents they continue to have to defend themselves (perhaps from charges about their personal lives—whether they are neglecting their families by serving in public office or whether separation from husbands means that they are sexually deviant—or even from attacks regarding their mental and physical capacity to serve). In a similar fashion, it is difficult for women to use an "above the political trenches" image, largely because they cannot afford, even as incumbents, to stop overt campaigning. In other words, because the credibility of women in politics is still so fragile, once attained, women who are incumbents must continue doing those sorts of things that allowed them to win in the first place.

It may be that many of the distinctions that exist between the campaign styles of men and women may one day be nonexistent. However, in the immediate future, the female candidate will continue encountering problems in creating a credible image because "traditional stereotypes about women and conventional expectations about political leaders do not blend together smoothly. Change will occur slowly as more women permeate political life and the image of women in leadership positions is assimilated in the public consciousness."53

CONCLUSIONS

In this chapter, we have examined an important, yet largely unstudied, element of elective politics—campaign style. In so doing, we considered style as sets of communication strategies that are employed by all candidates and noted the relationship of image and advancements in transportation and communication to their creation and maintenance.

The incumbency style was defined as a blend of symbolic and pragmatic communication strategies designed to make candidates be perceived by voters as not only good enough for the office sought but appear as if they already possess the office. Fifteen different yet complementary strategies were examined. In a similar manner, we analyzed the challenger style, defining it as a series of communication strategies designed to persuade voters that change is needed and that the candidate is the best person to bring about change. Then seven different yet complementary strategies were discussed.

Finally, we considered the campaign styles of the contemporary political woman and noted that because conventional images of political leaders do not yet match the dominant stereotypes about women they are unable to employ some of the strategies that are important to incumbents and challengers.

NOTES

1. Bruce E. Gronbeck, "The Functions of Presidential Campaigning," *Communication Monographs* 45 (November 1978): 268–80.

2. James Tobin, *The People's Choice* (Detroit: Detroit News, 1978), p. 3.

3. Ibid.

4. Irwin Silber, *Songs America Voted By* (New York: Stackpole Books, 1971), p. 34.

5. Kenneth E. Boulding, *The Image* (Ann Arbor: University of Michigan Press, 1961), p. 6.

6. Thomas E. Patterson, *The Mass Media Election* (New York: Praeger, 1980), p. 134.

7. Susan Hellweg, "An Examination of Voter Conceptualizations of the Ideal Political Candidate," *Southern Speech Communication Journal* XLIV (Summer 1979): 373–74.

8. Garrett J. O'Keefe, "Political Campaigns and Mass Communication Research," in *Political Communication: Issues and Strategies for Research,* ed. Steven H. Chaffee (Beverly Hills: Sage, 1975), pp. 147–48.

9. Robert Webb, "America May Rediscover Its Moral Roots," *Cincinnati Enquirer,* July 11, 1982, F1.

10. Jacob J. Wakshlag and Nadyne G. Edison, "Attraction, Credibility, Perceived Similarity, And The Image Of Public Figures," *Communication Quarterly* 27 (Fall 1979): 27. See also Dan Nimmo and Robert L. Savage, *Candidates and Their Images: Concepts, Methods and Findings* (Pacific Palisades, Calif.: Goodyear, 1976). For one of the important early studies on the construct labeled source valence, see V. J. Lashbrook, "Leadership Emergence and Source Valence: Concepts in Support of Interaction Theory and Measurement," *Human Communication Research* 1 (Summer 1975): 308–15.

11. Wakshlag, "Attraction, Credibility, Perceived Similarity," pp. 27–28.

12. Hellweg, "Ideal Political Candidate," p. 382.

13. Frederick Williams, *The Communications Revolution* (Beverly Hills: Sage, 1982), esp. pp. 183–99.

14. Ibid., p. 37.

15. Ibid.

16. Edgar E. Willis, "Radio and Presidential Campaigning," *Central States Speech Journal* XX (Fall 1969): 187.

17. Ibid., p. 191.

18. Ibid.

19. Williams, *Communications Revolution,* pp. 17–39.

20. Ibid.

21. Theodore H. White, *The Making of the President, 1968* (New York: Atheneum, 1969), p. 154.

22. For a discussion of the potential of what he terms "push-button government," see Williams, *Communications Revolution*, pp. 183–99.

23. W. Lance Bennett, "The Ritualistic and Pragmatic Bases of Political Campaign Discourse," *Quarterly Journal of Speech* 63 (October 1977): 228.

24. Keith V. Erickson and Wallace V. Schmidt, "Presidential Political Silence: Rhetoric and the Rose Garden Strategy," *Southern Speech Communication Journal* XLVII (Summer 1982): 402–21.

25. R. F. Fenno, Jr., *Home Style: House Members in Their Districts* (Boston: Little Brown, 1978), p. 211.

26. Robert E. Denton, Jr., *The Symbolic Dimensions Of The American Presidency* (Prospect Heights, Ill.: Waveland Press, 1982), p. 58.

27. Theodore H. White, *Breach of Faith* (New York: Atheneum, 1975), p. 322.

28. Dan D. Nimmo, *Popular Images of Politics* (Englewood Cliffs, N.J.: Prentice-Hall, 1974), p. 92.

29. John Louis Lucaites, "Rhetoric And The Problem Of Legitimacy," in *Dimensions Of Argument: Proceedings of the Second Summer Conference on Argumentation*, eds. George Ziegelmueller and Jack Rhodes (Annandale, Va.: Speech Communication Association), pp. 799–807.

30. Murray Edelman, "The Politics of Persuasion," in *Choosing the President*, ed. James David Barber (Englewood Cliffs, N.J.: Prentice-Hall, 1974), p. 171.

31. Denton, *Symbolic Dimensions*, p. 61.

32. Edelman, "Politics of Persuasion," p. 171.

33. William R. Brown, "Television and the Democratic National Convention of 1968," *Quarterly Journal of Speech* LV (October 1969): 241. For a more extensive treatment of pseudoevents, see Daniel J. Boorstin's classic, *The Image* (New York: Atheneum, 1980). Originally, the book was published under the title *The Image or What Happened to the American Dream* in 1961.

34. Ron Alridge, "Local News Stations Help Cast Byrne in Her Own Image," *Chicago Tribune*, April 8, 1982, sec. 3, p. 17.

35. Theodore H. White, *America in Search of Itself* (New York: Harper & Row, 1982), p. 296.

36. Ibid., p. 295.

37. Frank Kessler, *The Dilemmas of Presidential Leadership: Of Caretakers and Kings* (Englewood Cliffs, N.J.: Prentice-Hall, 1982), p. 313–14.

38. Dan Nimmo and James E. Combs, *Subliminal Politics: Myths & Mythmakers In America* (Englewood Cliffs, N.J.: Prentice-Hall, 1980), p. 78.

39. Ibid.

40. Barry Brummett, "Towards a Theory of Silence as a Political Strategy," *Quarterly Journal of Speech* 66 (October 1980): 289–303.

41. "The President," *Newsweek*, August 28, 1972, p. 15. See also Judith S. Trent, "Image Building Strategies in the 1972 Presidential Campaign,"

Speaker and Gavel 10, (January 1973): 39–45; and for a discussion of the use of surrogate speakers, see Chapter 6.

42. Ellen Reid Gold and Judith S. Trent, "Campaigning for President in New Hampshire: 1980," *Exetasis* VI (April 1980): 7.

43. Nelson W. Polsby and Aaron Wildavsky, *Presidential Elections* (New York: Charles Scribner's Sons, 1976), p. 165.

44. Judith S. Trent and Jimmie D. Trent, "The Rhetoric of the Challenger: George Stanley McGovern," *Central States Speech Journal* XXV (Spring 1974): 16.

45. Ibid., p. 17.

46. Ibid.

47. Gold and Trent, "Campaigning for President," p. 9.

48. Ruth B. Mandel, *In the Running* (New Haven: Ticknor & Fields, 1981), p. 31.; for a statistical profile of political women (officeholders) as compared with their male counterparts, see Marilyn Johnson and Susan Carroll, "Statistical Report: Profile of Women Holding Office, 1977," in *Women in Public Office: A Biographical Directory and Statistical Analysis,* 2nd ed., compiled by the Center for the American Woman and Politics (Metuchen, N.J.: Scarecrow Press, 1978).

49. Mandel, *In The Running*, p. 17.

50. Ibid., p. 18.

51. Ibid., p. 42.

52. Ibid., esp. pp. 231–49.

53. Ibid., p. 62.

4

Communicative
Mass Channels
of Political
Campaigning

NO OTHER NATION IN THE WORLD CON-
SUMES SO MUCH MASS COMMUNICATION.
BY 1980 WE WERE BUYING 62 MILLION
DAILY NEWSPAPERS AND HAD 1,700 VARIE-
ties from which to choose. Our radios were on five hours a day,
and almost 10 million of us were subscribing to weekly news
magazines. However, the medium we devour to a greater extent than all others is television. Almost 99 percent of all
households have one television set, and approximately 50 percent have two or more, making television more plentiful than
home telephones or automobiles.[1] More striking, however,
than the number of television sets owned is the frequency of
their use. Television is the major source of entertainment and
information, the primary leisure time activity. We have our
sets turned on over six hours every day and spend 40 percent of
our time watching it.[2] In other words, it is a dominant force in
the lives and environments of most of the public, a fact that
was called to our attention in a well-known study conducted in
1978. When the Roper organization surveyed citizens to learn
which medium they relied on to tell them what was going on in

the world, researchers found that television was the primary as well as the most credible source of information.[3]

Not only is U.S. mass media consumption unequaled, in no other nation is it so inextricably linked to the electoral process. Mass communication has become the center stage for all major political events. For example, daily newspapers and weekly magazines keep political people and issues in our minds as they frequently report the result of the latest poll taken to measure how individuals feel about the president, governors, members of Congress, candidates, and specific issues and controversies. Radio programming is punctuated with five- and ten-minute news reports regarding some aspects of politics or with 30- and 60-second spot advertisements for candidates and local "vital" issues. But it is television that has most dramatically linked us to large-scale political campaign events such as presidential debates, national nominating conventions, primary victories and losses, candidates' gaffes, campaign trips, news conferences, election eve rituals and campaign speeches, biographies and commercials. It was television that brought Ronald Reagan to national political attention in 1964 as he delivered one of history's most financially successful speeches; just as 16 years later, television announced his election as president even as millions of citizens were still voting.* In short, the mass media and especially television have had a profound impact on the electoral process by connecting citizens and political campaigns.

In spite of this, the influence of mass communication on political behavior remains uncertain. Although media effect is one of the most studied areas in the social sciences, after 60 years of intense research, there are relatively few absolutes,

---

*On election night, 1980, even though people were still voting somewhere in virtually every state in the union, NBC television announced that Ronald Reagan would be the next president of the United States. Although the Reagan victory did not actually exist at 8:15 P.M. EST (not a single vote had been certified by the state canvassing agencies), the fact that everyone believed the network announcement demonstrates faith in the medium.

largely because the findings of one generation of scholars has been reversed by the next.

Thus the purpose of this chapter is to sort through the major theories, perspectives, hypotheses, and models that have been advanced regarding the media's role in or influence on political behavior and attempt to draw at least some general conclusions. In so doing, it may be helpful to understand that for some scholars the "theories" are not theories at all because they are not all unambiguous, deductive, and interrelated structures from which empirically ascertained and consistent laws or general principles have been derived. For our purposes in this chapter, however, theories come in various packages. Although most have been empirically derived, not all are unambiguously and deductively determined. Moreover, if we insisted that the theories presented here must account for or predict general principles, there would be relatively little to discuss. Few of the perspectives or hypotheses have provided the consistency needed for determining general laws or principles. In other words, when it comes to the question of the role of media in determining political behavior, there is no one grand theory. There are a number of partial theories or what (in another context) communication scholar Frank E. X. Dance refers to as particularistic theoretical bits and pieces,[4] but no single theoretical development that can account for or predict related phenomena. It is for this reason that we discuss a number of the major perspectives and approaches that have generated research. Whether or not multitheoretical conceptualizations are desirable or undesirable, the fact is that six decades of research have frequently led to conclusions that contrast with one another. This is one element to which we pay special attention as we proceed through the various theoretic approaches.

We define "mass" in a standard way as consisting of people representing all social, religious, and ethnic strata from all regions of the country. Moreover, they are anonymous (do not necessarily know one another) and therefore act not in concert but spontaneously as individuals. We use the terms "mass channels" and "mass media" interchangeably to refer to the primary means of mass communication (radio, television, newspapers, and magazines). While we would not deny the existence of other modes of mass communication such as books and motion pictures in the political campaign any more than we would refuse to recognize forms of "mini" communication such as posters, billboards, and campaign literature, they are simply not as important. The major perspectives have been generated from studies of radio, television, newspapers, and magazines.

Finally, it is important to understand that the focus of this chapter is not candidates and the campaign process but voters and the campaign process. The principles that are analyzed center around the effect of mass communication on the political behavior of citizens. As such, we will be concerned with the way researchers have answered such questions as: (1) to what extent do the media influence cognitions and behavior? (2) what are the primary mass communication models that have guided research? (3) what have been the effects of the media on the electoral process itself? (4) how do people use the media in the political process?

The chapter is organized chronologically in that the general conceptualizations from early and contemporary research compose separate sections. Within each, major studies are examined and any specific hypotheses or models that have been derived from them will be discussed. The conclusion focuses on a summary of principles regarding the influence of the media that are most important in understanding the nature of political campaign communication.

EARLY STUDIES

The media's influence on political behavior has been a subject of scholarly investigation since the 1920s. Although readers might question the need to be aware of anything other than the most recent research findings, many of the early studies have been of tremendous importance. In fact, their impact has been so profound, they are considered "classics," and the conclusions they articulated as well as the methods they employed influenced all who followed. Thus we will discuss each of the major perspectives as well as the general models or hypotheses that were derived from them during the 30-plus-year period in which they dominated mass communication research.

Hypodermic Effect

The assumption that the press is a powerful force in shaping public opinion had been around for centuries. In 1529, 50 years after the printing press had been introduced to England, King Henry VIII seized control of the printing industry. Licensed printers held their patents only if what they printed pleased him.[5] In the mid-1600s the Puritan establishment in Massachusetts Bay Colony maintained strict control over printing because they feared that a free press might threaten the government and promote religious heresies.[6] In 1722 the founder and editor of a Boston newspaper, the *New England Courant,* was jailed for three weeks because of his attacks on the government.[7] Years later, the press was thought to have been a powerful force in creating revolutionary fervor in the United States, for providing passion and visibility to the abolitionist movement, and for provoking Congress to go to war with Spain.

However, it was not until the 1920s and 1930s that researchers actually tried to determine the power of mass communication in shaping values and behaviors of citizens. The motivation to learn more about the ways in which media could influence the public was provided, in large measure, by Adolf Hitler's propaganda machine, which seemed to have captured the minds of the German people, the brilliant yet frightening movies of the Nazi mass rallies, and the use of the radio by Roberto Mussolini in Italy and Father Charles Coughlin in the United States to stir public support and sentiment for the fascists. The Information and Education Branch of the United States Army began recruiting social scientists to study the influence of media persuasion. As researchers analyzed the effects of propaganda films such as "The Battle of Britain" or the pro-German magazine, *The Galilean*, they confirmed what had been only assumed for centuries. The media really were powerful; they had the strength to not only change people's attitudes but to alter their behavior. And because citizens were often helpless to resist the persuasion of propaganda, they were easily "bamboozled." Moreover, according to the researchers, these effects occurred in all people because, despite individual attributes and characteristics, individuals responded in the same way when they received similar messages. Audiences were like mobs; there were no individual minds but only a group consciousness. Messages went directly from the media to the individual where they were immediately assimilated. "Messages were literally conceived of as being 'injected' into the mind where they were 'stored' in the form of changes in feelings and attitudes. Eventually such feelings or attitudes produced the behavior desired by the message source."[8] This is, essentially, what researchers called the hypodermic effect or the hypodermic needle model.

Although it may be difficult for us to subscribe to specific aspects of the hypodermic model, it must be viewed in terms of the context in which it was developed. The 1920s through the early 1940s was a time of worldwide social, political, and economic unrest, passion, and violence. Economic depression, the rise of fascism and Hitler, and the domination of the Nazis throughout much of Europe suggested irrational yet somehow controlled mass group behavior. It seemed entirely likely that people's minds were being manipulated by powerful propaganda devices. In the view of many who were studying it, the "mass media loomed as agents of evil aiming at the total destruction of democratic society. First the newspaper and later the radio, were feared as powerful weapons able to rubber-stamp ideas upon the minds of defenseless readers and listeners."[9]

By the late 1930s, the hypodermic effect was widely enough accepted (even by those social scientists not involved in the government propaganda research program) to be applied specifically to the electoral process. One of the first systematic attempts to determine the political impact of the press was undertaken in 1937. Harold Gosnell studied the relationship of social and economic characteristics and newspaper-reading habits to election returns in several Chicago neighborhoods and found that the endorsements of newspapers could influence the way readers voted.[10] Thus social scientists were provided with additional proof of the seemingly unlimited power of the media to persuade.

Limited Effects or the Social Influence Model

Although the work of many of the army's psychologists and sociologists who were studying the effects of propaganda continued to reflect the hypodermic thesis, by the early 1940s, the findings of some researchers began to challenge the idea that the media were so potent that the public was mesmerized by them. One of the most important challenges occurred when three social scientists from Columbia University's Bureau of Applied Social Research, Paul Lazarsfeld, Bernard Berelson, and Hazel Gaudet, studied the 1940 presidential campaign and discovered (much to their surprise) that campaign propaganda had little impact on the way the electorate had voted. This study and others that followed began to build a competing explanation for media influence, one that was in stark contrast to the presumption that people were unable to control their own destinies or the destiny of the nation. It was, of course, a much more comforting thought than the hypodermic thesis because it provided reassurance that in the United States individual rationality and society's sense of order could not be overthrown because of the seizure or control of the media by a demagogue or someone who had gone insane.

The 1940 study began to form what became known as the social influence model. Twenty years later, mass communication scholar, Joseph Klapper, in summarizing the conclusions of the work done on the impact of the media during the 1940s and 1950s, concluded that media effects are limited and even in cases where they do occur, are mediated by other factors.[11] Thus he coined the term "limited effects model," a label that obviously stands in direct contrast with the earlier hypodermic perspective.

To understand this shift, it may be best to take a closer look at those studies that are regarded as the classics and that collectively influenced generations of mass communication scholars and their view of media and politics.

The first study by Lazarsfeld, Berelson, and Gaudet was conducted in Erie County, Ohio, a section of northern Ohio fairly equally divided between a city and farmland. Lazarsfeld and his colleagues wanted to measure the repercussions of campaign press coverage during a presidential election. At the outset, they divided potential political effects into three categories: first, they believed the media could arouse public interest in the campaign and encourage voters to seek out more information about the candidates and issues; second, they reasoned that the press could reinforce existing political beliefs to make them stronger and more resistant to change; and third, they hypothesized that the media were powerful enough to convert attitudes, changing voters from supporting one candidate or party to supporting the opposition.

From May to November, a member of the research team interviewed someone each month in every twentieth house or apartment in the county. In total, 600 people were questioned about political parties, candidates, issues, and the news. Interviewers kept carefully structured records of each talk, and from these records Lazarsfeld and his colleagues were able to reconstruct how Erie County citizens made their decision between Franklin Roosevelt and Wendell Wilkie. The results were published four year later in a book called *The People's Choice*.[12]

Although Lazarsfeld and his colleagues believed that their research would confirm the prevailing thesis that the media were capable of controlling individual thought processes, they instead found that very few people changed their vote in response to the campaign propaganda and that those who changed did not attribute their conversion to media information. Specifically, they learned that:

1) people who read or listened to a substantial amount of campaign media coverage were more likely to become more interested in the election; but
2) their interest and activation were selective in that they tended to seek out stories that were consistent with prior political attitudes; and
3) those relatively few who did change their minds, did so not because of attending to the media directly but by the filtering of information to them from people in the community whom they respected. Such people were perceived to be highly active, highly informed, interested in politics, and therefore more likely than others to read or listen to media coverage of the campaign. These individuals were labeled "opinion leaders."

In the largest sense, the results of the Erie County study were not as important as the two explanations that Lazarsfeld and his colleagues offered for their findings. The explanations formed the cornerstone of the social influence theory. The researchers maintained that if a message presented by the media is in conflict with group norms it will be rejected. "Since groups have opinion leaders who transmit mass media information to individuals who do not attend to the media, these leaders influence whatever opinion change takes place in the followers; media messages do not have direct impact."[13] The

131

second explanation given for their findings was that people are selective in those campaign messages to which they attend. They only listen to or read messages that are most consistent with their own beliefs, attitudes, and values. In other words, voters use the content of the media to support or reinforce the voting conclusions they would have reached because of their social predispositions. Interestingly, the concept of selective exposure was based on an analysis of only 122 persons who by August had not yet decided for which candidate they would vote. While 54 percent of those people with a Republican predisposition exposed themselves to Republican material and 61 percent with a Democratic predisposition exposed themselves to Democratic material, 35 percent of the Republicans and 22 percent of the Democrats did expose themselves to material from the other party—material that presumably was inconsistent with prior beliefs or social predispositions.

These percentages were never explained and the concept of selective exposure became a widely accepted phenomenon not only for the sociologically oriented voter studies but also by psychologists who eventually incorporated it into a series of studies regarding involuntary and voluntary exposure to information to reduce psychological dissonance.[14]

The second of the classic studies conducted by the Columbia group was also staged in a single location. In 1948 Paul Lazarsfeld, Bernard Berelson, and William McPhee went to Elmira, New York to determine voter behavior during the presidential campaign. The Elmira results, published in 1954 in *Voting*, supported the Erie County findings that campaign press coverage converted few voters and that information was disseminated from opinion leaders.

The third single-location study was mounted in Decatur, Illinois and was reported by Elihu Katz and Lazarsfeld in the book *Personal Influence*. The researchers interviewed 800 women regarding "four arenas of everyday decision: marketing, fashions, public affairs, and movie-going" and for each arena asked respondents "not only about themselves and their own behavior but about other people as well—people who influence them, and people for whom they are influential."[15]

Essentially, the results of the Decatur study confirmed the social influence model, although they also produced a more precise conceptualization of "the two-step flow of communication." The idea that had been hypothesized from the Erie County data suggested that "ideas often flow from radio and print to the opinion leaders and from them to the less active sections of the population."[16] However, in Decatur, the Columbia group wanted to compare the media behavior of opinion leaders and nonleaders "to see whether the leaders tend to be the more exposed, and the more responsive group when it comes to influence stemming from the mass media."[17] They discovered that the women they studied were willing to admit that they were influenced by other women, that leadership varied by topic, that leaders for each topic had different social and psychological characteristics, and that no single leader exercised control over the political beliefs of others. However, their most important finding, in terms of media impact on the electoral process, was that "opinion leaders were not more likely than followers to attribute influence upon their beliefs or opinions to the mass media."[18] Thus as a result of the third Columbia study, the role of the media was reduced even further in the minds of most social scientists. It appeared as if no group sizable enough to be measured was persuaded by media messages during a political campaign.

In 1952 another group of researchers began examining voters' behavior. Using the 1952 presidential election as their base, the University of Michigan Survey Research Center* (SRC) soon replaced the Columbia group as the dominant research force in large-scale voting studies. Methodologically as well as conceptually, the work of the Michigan group represented a major shift in the effort to examine voters and their behavior.[19] For example, the SRC relied on panels of potential

---

*Now called the Center for Political Studies, Institute for Social Research, the University of Michigan.

voters based on national probability samples rather than a single community. In focusing on national behaviors, they moved away from sociological explanations (the emphasis on traditions, structure, composition, and the sociological nature of major institutions within single communities), which the Lazarsfeld group had presumed were the reasons for voters' predispositions. Instead, the Michigan researchers sought cognitive and attitudinal reasons for voting decisions. They asked citizens to indicate their party affiliation (Columbia had studied parties only in terms of social predispositions that led voters to choose one candidate over another). Thus with party identification as a key factor in explaining voters' attitudes and evaluation of candidates, the idea of interpersonal communication and the two-step flow conceptualization as the primary means of information diffusion was relegated to a "relatively unimportant position in the SRC model."[20]

However, in one important respect, the early SRC studies did not differ from their Columbia counterparts. In spite of the fact that in 1952 television played a role in the presidential primaries, in the nominating conventions, and in the general advertising campaigns of at least one of the candidates, the Michigan researchers concluded that the impact of the mass media on the electoral process was minimal.[21] In fact, in the *American Voter* (a book based on the data collected in 1952 and 1956), the researchers indicated that it was party identification and not television that was the important factor in the development of political cognitions, attitudes, and behavior.[22]*

Finally, in 1963 undoubtedly in an attempt to revitalize a theory that was being challenged by many, Lazarsfeld and his colleagues described a modification of the two-step flow. In the new conceptualization, information from the media was relayed from one opinion leader to another before it was passed on to followers. The revision became known as the "multistep flow" and because more people were added to the transmis-

---

*SRC studies dealt only minimally with the mass media until the 1974 election.

sion process, the persuasive power of the media was viewed as even less significant than it had been before. Moreover, information not only traveled from opinion leader to opinion leader, any one of these people could act as a "gatekeeper" and thereby prevent a follower from even being exposed to part of the information. In other words, opinion leaders functioned not only as conveyers of information among each other and finally to their respective "audiences" they determined just what information would be transmitted.

Although gatekeeping was discussed by Lazarsfeld in relationship to the multistep flow in 1963, the idea was not new. As early as 1950, one study had examined the selection and rejection of messages by gatekeepers. One of the key findings confirmed in many studies that followed was that when media gatekeepers made decisions, they did not have the audience in mind.[23]

Essentially, a gatekeeper is any person in the news-gathering process with authority to make decisions affecting the flow of information to the public. "The image is precisely that of a turnstile gatekeeper at a sporting event—he examines the qualifications of each person in line, and decides whether or not to let him in. The difference is that what gets let in or left out is not a person, but a piece of news."[24] One of the reasons the gatekeeping function has received so much attention is that there are a variety of people in the media who must make decisions regarding the presentation of information and news. Examples include telegraph and wire service editors, reporters, film editors, headline writers, radio and television producers, news program anchors and commentators, and even other media (small newspapers and radio and television stations frequently take their news from the larger and more established media). Thus given the wide spectrum of people who daily determine which of the many possible news items the public will be presented, it is little wonder that gatekeeping has been the subject of scholarly investigation as well as public consternation. Undoubtedly the most famous attack against media gatekeepers was leveled in 1969 by Vice-President Spiro Agnew. One of the broad areas of his criticism concerned the similarities of the various media decision makers. In an address before the Midwest Regional Republican Committee in Des Moines, Iowa, Agnew charged that:

> A small group of men, numbering perhaps no more than a dozen "anchormen," commentators and executive producers, settle upon the 20 minutes or so of film and commentary that is to reach the public. . . . We do know that, to a man, these commentators and producers live and work in the geographical and intellectual confines of Washington, D.C. or New York City—the latter of which James Reston terms the "most unrepresentative community in the entire United States." . . . We can deduce that these men thus read the same newspapers, and draw their political and social views from the same sources. . . . The upshot of all this controversy is that a narrow and distorted picture of America often emerges from the televised news.[25]

Whether or not Agnew's charges were true, they did provoke public discussion as well as a good deal of media response. In addition, gatekeeping continued to be a subject of scholarly investigation throughout the 1960s and 1970s.[26]

In summarizing the major ideas advanced by the early studies of media influence, it is tempting to conclude that in spite of the label of some of them as classics, almost four decades of investigation has little relationship to contemporary theory. Researchers went from one extreme to the other; first media propaganda was the harbinger of all that was evil and then, it had little impact at all. Effects were seen primarily on a one-dimensional level—persuasion. The informational or cognitive function was largely ignored because of the dominance of selective exposure, a concept with little empirical validation then and clearly inadequate now.[27] Moreover, investigators were so intent on confirming the basic tenets of the social influence model that they ignored media effect in such important areas as voter turnout, political activation, and informa-tion seeking. The studies were conducted at a time in which home television sets were far less plentiful than they are today, and so the medium was viewed as having little direct influence on political behavior. Radio and newspapers were important only in their role as reinforcers rather than opinion formers, thus suggesting that voters were limited perceptually by their past.

However, in spite of all this, the early studies remain an important part of our media research heritage for at least four reasons. First, they pointed the way toward research method-ologies that were more sophisticated than those that had been used. Moreover, the Columbia studies were the last massive single-community analysis for many years. And the Michigan studies of the national electorate continue to provide the most authoritative source of election data available. Second, the so-cial influence model did rescue social scientists from the mass media hysteria symbolized by the hypodermic thesis. Third, al-though the Columbia studies may have carried the sociological explanation of voters' behavior to the extreme, they did begin the path toward the study of mass media and interpersonal re-lationships, obviously an important area of political campaign communication. Finally, the limited effects theory served as a catalyst for later scholars who would challenge the idea that the mass media had little impact on voters' behavior or the electoral process. Indeed, the sheer attempt to disprove the theory may well have led to the multiperspectivism that char-acterizes contemporary mass communication research.

CONTEMPORARY STUDIES

Just as the hypodermic thesis reflected society's turmoil and the social influence model depicted a quiet, reflective peo-ple not swayed by campaign propaganda, the mass media re-search of the 1960s and 1970s was a product of or at least representative of its time. If the decade of the 1950s is described by such words as quiet, inactive, or dull, the following years can be characterized as disquieting, tumultuous, and wild. While the federal bureaucracy grew in size and influence, so did citizen involvement in public affairs. Beginning with the civil rights struggle, which brought local groups together to form national organizations, a number of large-scale political and social movements appeared on the national scene. Each of them demanded new social and economic legislation to ensure equality and to guarantee their rights as citizens to help formulate national and international policy. However, each of them also needed various forms of mass communication not only to recruit, organize, and maintain their movements but to publicize their demands by drastic and frequently passionate actions.

The changes in society and the escalation of the social movements corresponded to alterations in the mass media system. It too was growing, largely because of the widespread use of television. More people owned television sets, and it was beginning to replace interpersonal conversations and meetings as a leisure time activity.[28] Television was becoming the most revolutionary branch of journalism. While in the 1950s, television news was typically read by one person seated in front of a wall map, during the next 20 years it became a drama featuring live coverage of national and international events. The sit-ins and marches of the social movements, the urban riots and burning of U.S. cities, the funeral of a young president and the assassination of his alleged killer, the bloody battles of the war in Vietnam all contributed to the transformation of U.S. news gathering and of those social scientists who studied it.[29]

It was in this atmosphere that many mass communication scholars began to question the basic tenets of the social influence model. Although they had no one holistic theory with which to replace it, maintaining that the media had little influence on or played no major role in the electoral process appeared a direct denial of what was happening all around them.

138

A few researchers looked to the reigning paradigm for new explanations. For example, one study in 1962 indicated that uninvolved voters are susceptible to attitude change if any new information reaches them,[30] and another showed that under certain conditions, it is possible for large audiences to get information directly from the media without the intervention of an opinion leader, suggesting that mass communication does not always work in a two-step flow.[31] However, the most important break with the social influence model occurred when social scientists, Jay G. Blumler and Denis McQuail, discovered in a study of the 1964 British parliamentary election that "regular viewers of television news developed significantly different perceptions of the Liberal and Conservative parties."[32] Clearly, it was possible for media to do more than simply reinforce the status quo.

Beginning roughly about the time that the work of Blumler and McQuail appeared to suggest a new perspective for viewing media influence in politics, other theories or quasi theories were being articulated. In the remainder of this section, we discuss the basic assumptions or tenets of four of the most important approaches undertaken during the 1960s and 1970s.

Diffusion of Information

One of the approaches that bridges the gap between the limited effects model and the contemporary conceptualizations is the diffusion of knowledge perspective. It is related to the research that characterizes social influence theory largely because it was initiated in that era and because it acknowledges the importance of interpersonal communication to the dissemination of information. However, it differs from that theory in at least two important respects. First, diffusion research maintains that under certain conditions, media transmission of information will have a direct impact on individuals and can produce changes in their knowledge or even their behavior. Interpersonal communication occurs after the mass media transmit information about news events and is therefore only a response to media reports.[33] The second way in which diffusion research is distinct from social influence is that it does not study attitude changes in voting behavior during political campaigns but focuses instead on the influence of the mass media on the acquisition of political cognitions. In other words, diffusion research is concerned with such topics as knowledge of campaign issues, candidates, and general public affairs. It is also used to investigate possible stages of information dissemination, how specific groups within society become aware of particular political matters, what factors contribute to the acceptance or rejection of political ideas, and what conditions mediate the flow of information about events.

Although diffusion has been defined in a variety of ways, generally, conceptualizations of it in communication research capitalize on the idea of movement—the spread of adoption of new ideas (innovations) through time and space from one individual or group of people to another. In spite of the fact that diffusion research and the resulting diffusion model have roots in the physical sciences, it is employed by a number of disciplines within the social sciences. In the area of our interest, much of the early important work was done by Everett Rogers. In his 1961 book, *Diffusion of Innovations*, and in his later work with Floyd Shoemaker, Rogers discovered a multistage process of innovation diffusion. The four stages are: 1) information or knowledge; 2) persuasion; 3) decision or adoption; and 4) confirmation or reevaluation. In other words, new information is transmitted through society (or from person to person) in a particular sequential pattern. While it can be argued that these stages will not always be either separate or sequential under some conditions for some people, according to Rogers and Shoemaker, the media are important primarily in the first or information stage, where an interest in, awareness of, and understanding of the innovation can be created. Interpersonal communication is important during the last three stages as people seek confirmation or interpretation of the information they have received from the mass media.[34]

To support the view that the media were the predominant sources of information about political news events, early diffusion research in political communication was designed to measure the extent to which messages were transmitted. For example, it was discovered that the media informed most people about the death of Senator Robert Taft, President Eisenhower's decision to seek reelection, the dropping of Senator Thomas Eagleton as the Democratic vice-presidential candidate, and the assassination of John Kennedy.[35] To a large extent, much of the diffusion research even during the 1970s continued to be concentrated on the extent and veridicality of information flow. Thus researchers appeared to be more interested in the attention arousal and information-seeking characteristics of the first stage of the process rather than the later adoption or persuasion stages.[36] In fact, after one recent review of the diffusion approach to political communication studies, it was noted that "except for news dissemination studies, the current political communication literature explicitly making use of the diffusion perspective is as yet small in volume."[37]

In considering the diffusion approach solely in terms of information it may provide about the relationship of media to elective politics, what are the possibilities for the future? While mass communication scholars readily acknowledge that the approach has not yet lived up to its potential, one of them, Steven H. Chaffee, urges a research program in which a virtually universal scheme is developed for categorizing different types of diffusion items according to the type of communication that transmits them, the type of person most receptive to them, and determining the way in which items are relevant from the perspective of the political system.[38] In a similar vein, Robert L. Savage, after reviewing the political diffusion literature, writes that scholars should investigate such questions as: Are diffusing messages causes or effects of human actions?

What latent and/or dysfunctional consequences follow from existing diffusion patterns? Savage then wonders if political communication scholars have used the diffusion approach for all relevant forms of political information.[39] Finally, after analyzing the basic assumptions of the diffusion model, authors Sidney Kraus and Dennis Davis suggest that it should be supplemented by stipulating specific patterns of media use and perception to understand better the conditions that mediate the flow of information.[40]

Thus while the diffusion of information perspective helped redirect the focus of media/political research away from the unidimensional thrust of the social influence model, its potential has yet to be realized.

Uses and Gratifications

A crucial assumption of the uses and gratifications perspective is that a wide range of motives exists for using the mass media and that an individual's media requirements are dictated by such factors as their social roles, situations, or personalities. In other words, media audiences should not be thought of as huge collectivities who watch television shows, attend movies, and read newspapers and magazines for the same reasons.[41]

In one sense, the uses and gratifications perspective is similar to some of the other research approaches discussed in this chapter in that there is really no single theory. We do not mean to imply that the perspective is atheoretical but simply that there are numerous theoretical bits and pieces that compose the perspective. However, as one of its principle advocates, Jay G. Blumler, has argued, the various theories about the phenomena "share a common field of concern, an elementary set of concepts indispensable for intelligibly carving up that terrain, and an identification of certain wider features of the mass communication process with which such core phenomena are presumed to be connected."[42]

Although a diverse range of research has been conducted under the uses and gratifications paradigm, essentially it has been concerned with determining those uses people make of the mass media in the circumstances of their own lives as well as the gratifications they seek and receive from such consumption.

To an extent, part of the popularity of the approach is that it has served as a means of integrating ideas of massive effects (the hypodermic thesis) with limited effects (the social influence model) to form a middle-ground position where the audience is viewed as active, thinking receivers who are neither susceptible to all persuasive media messages nor impervious to them. In fact, it has been argued that it is in this role as an integrative component in an effects model "that the uses and gratifications perspective offers its greatest promise to the study of political communication."[43]

Not only, however, is the approach used for its bridge between the effects models, it has the additional benefit of allowing researchers to study more than just effects—to get at the functions mass media may provide during a political campaign. While some of these functions may be obvious (we read a newspaper account of a candidate's speech to gain more information about the candidate and the campaign), others may be latent (we watch a television commercial about a candidate so that we have enough information about the campaign to maintain our social status as an informed citizen). In other words, the functions served by the media during a campaign are not necessarily what they appear to be. Information or cognitive gain may serve many important purposes for the individual and the uses/gratifications perspective provides a way to examine them.

Although the uses and gratifications paradigm has been especially popular since the 1970s, research conducted under its label goes back as far as the beginning of World War II when studies were published that dealt with the use of radio for entertainment purposes. Similarly, during the following two decades, when commercial television became important, the approach was used to generate data regarding entertainment programming. It was not until the landmark Blumler and McQuail study, published in 1969, that the perspective came into major use in examining political campaigns. In fact, it was this investigation of the 1964 British election that really spelled out the basic assumptions for researchers in political communication. Other studies followed, and in 1974 Blumler and Katz summarized much of the research the perspective had stimulated in *The Uses of Mass Communication.*

In spite of the fact that multiple studies have been conducted under the uses and gratifications paradigm, there is not only the lack of one coherent theory, there is still little agreement about such basic tenets of the perspective as defining what is meant by an active audience, deciding on the difference between needs and motives, or even more important, determining what the specific motives or gratifications are. For example, Blumler and McQuail suggested eight different motivations: using the political content of the media for vote guidance; reinforcement of decisions already made; general surveillance of the political environment; excitement; or because they anticipated using the information in future interpersonal communication situations; and not using or avoiding political messages because of feelings of alienation; partisanship; or because they did not need it for relaxation.[44] However, later researchers have claimed only three motives, which cluster around:

1) cognitive or informational needs
2) diversion needs (including relief from boredom and the constraints of daily routines imposed by the typical or "light" entertainment shows and even the excitement generated by political election campaigns
3) personal identity needs or functions (using the media materials to give added importance to one's own life).[45]

In considering the uses and gratifications perspective in terms of its utility to political campaigns, what can we conclude? Current studies can be classified into such groups as those that attempt to determine audience motives or the antecedents of motives, those that examine the media's ability to provide audience satisfaction, those that explore the linkages between motives and media use, and those that investigate the political effects of the media.[46] Although individual studies in these groups have been valuable in adding to our knowledge about media use and political effect, unanswered questions remain largely because there is so little agreement on the theoretical constructs that have guided individual research. In fact, "even the seemingly straightforward concept of 'media use' has widely varied meanings, including exposure time, intake of various types of media content, and what the person expects to get from the media."[47]

Thus while the uses and gratifications perspective has itself served a useful function by continually illustrating that people do pay attention to the political content of the media, the solidification or consolidation of basic tenets could enhance the value of this approach to political communication research.

Agenda-Setting Hypothesis

Undoubtedly, the most popular contemporary approach for studying the relationship of media and politics is the agenda-setting hypothesis. It has generated more research than any of the others. It clearly separates the persuasive and informational communicative functions of the media. It comes closer than any of the other approaches to reaffirming the early basic assumption that the media do have a great deal of influence on politics; the media may not dominate, but they do have a significant impact on what we think about (our focus of attention). Finally, the perspective is important for another reason. The most frequent site for agenda-setting research has been election campaigns, and this has not been the case with either the diffusion of information or uses and gratifications perspectives.

The underlying assumption of agenda-setting was first articulated by a political scientist, Bernard C. Cohen, in 1963. Cohen argued that the press may not be successful in telling its readers what to think, but "it is stunningly successful in telling its readers what to think about. . . . The editor may believe he is only printing the things that people want to read, but he is thereby putting a claim on their attention, powerfully determining what they will be thinking about, and talking about, until the next wave laps their shore."[48]

Just two years later, empirical verification of Cohen's ideas began to appear. In a study of the 1964 presidential campaign, researcher Jack McLeod found that the stories from two newspapers revealed clear differences in their reports of two issues in the campaign, federal spending policies and control of nuclear weapons. Specifically, the study revealed that respondents who read the paper that provided a good deal of coverage to nuclear control (the Democratic issue) ranked it higher than they did the economic issue. Correspondingly, those who read the paper that focused on spending policies (the Republican issue) ranked it higher than they did nuclear control.[49] In 1972 Maxwell McCombs and Donald Shaw explored the power of the press to set the agenda by studying the 1968 presidential campaign. Specifically, they hypothesized that "the mass media set the agenda for each political campaign, influencing the salience of attitudes toward the political issues."[50] Before the election, the researchers interviewed 100 people in five precincts in Chapel Hill, North Carolina who had not yet decided whether they were going to vote for Hubert Humphrey, Richard Nixon, or George Wallace. The undecided voters were the only people interviewed on the presumption that they would be the most receptive to campaign information. McCombs and Shaw compared what voters said were the key issues in the campaign with the amount of space devoted to those issues in the particular medium used by the voters. They found a strong relationship between the emphasis given by the medium to specific campaign issues and the judgment of voters relating to the salience and importance of those issues. A third study, this time a national one conducted from 1964 to 1970, compared what people identified as the most important problems facing the United States (according to data from Gallup Polls) with listings of the content of news magazines. The researcher, G. Ray Funkhouser, concluded that "the average person takes the media's word for what the 'issues' are, whether or not he personally has any involvement or interest in them."[51]

In these three studies and many others that followed them, the agenda-setting functions of the mass media appear to have gained wide acceptance from social scientists. While the perspective does not suggest that media have the all-powerful attributes envisioned by the hypodermic thesis, the media do set public priorities, just by paying attention to some issues while ignoring others. They determine which issues are important and in this way play an important role in structuring our social reality. In other words, we not only learn about issues through the media, we learn how much importance to give to them because of the emphasis placed on them by the mass media. Thus researchers have demonstrated the legitimacy of Cohen's 1963 argument that although the media may not be powerful enough to tell people what to think, they are powerful enough to tell us what to think about.

For our purposes, the agenda-setting perspective is significant because it has illustrated "how significant communication variables can be operationalized and linked to concrete political processes such as election campaigns."[52] It has stimulated a good deal of research (although few consistent conclusions) on such important areas as the distinct agenda-setting roles of newspapers and television, the differences between the intrapersonal agenda (operationalized in most studies in terms of what each individual considers personally most important) and the interpersonal agenda (what each individual talks about most often with others), and the length of time required for agenda-setting effects to manifest themselves in the public agenda.[53] However, the primary disadvantage of the concept, like most of the others we have summarized, is that in the largest sense it is still a concept and not a theory. It is not a universal influence. Agenda-setting effects "often have been demonstrated, but they are not of consistent and major magnitude in all circumstances."[54] In other words, there are contingent conditions such as the nature of the issues and the characteristics of the media's audience that constrain or enhance the function. Until researchers are able to more consistently document the nature of those conditions or variables—when they will occur, why they occur, and the extent to which their presence will be of concern—there is not a theory of agenda setting, only a concept regarding the focus of public opinion.

However, the future for this perspective looks bright because not only has recent research been extended to include agenda items such as political candidates, their images, and politics itself, researchers are beginning to concentrate on the specification of those contingent conditions that will start the process of creating a theory of agenda-setting.

Reconceptualization of the Classics

Although not a complete perspective like information diffusion, uses and gratifications, or agenda-setting, we nonetheless conclude this section with a brief summary of the major tenets of a study that, while modeled after those of the Columbia Bureau of Applied Social Research, came to opposite conclusions.

In an effort to provide a body of knowledge that would "contribute to an understanding of election coverage and the American voter,"[55] Thomas E. Patterson implemented the "most comprehensive panel survey ever conducted for the study of change during a presidential campaign."[56] The study and its results were described in the book, *The Mass Media Election.*

Although the Patterson investigation resembled the earlier work of Lazarsfeld and Berelson, there were major differences that are important to our consideration of political campaign communication in two respects. The first concerns the overall design of the study, and the second relates to the conclusions. We will begin by comparing designs.

In each of the Columbia studies, respondents were interviewed a number of times to determine if their attitudes were changing as the presidential campaigns were proceeding. Panel surveys were the single source of data for findings. Moreover, each of the Columbia studies interviewed 600 to 800 potential voters, and each was conducted in a single community. By contrast, the design of the 1976 study was more comprehensive. First, more people were interviewed (1,236). Second, they were interviewed in seven waves (five face-to-face interviews and two over the telephone), which were timed to correspond with each of the important intervals and stages in the campaign (just before the New Hampshire primary, after the early primaries, after the final primaries, after the conventions, before the general election, after the first and second presidential debates, and after the election). Third, respondents represented two communities that had substantially different populations and media (Erie, Pennsylvania and Los Angeles, California). Finally, data collected from repeated interviews represented only one of the sources of evidence. The other was a content analysis of election year political news stories that appeared on evening newscasts of the three major television networks, two news magazines, two national newspapers, and two local newspapers (one in each of the selected cities). The content analysis was conducted from January until after the general election in November, and the interviews began in February and also concluded when the election was over. In short, the Patterson study was not only a more ambitious undertaking than any of the Columbia efforts had been, it was the largest project attempted in the intervening years—years in which research regarding the influence of mass communication was beginning to illustrate that the media were not passive entities in the political process.

As we discussed earlier, the primary conclusion derived from the Lazarsfeld/Berelson work was that the media did not play a major role in determining voters' attitudes during a presidential campaign. In fact, media messages were far less important than the messages relayed through interpersonal communication channels. Political opinions were determined by party and social affiliations, and therefore if the media were not absolutely powerless they were of minor importance in influencing how people voted. However, in reporting the results of his 1976 investigation, Patterson argued that the presidential campaign is essentially a mass media campaign. He felt that for the "large majority of voters, the campaign has little reality apart from its media version."[57] In other words, far from being an unimportant factor, media are a significant part of the campaign process itself. As a matter of fact, virtually each of the conclusions from the 1976 study contradicted those articulated by the Columbia researchers. Among the conclusions Patterson discussed, the following three are particularly important for us:

1) Although the media do not change attitudes, they do influence because people rely on them for information, thereby placing media in a position to influence perceptions;
2) The stories that voters see in newspapers and watch on television "affect what they perceive to be the important events, critical issues, and serious contenders; [media] will affect what they learn about the candidates' personalities and issue positions";[58] and
3) Thus the power of the press "rests largely on its ability to select what will be covered and to decide the contest in which these events will be placed."[59]

150

Therefore, the Patterson investigation of the ways in which voters were influenced by the media is especially important. First, it firmly dispelled the long-term myths created by the Columbia studies and, second, it provided the comprehensive data necessary for updating and solidifying our knowledge of the ways in which voters, candidates, and the mass media interact with each other in contemporary political campaigns.

CONCLUSIONS

As we have seen, beliefs regarding the political influence and power of the mass media have come almost full circle during the 60 years researchers have been studying them. First, it was believed that the media were all-powerful. Then their power was seen as limited and of secondary or minor importance. In each instance, conclusions were frequently based on substantial evidence but gained prominence because they reinforced the dominant attitudes and context of the time in which they were articulated. The effective use of propaganda in the 1930s and the early 1940s convinced researchers that the power of the media was massive. Indeed, the media were virtually unlimited in the ways they could change attitudes and produce behavior modification or conformity. Whereas in the 1950s, the opposite viewpoint was held because in the context of those years it seemed difficult to subscribe to the belief that U.S. citizens could be reduced to puppets who would follow the ravings of any demagogue. Moreover, it must be remembered that when the classic Columbia studies were undertaken (during the 1940 and 1948 presidential elections), television was not yet a real factor in politics or in the environment of voters. However, by the time of the 1960 presidential campaign, television was on its way to becoming a political force. Both candidates were using the medium for spot commercials, and their precedent-setting debates broke all previously established viewing records. When over 100 million people watched the debates and subsequently talked about their perceptions and reactions to the candidates, it became increasingly difficult for social scientists to deny that media, particularly television, had any impact.

Thus as the context/environment changed, some researchers began to question the limited effects model just as 20 years earlier they had challenged the validity of the hypodermic thesis. Eventually, most conceded that the media possessed some influence—even if they did not create massive changes in voting behavior. Some acknowledged the media's ability in the transmission and diffusion of information regarding candidates, issues, or the campaign itself. Other researchers suggested that people use the media for a variety of political reasons: for information, entertainment, increasing the range of topics for social exchange and acceptability, meeting expectations of peer groups, or for intrapersonal communication. And there were those who argued that the media are important because of their power to determine what information or news would be presented. Thus by the middle of the 1970s, many social scientists had begun to believe that media influence in the electoral process could not be ignored. Finally, in 1976 a study was undertaken that provided enough data to confirm many of the trends evident throughout the decade.

Thus when we asserted at other points in this chapter that beliefs regarding the influence of the media had come full circle, we were not exaggerating. But do these perspectives from mass media research contribute to the understanding of campaign communication? We think they can and suggest six principles of campaign communication that can be drawn from them.

The first of these principles is that the most important effect of media influence is not direct persuasion but providing information that affects perception and may ultimately persuade. Persuasion theorists have consistently determined that a "one-shot" persuasive effort or message does not change attitudes—at least does not change attitudes from one extreme to the other. There may be behavior modification or conformity when conditions include threat, punishment, or even reward, but not internalized attitude change. And it is naive to assume that it is any different in the context of a political campaign. Instead, persuasive information about a candidate, about the issues for which the candidate stands, even information regarding the candidate's background and personality affect perception and thus help to draw attention to the candidate and campaign and may even influence later perception. Therefore, we conclude that the media are important to and powerful in a political campaign not in necessarily changing votes because of a single message but in drawing attention to candidates and thereby providing information for a full range of attitude formulations (including reinforcement, reformulation, and repositioning).

The second principle is simply that the contemporary candidate needs the mass media, in part because voters have expectations regarding the media's role in providing information about the candidate and the campaign. Citizens rely on newspapers and newscasts to tell them about candidates, issues, and the campaign itself. Moreover, candidates have found that they can efficiently reach potential voters only through the mass media.

The third principle is that the media have tremendous power in determining which news events, which candidates, and which issues are to be covered in any given day. Thus a candidate's campaign must be focused, in large measure, around those sorts of issues, photographic opportunities, and events that will draw media attention. Whether these are pseudo-events or real, pseudoissues or real, modern candidates do those things that will "play" to the media—that will call attention to themselves and their campaigns. Perhaps more important, because of the media, candidates do not do some things and do not discuss some issues. Often what they fail to do is just as important as what they do.

The fourth principle may be less obvious. Although candidates attempt to use the media for their own purposes, they are not always able to control it. While a candidate can send a press release, its use is not guaranteed. Although an appearance at the state fair is planned, there is no assurance the event will be used in the evening newscasts. It may well be that election coverage will focus on an opponent or on yesterday's gaffe. Moreover, media have the power to penetrate even the most expertly contrived image—the newspaper reporter catches the wording of the answer to a question, or the television camera records unplanned nonverbal behavior. The point we make is simply that candidates may spend most of their campaign resources on the media, they may depend on them to present persuasive information regarding their candidacies, but with the exception of their own advertisements, they cannot control the media.

The fifth principle is that mass media influence is important to our knowledge or appreciation of the electoral process itself. The media allow us to witness political events, they teach and instruct, thereby adding to our expectations about the democratic process. While this may increase or decrease our liking for particular candidates, issues, or campaigns, it does provide a sense of involvement as we affirm (or deny) our role as citizens.

Finally, we believe that the influence or power of the media has contributed mightily to the many changes in the electoral process. For example, the surfacing and primary stages of the campaign have become more important to the final outcome, receive more precise and planned attention by candidates, and generate more excitement and enthusiasm from the general public than before television entered the political arena. This has happened because the media treat these preliminary events in much the same manner as they treat the later stages. In fact, because of high media involvement, the first two stages have replaced not only the attention-getting power of the nominating conventions and the general election, they have also seized much of their legitimate power.

In the largest sense, we conclude this chapter as we began it—convinced that the mass media (especially television) have a tremendous impact on political campaign communication.

NOTES

1. Frederick Williams, *The Communications Revolution* (Beverly Hills: Sage, 1982), p. 44.

2. Ibid., pp. 139–51.

3. Roper Organization, *Public Perceptions of Television and Other Mass Media: A Twenty-Year Review, 1959–1978* (New York: Television Information Office, 1979).

4. Frank E. X. Dance, "Human Communication Theory: A Highly Selective Review and Two Commentaries," in *Communication Yearbook II*, ed. Brent D. Ruben (New Brunswick, N.J.: Transaction Books, 1978), pp. 7–22.

5. Peter M. Sandman, David M. Rubin, and David B. Sachsman, *Media* (Englewood Cliffs, N.J.: Prentice-Hall, 1972), p. 20.

6. Ibid., p. 23.

7. Ibid., p. 25.

8. Sidney Kraus and Dennis Davis, *The Effects of Mass Communication on Political Behavior* (University Park: Pennsylvania State University Press, 1976), p. 117.

9. Elihu Katz and Paul F. Lazarsfeld, *Personal Influence* (New York: Free Press of Glencoe, 1955), p. 16.

10. Harold F. Gosnell, *Machine Politics Chicago Model* (Chicago: University of Chicago Press, 1937).

11. Garrett J. O'Keefe, "Political Campaigns And Mass Communication Research," in *Political Communication: Issues and Strategies for Research*, ed. Steven H. Chaffee (Beverly Hills: Sage, 1975), p. 133.

12. David Blomquist, *Elections and the Mass Media* (Washington, D.C.: American Political Science Association, 1981), pp. 4–6.

13. Kraus and Davis, *Effects of Mass Communication*, p. 117.

14. For a discussion of the methodological difficulties of the selective exposure concept, see, for example, Lee B. Becker, Maxwell E. McCombs, and Jack M. McLeod, "The Development of Political Cognitions," in *Political Communication: Issues and Strategies for Research* ed. Steven H. Chaffee (Beverly Hills: Sage, 1975), pp. 28–31; Kraus and Davis, *Effects of Mass Communication*, pp. 51–54; and David Sears and Johnathan Freedman, "Selective Exposure to Information: A Critical Review," *Public Opinion Quarterly* 31 (Summer 1967): 194–213.

15. Katz and Lazarsfeld, *Personal Influence*, p. 138.

16. Ibid., p. 309.

17. Ibid.

18. Kraus and Davis, *Effects of Mass Communication*, p. 120.

19. Becker, McCombs, and McLeod, "Development of Political Cognitions," p. 32.

20. Ibid., p. 33.

21. Kraus and Davis, *Effects of Mass Communication*, p. 53.

22. Angus Campbell et al., *The American Voter* (New York: John Wiley & Sons, 1964).

23. David M. White, "The 'Gate Keeper': A Case Study in the Selection of News," *Journalism Quarterly* 27 (Fall 1950): 383–90.

24. Sandman, Rubin, and Sachsman, *Media*, p. 103.

25. Ibid., p. 109.

26. See, for example, Lewis Donohew, "Newspaper Gatekeepers and Forces in the News Channel," *Public Opinion Quarterly* 31 (Spring 1967): 62–66; Jean S. Kerrick et al., "Balance and the Writer's Attitude in News Stories and Editorials," *Journalism Quarterly* 41 (Spring 1964): 207–15; and G. A. Donohue, P. J. Tichenor, and C. N. Olien, "Gatekeeping: Mass Media Systems and Information Control," in *Current Perspectives in Mass Communication Research*, eds. F. G. Kline and P. J. Tichenor (Beverly Hills: Sage, 1972).

27. Studies in the late 1960s and in the 1970s have consistently indicated that voters use the media for purposes other than reinforcement of their views. Moreover, other studies have shown that there are cases wherein voters prefer messages that contradict their views. Finally, with the decline of party affiliation, there is reason to believe that voters are not holding onto preconceived political beliefs but enter a campaign season with a willingness to be persuaded on issues. Steven Chaffee and Michael Petrick call the concept of selective exposure "too simplistic." See their book, *Using The Mass Media* (New York: McGraw-Hill, 1975), p. 141.

28. Kraus and Davis, *Effects of Mass Communication*, p. 123.

29. Blomquist, *Elections and the Mass Media*, p. 7.

30. Ibid.

31. Ibid.

32. Ibid., p. 8. See also Jay G. Blumler and Denis McQuail, *Television in Politics* (Chicago: University of Chicago Press, 1969).

33. Kraus and Davis, *Effects of Mass Communication*, p. 126.

34. Ibid., p. 128.

35. Ibid., p. 127.

36. Robert L. Savage, "The Diffusion of Information Approach," in *Handbook of Political Communication*, eds. Dan D. Nimmo and Keith R. Sanders (Beverly Hills: Sage, 1981), pp. 104–7.

37. Ibid., p. 107.

38. Steven H. Chaffee, "The Diffusion of Political Information," in *Political Communication: Issues and Strategies for Research* ed. Steven H. Chaffee (Beverly Hills: Sage, 1975), p. 125.

39. Savage, "Diffusion of Information Approach," p. 115.

40. Kraus and Davis, *Effects of Mass Communication*, p. 130.

41. Jay G. Blumler, "The Role Of Theory in Uses and Gratifications Studies," *Communication Research* 6 (January 1979): 21.

42. Ibid., 11–12.

43. Jack M. McLeod and Lee B. Becker, "The Uses and Gratifications Approach," in *Handbook of Political Communication* eds. Dan D. Nimmo and Keith R. Sanders (Beverly Hills: Sage, 1975), p. 71.

44. Ibid., p. 87.

45. Blumler, "Theory in Uses And Gratifications," p. 17.

46. McLeod and Becker, "Uses and Gratifications Approach," pp. 86–94.

47. Ibid., p. 94. While we have presented many of the major problems theorists have articulated regarding the uses and gratifications perspective, we have not discussed the charge that it is grounded in functionalism. For an excellent discussion of its functionalist roots and a critique of the approach itself, see David L. Swanson, "Political Communication Research and the Uses and Gratifications Model: A Critique," *Communication Research* 6 (January 1979): 37–53.

48. Bernard C. Cohen, *The Press and Foreign Policy* (Princeton: Princeton University Press, 1963), p. 13.

49. Kraus and Davis, *Effects of Mass Communication*, p. 216.

50. Maxwell E. McCombs and Donald L. Shaw, "The Agenda-Setting Function of Mass Media," *Public Opinion Quarterly* 36 (Summer 1972): 177.

51. G. Ray Funkhouser, "Trends in Media Coverage of the Issues of the '60s," *Journalism Quarterly* 50 (Autumn 1973): 538.

52. Kraus and Davis, *Effects of Mass Communication*, p. 214.

53. Maxwell E. McCombs, "The Agenda-Setting Approach," in *Handbook of Political Communication*, eds. Dan D. Nimmo and Keith R. Sanders (Beverly Hills: Sage, 1975), pp. 127–30.

54. Ibid., p. 131.

55. Thomas E. Patterson, *The Mass Media Election* (New York: Praeger, 1980), p. 8.

56. Ibid., p. viii.

57. Ibid., p. 3.

58. Ibid., p. 95.

59. Ibid., p. 53.

Part II
Practices of Political Campaign Communication

5

Public
Speaking in
Political
Campaigns

*T*HIS CHAPTER WILL FOCUS ON WHAT IS PER-
HAPS THE MOST FUNDAMENTAL COMMUNI-
CATION PRACTICE IN ANY CAMPAIGN, PUBLIC
SPEAKING. IN THE FIRST SECTION, WE WILL
examine the factors that enter into a candidate's decision to
speak. Decisions on where and when to speak and what to say
to a given audience are not made randomly but are often the
result of considerable thought and planning on the part of candidates and their staffs. In the second section, we will inspect
the use of stock or modular speeches. This practice is a common one utilized by candidates running for virtually every office. As we will see, it is an effective means of handling the
massive speaking demands placed on candidates for public office. In the third section, we will discuss the practice of political speechwriting. Candidates are using speechwriters more
today than ever before; any examination of public speaking
practices in political campaigns must consider the use of
speechwriters. Similarly, many candidates today are making
extensive use of advocates or surrogates. These "substitutes"
for the candidate may be heard in person by as many people, if

not more, than those who actually hear the candidate. Hence, any examination of public speaking practices in contemporary campaigns that does not consider the use of surrogate speakers would be less than complete.

THE DECISION TO SPEAK

Perhaps the most important resource available to any campaign is the time of the candidate. That time must be used wisely. Decisions to use the candidate's time for public speeches are made out of self-interest, as the candidate attempts to influence the maximum number of voters. Hence, it is vital that candidates and their staffs do an effective job of analyzing voter audiences to best utilize the candidates' time. Essentially candidates face two tasks: first, to determine whom they should address and, second, to determine what messages should be presented to those they address.

Audiences

Since 1946 when Jacob Javits, then running for a seat in the House of Representatives, employed the Elmo Roper Organization to make opinion polls of his constituency to determine better what issues he should develop in his campaign,[1] political campaigns have increasingly relied on two tools to assist them in analyzing audiences. The first is studies of past voter statistics, and the second is the public opinion poll. As we have seen in earlier chapters, these tools have blossomed in recent years because of improvements in computer technology.

Local and national candidates make use of past voter statistics to analyze audiences. Yet these statistics play a more vital role in the campaigns of local candidates than they do in the campaigns of national or major statewide contenders. Indeed, there is no more valuable campaign aid to the local candidate than accurate voter statistics. Though voter statistics may serve many potential purposes, their chief function is to pinpoint, on a precinct-by-precinct basis, where candidates should be concentrating their efforts. This knowledge enables candidates to determine what speaking invitations should be accepted and in what areas of the district their staffs should attempt to arrange speaking opportunities and otherwise concentrate.

Though the same principles apply for national figures and local figures, in practicality major national or statewide figures are rarely able to aim their speeches or campaign materials to a specific precinct. The size of their constituency and the extensive media coverage they receive, often prohibit tailoring a given speech to a specific precinct, as can the local candidate dealing with a smaller constituency. The local candidate, far more than counterparts seeking national or statewide office, must know precisely, down to the precinct, the nature of the constituency. Because their constituencies are smaller, in many instances the local candidate can knock on every door in the district, or at least on every door in those precincts that are deemed most valuable. When a statewide candidate like "Walking Joe" Teasdale, former governor of Missouri, walks across his state he is doing so primarily for media coverage.

Local candidates, however, will not receive the media exposure of the gubernatorial candidate. Rather, their walks in the district can put them face-to-face with a large percentage of their constituency. The act is real rather than symbolic. To be effective, the local candidate must know which areas of the district in which to walk, speak, and otherwise campaign. Accurate voter statistics are an acute concern for local candidates who can meet a substantial portion of their constituency, can express their concern for voter problems face-to-face, and whose limited financial resources must be used with maximum effect.

Typically, candidates direct their efforts primarily toward precincts where their party traditionally runs well and those where ticket-splitting commonly takes place. It is in these two areas that candidates should concentrate the majority of their speaking efforts. That may even mean actively soliciting speaking engagements in these areas, when none are forthcoming. It means consistently giving preference to these regions when simultaneous speaking opportunities arise in two or more sections of the district. Local candidates can think in precinct terms. National or statewide candidates use the same process but must think more in media market and electoral vote terms.

Utilizing past voter records and computers to help analyze the data, state and local political organizations will often provide candidates with a precinct-by-precinct breakdown of their district. The materials a candidate receives might be similar to the two examples shown in Table 1. These examples are modeled after materials provided Republican candidates in the cities of Hamilton and Fairfield, Ohio during the 1980 elections. Using the table provided, can you determine whether a Republican candidate should speak in these precincts?

The first precinct is one in which a Republican candidate should actively speak and campaign since it is a heavily Republican precinct. Note that every one of the nine Republicans on the ballot in the last two elections has won. If a Republican had lost, the figures in the difference column would have a minus in front of them. Rather, as you can see, Republican candidates have consistently carried this precinct by a minimum of 330 votes and in some cases by as many as 674 votes. The average Republican percentage in this precinct in 1976 was 73.8 percent, and in 1978 it was 71.4 percent. Out of 53 precincts in the district, this precinct turned in the highest average Republican percentage in 1978 and the second highest in 1976. Moreover, there is comparatively little ticket-splitting in this precinct. In 1976 it ranked nineteenth among 53, but that was because of a comparatively unpopular Republican state senator who drew "only" 66 percent of the vote. In 1978 every Republican drew between 69 and 72 percent of the vote, and this precinct ranked

53 out of 53, or dead last, with only 2.6 percent of the voters splitting their tickets.

The second precinct is also one in which a Republican candidate should actively speak and otherwise campaign. It too is Republican, although not nearly so heavily as the first. Examining the difference figures indicates that although Republicans have consistently won this precinct, on several occasions the margin of victory has been under 75 votes. Also note that the average Republican vote in the precinct dropped sharply between 1976 and 1978, from 66.3 to 59.1 percent. Notice particularly that in 1976 the Republican congressman carried 76 percent of the vote, but in 1978 that dropped sharply to 61 percent. In 1976 the Republican senatorial candidate carried 69 percent of the vote, but in 1978 the other Republican senatorial candidate barely won, with 52 percent of the vote. Though this district is Republican, some Democratic candidates have done well in it and seem to be growing stronger.

Additionally, this is typically a precinct with considerable ticket-splitting. In 1976 over a fifth of the district split their tickets, making this the third highest ticket-splitting precinct among the 53 in this district. In 1978 the incidence of ticket-splitting was still high, ranking this precinct twenty-second out of 53, clearly in the top half. Finally, this is one of the largest precincts in the district. In 1976 the total vote in this precinct was the largest in any precinct, and in 1978 it was the seventh largest.

Thus, although Republican, this precinct is one in which Democratic candidates seem to have been making gains and appear to be on the verge of winning elections. It is a precinct with many ticket-splitters and one of the largest in the district.

Using figures such as these, local candidates determine where they wish to speak. Typically, they will write off about 30 percent of the district as hopeless. The first precinct we just analyzed, for example, would be a hopeless precinct for a Democratic contender. Candidates then target the remaining 70 percent, those precincts where their party runs strong or

TABLE 1. PRIOR ELECTION RESULTS

	1976 U.S. Pres.	1976 U.S. Sen.	U.S. Hse.	St. Sen.	St. Hse.	St. Aud.	1978 U.S. Sen.	1978 U.S. Hse.	St. Sen.	St. Hse.	Avr. R%	Rank	Total Vote	Rank	Ticket-Splitting R%	Rank
Sample Precinct 1																
Hamilton City: Ward 1, Precinct 6																
Rep.	784	789	860	686	761	629	613	614		631						
Dem.	276	266	186	356	292	239	254	264		250	73.8	2	(1976) 1,065	9	16.4	19
Other	5						16									
Total	1,065	1,055	1,046	1,042	1,053	868	883	878		881						
R. pct.	74	75	82	66	72	72	69	70		72	71.4	1	(1978) 883	2	2.6	53
D. pct.	26	25	18	34	28	28	31	30		28						
Diff.	508	523	674	330	469	390	359	350		381						
Sample Precinct 2																
Fairfield City: Ward 4, Precinct 1																
Rep.	1,096	1,174	1,283	1,091	938	429	418	480		489						
Dem.	660	538	400	589	755	364	344	301		309	66.3	19	(1976) 1,756	1	22.8	3
Other																
Total	1,756	1,712	1,683	1,680	1,693	793	805	781		798						
R. pct.	63	69	76	65	55	54	52	61		61	59.1	23	(1978) 805	7	9.0	22
D. pct.	37	31	24	35	45	46	48	39		39						
Diff.	436	636	883	502	183	65	74	179								

Total no. of precincts:
Hamilton-Fairfield—53.

Title of Report (Legislative)

Other   The vote for all other party votes in the precinct for a particular office.

Total   The total vote in the precinct for a particular office. Obtained by adding the Republican, Democratic, and other vote.

R. pct.   The Republican percentage in the precinct for a particular office. Obtained by dividing the Republican vote by the total vote in the precinct.

D. pct.   The Democratic percentage in the precinct for a particular office. Obtained by dividing the Democratic vote by the total vote in the precinct.

Diff.   The difference between the Democratic and Republican vote for a particular office. A minus sign (−) indicates Republican vote less than Democratic vote.

Columns 2–7
1976 Election Results

Columns 8–11
1978 Election Results

Column 12
Average R%   This is the average Republican percent in the precinct.

Column 13
Rank   This is the rank order number of the particular precinct in terms of Republican percentage in the total district. The precinct with the highest Republican percentage in the district is number 1.

Column 14
Total Vote   This is the maximum number of votes cast in this precinct since 1972.

Column 15
Rank   This is the rank order number of the precinct in the district in terms of total votes cast.

Column 16
Ticket-Splitting R%   This is the percent of ticket splitting in the precinct. It was calculated by subtracting the lowest Republican percent from the highest Republican percent in the precinct.

Column 17
Ticket-Splitting Rank   This is the rank order number of the precinct in terms of ticket splitting. The precinct with the highest percentage of ticket splitting in the district is number 1.

Total number of precincts: Hamilton-Fairfield Legislative Report—53.

where ticket-splitting is common. Precinct two, for example, might well have been targeted by both Republican and Democratic candidates during 1980; though Republican, Democrats have twice come within 75 votes of winning it. And it is a large precinct with heavy ticket-splitting. National and statewide candidates operate on the same premise. They too target about 70 percent of their constituency. Typically, presidential candidates target states and media markets within states, rather than precincts, and choose to speak and campaign accordingly.[2]

Messages

The second primary tool of audience analysis is the public opinion poll. Polls help candidates develop their messages. But polls are utilized differently by local and major candidates. Accurate voter statistics down to the precinct level are of acute concern to the local candidate but often of lesser concern to the major candidate. However, the public opinion poll is of more concern to major candidates but often of lesser concern to the local candidate. Typically, the explanation for this different emphasis on the use of polls involves two distinctions between local and major candidates. First, the major candidate can normally afford a polling service and may also be helped by national polls such as those of Gallup and Harris. Candidates for Congress and statewide and national offices all utilize polling services. Occasionally, contenders for the state legislature may also make use of polls. Frequently, state legislative candidates and contenders for local offices such as sheriff, county or city recorder, clerk, or engineer cannot afford polling services.

Second, even if the local candidate could afford polls, the essentially administrative nature, rather than policy-making nature, of most local offices tends to minimize the distinctions between the viewpoints of local candidates. Issues of policy, which sharply divide candidates for major office, often are not at stake in local elections. This is not to say that there is no opportunity for policy making at the local level. Rather, it is to suggest that while major campaigns almost invariably involve clashes over policy issues, many local campaigns are waged for positions with comparatively little policy-making responsibilities. Hence, there is often little distinction between candidates on the basis of issues and less need for polls.

Issue polls are designed to determine what concerns are uppermost in the minds of the voters. They serve major candidates as a *topoi*, or topics, system. In addition to suggesting topics upon which to speak, they indicate voter opinions and beliefs. As we have noted earlier, candidates rely on polling services when they develop positions on issues.

Using polls to determine important issues makes good sense. Using polls, instead of solid study, research, and good judgment, to determine what to say about the public's concerns is a questionable procedure. Writing in 1954, when polling was first developing as a major campaign tool, former President Harry Truman asked:

> I wonder how far Moses would have gone if he'd taken a poll in Egypt? What would Jesus Christ have preached if he'd taken a poll in Israel? Where would the Reformation have gone if Martin Luther had taken a poll? It isn't polls or public opinion of the moment that counts. It is right and wrong leadership—men with fortitude, honesty and a belief in the right that makes epochs in the history of the world.[3]

Most political candidates probably agree with the implications of Truman's remark that although the polls can help determine what absorbs the public's attention, they should not be used to dictate the candidate's approach to an issue. Despite the undesirability of this use of polls, no doubt the practice will continue.

Typically, the candidate's polls will be able to rank order issues of concern among specific constituencies such as older voters, women voters, or middle-income voters. The degree to which the polling data are broken down and analyzed depends

169

on the candidate's needs and the finances available. A national campaign will break down the polling data extensively, determining, for example, what issues are of concern on such bases as geography, economics, race, religion, and party. As candidates speak, they can adapt subject matter to insure they are addressing the major concerns of the groups to whom they are speaking.

Polls also provide candidates with feedback on messages. Candidates often reposition their stands on issues as a consequence of that feedback.

Competency and Format

Most individuals who run for major public office feel comfortable in front of an audience.[4] Most have had extensive prior public speaking experience, and many have also had both formal and informal training.[5] If prospective candidates are apprehensive about the speaking demands of their races, they might well prepare by seeking the advice of competent professionals. Many candidates utilize the services of speech coaches. Both the Republican and Democratic national committees, as well as many state and local party committees, provide speech training in their candidates' schools.

If candidates are uncomfortable with some speaking formats, they and their staffs might attempt to place them in formats where they do not feel uncomfortable. If, for example, they are uneasy delivering formal speeches, perhaps their formal speeches could be kept brief and be followed by extensive question-and-answer periods. The type of training and formats utilized by candidates varies on an individual basis, but should not be ignored. A frank and realistic assessment of the candidate's speaking abilities, no less than assessments about where and when to talk and what to talk about must enter into the candidate's decisions to speak.

THE SPEECH

During the 1980 primaries, the *New York Times* wrote:

Candidates for the Presidential nomination in both major parties make hundreds of speeches in their campaigns, speeches that vary in content depending on where they are given and the audience addressed. But every candidate has a body of material, usually presented in every speech, that varies little from audience to audience. This material represents the heart of his message to the voters as he moves around the country.[6]

The *Times* was describing what political speakers call their "stock speeches," and what their speechwriters might also call their "module speeches." The great demand to speak that is placed on contemporary political figures has caused most of them to resort to the use of stock or module speeches. The demand to speak is also one of the principal reasons used by candidates to justify the use of speechwriters. In this section, we will examine the use of stock speeches, and in the next section we will examine the practices of political speechwriters.

Need and Justification

Speechmaking is fundamental to political campaigning. The politician cannot reasonably expect to campaign without continually facing audiences. Even the candidate for city council in a small community must constantly speak. Typically, such a candidate is called upon to make several major speeches during the campaign, at such events as the local League of Woman Voters' "Meet The Candidates Nights," or at the Rotary Club's monthly meeting. Moreover, these candidates must be continually speaking, often three or more times an evening throughout the final weeks of the campaign, to smaller groups of citizens. Campaign coffees, teas, church socials, and similar activities crowd the calendars of most candidates. It is not unusual for local candidates to find themselves confronting the prospect of a hundred or more speeches during the last four to six weeks of a campaign. Similarly, as we will see in the next section, candidates for more important local, state, and federal offices face situations where they must speak 30 or more times a week. Because of these demands, most candidates make use of a stock speech, and if possible, the services of speechwriters.

Speech Modules

Although the phrase "stock speech" has entered the vocabulary of most politically aware citizens, it is a misnomer. We tend to think of it as a speech that is delivered time and time again with little change. We think of it as unvarying, set, well established. Yet if you read the *New York Times* description of stock speeches that opened this section carefully, you may recall that the *Times* noted that stock speeches "vary in content depending on where they are given and the audience addressed." They are not altogether set and established. Candidates do not give the identical speech time after time after time, regardless of the audience, occasion, or the actions of their opponents. Rather, they adapt to these factors.

How do the candidates adapt, given the heavy demands on time? They do so by making use of "speech modules." A speech module is a single unit of a speech. Typically, candidates will have a speech unit, or module, on each of the 10 to 20 issues on which they most frequently speak. Each module is an independent unit that can be delivered as a three-to-seven minute speech on the issue. The length of each can be varied simply by adding or subtracting examples, statistics, illustrations, or other support materials. Typically the organization of each module is similar and will be readily recognized by many students of public speaking.

Each module opens with some attention-gaining device, and then candidates quickly move to a discussion of a problem. Having sketched the problem, they then present their policies as an appropriate solution to the problem. If more time is available, they might then vividly describe or visualize what would happen if they are elected and their policies carried out. Thus the typical speech module is designed to: (1) gain attention, (2) describe a problem, (3) present a solution, and (4) visualize the solution. The first three of these steps are characteristic of virtually every speech module the candidate presents. The final step may not be necessary. It may be implicit from the discussion of the problem and the solution and hence not warrant explicit treatment. The following is an example of a speech module used by Ronald Reagan during the 1980 primaries.

Despite the protests about all the problems he inherited, Jimmy Carter came into office with the economy expanding, with inflation reduced to less than 5 percent, and with the dollar a relatively stable measure of value. In 36 months he has tripled the rate of inflation; the prime interest rate has risen to the highest level since the Civil War; the price of gold has risen from $125 an ounce to more than $600 and fluctuates up there at that level which measures the extent to which international confidence in the dollar has fallen. And that is the indication of the collapse of confidence of economic policies in the Carter Administration.	Attention Startling statements used to 1 gain attention 2 initially develop the problem

After last summer's Cabinet massacre, the departing Secretary of the Treasury confessed that the Carter Administration did not bring with it to Washington any economic philosophy of its own. So the President and his counselors embraced the only economic philosophy they could find at hand—the warmed-over McGovernism of the Democratic platform of 1976.

<u>Problem</u>
Developed in chronological order

Together Mr. Carter, his Democratic Congress and his first choice for chairman of the Federal Reserve proceeded on the premise of parallel lanes of national prosperity, Federal deficits and easy money. Pursuing this course together, they made a shambles of our national economy wiping out in three years' time tens of billions of dollars of value in our private pensions, savings, insurance, stocks and bonds.

I suggest that when one administration can give us the highest inflation since 1946, the highest interest rates since the Civil War, and the worst drop in value of the dollar against gold in history, it's time that administration was turned out of office and a new administration elected to repair the damage.[7]

<u>Plan</u>
Reject Carter and elect Reagan

<u>Visualization</u>
Not explicit

In this module, we see an independent speech unit or module on the Carter administration's conduct of economic affairs. The passage stands by itself. It also could be linked very easily into another module with a simple transition. In fact, this is precisely what Reagan did. Following the quoted passage he would normally add: "But when we consider what lies ahead in this new decade, the damage done to the national economy is insignificant alongside the damage done to our national security."[8] At this point he would present his modular on national security.

Economy Module		Security Module
Attention		Attention
Problem	Transition	Problem
Plan		Plan
Visualization		Visualization

These happen to be the two modules Ronald Reagan used most frequently during the 1980 primaries. Because the economy and national security are issues that vitally affect all citizens, they were appropriate to use with most audiences. But let us imagine for a moment that Reagan was speaking to a group of voters during the New Hampshire primary. The primary was being held in the dead of winter, in one of the coldest states in the union. He might reasonably expect, and his polls might suggest, that the high cost of energy and fuel oil was uppermost in the minds of his audience.

Having already prepared a module on energy, it would be a rather minor adjustment for Reagan to present his initial module, for New Hampshire like all the nation was suffering economically, and this was Reagan's major issue. Then, adapting to this audience and the occasion and timing of the speech, he might choose to speak about energy, not national defense. He could do so by:

Economy Module

Attention	Transition	
Problem		
Plan	But when we consider what lies ahead in	Energy Module
Visualization	this new decade, the damage done to the	
	national economy is insignificant along-	Attention
	side the damage done to our energy pro-	Problem
	grams.	Plan
		Visualization

Most candidates will develop key modules at the outset of the campaign, occasionally adjusting them as the need arises. Additionally, they will add modules as the need arises. Then, depending on the audience, the occasion, and any other relevant factors, they will determine what modules to use for a given speech. Often, as with Reagan and the national economy, the same module is used in many speeches. Yet each speech is in fact tailored to the specific audience and occasion.

Speechlike Opportunities and Modular Speeches

One of the principal advantages of developing a basic speech through modules is that the modules can then be used by the candidate in many speechlike situations. Often candidates desire to appear on interview shows such as "Meet the Press," or talk shows such as "Phil Donahue." Opportunities such as these must be weighed like any other opportunity to speak. However, because they do offer free exposure, many candidates, especially those operating on a limited budget, attempt to utilize them. Almost every media market has local radio talk shows and television shows, so that these decisions are not unique to national contenders.

If candidates have already prepared speech modules on most major topics, they are likely to do well on these shows. The module, which can be varied in length, lends itself to use in these formats. Candidates can accept such invitations with a minimum of preparation and be confident that they are unlikely to be caught ill-prepared. Moreover, they can be certain

176

that their remarks will be consistent with those they have made throughout the campaign.

Occasionally, if a module is done especially well, it can also be turned into an effective television or radio spot. Since the module can stand alone and its length can be varied, it is easy to adapt to a commercial. Often media advisors wish to show their candidate in "the real world," talking to "real people." The speech module lets them do just that. Every Republican presidential candidate since Richard Nixon in 1968 has made use of modules excerpted from their acceptance address in precisely this fashion.

POLITICAL SPEECHWRITING

The use of speechwriters by political figures dates back to ancient Greece and Rome when men such as Julius Caesar and Nero received aid in preparing their speeches. In the United States, the use of speechwriters has been a feature of our politics since our nation's inception. George Washington had at least four different speechwriters, including Alexander Hamilton. Amos Kendell, a former editor of the *Kentucky Argus* newspaper and a close personal confidant of Andrew Jackson, was called by one of Jackson's critics, "the President's thinking machine, and his writing machine, ay, and his lying machine."[9]

Abraham Lincoln frequently called upon his secretary of state, William Seward, for advice on public speeches. Lincoln's successor, Andrew Johnson, had grown up on the frontier and did not learn to read and write until meeting and courting his wife, a teacher. Not surprisingly, he too sought a speechwriter. This rough-hewn president found his man in George Bancroft, perhaps the most erudite and distinguished historian of the day.

Although both presidents Calvin Coolidge and Herbert Hoover made use of the same speechwriter,[10] it was not until the administration of President Franklin Delano Roosevelt that the public at large became fully aware of the pervasive use of speechwriters by political figures. Roosevelt used a variety of individuals to provide him with aid in preparing speeches. Typically, Roosevelt drew upon both subject matter experts, often cabinet members, and stylists, such as authors Robert Sherwood and John Steinbeck.

Justification and Implications of Political Speechwriting

Since Roosevelt, the public has been aware that political figures often use speechwriters. Today no national or state-wide campaign is run without them. The vast majority of candidates running for Congress utilize speechwriters, and so do many candidates running for lesser office. Incumbents, whether presidents, Congress members, mayors, state representatives, or town council members, almost invariably delegate some of their speechwriting chores to paid staff members. The staff member's title may be "assistant to," or "press secretary," but part of the job responsibility is speechwriting. Similarly, challenger candidates normally hire a "wordsmith" to help with speeches, press releases, and similar tasks right after hiring a campaign manager.

Though the public has accepted leaders who make use of speechwriters, somehow we remain vaguely troubled by the thought that those who aspire to lead us often do so by mouthing the words of others. Traditionally, there have been two basic justifications for using speechwriters.

First, candidates face such extensive demands on their time that it is impossible to fulfill those demands without speechwriters. In 1948 while governing the nation and running for reelection, President Harry Truman delivered 73 speeches in one 15-day period.[11] In 1952 during the final months of the campaign, the Republican and Democratic presidential and vice-presidential candidates delivered a combined total of nearly 1,000 speeches.[12] In 1960 John Kennedy delivered 64 speeches in the last 7 days of the campaign.[13] In 1976 Jimmy Carter delivered 2,100 speeches while running for president.[14] These demands are not unique to presidential candidates. In 1954 Orville Freeman, running for governor of Minnesota, found himself facing over 120 speaking situations for which he felt the need for advanced preparation.[15] This number does not include the many countless situations in which he spoke with little preparation. In 1970 Nelson Rockefeller delivered over 300 speeches in his campaign for the governorship of New York.[16] A recent survey of candidates for Congress indicates that they spoke approximately four times a day.[17] Thus candidates at all levels simply cannot prepare for the many speeches they must make, while simultaneously fulfilling other responsibilities as candidate, breadwinner, and family member, without the help of a speechwriter. This justification is a compelling one.

Though the public is aware of speechwriters and understands the time demands that justify their use, it remains slightly troubled by the practice of one person writing the words of another. A second reason candidates use speechwriters is because they believe the writer will produce a good speech. Speechwriters possess unique skills. If their skills can be marshalled on behalf of the candidate, the result will be a stronger speech, and to that extent, an increased likelihood of election. But this justification raises troubling questions.

One critic has suggested that "the essential question is how much borrowing is ethical?"[18] There is, he suggests, a continuum of help that one can provide to a speaker. On one end of the continuum, few people would find anything wrong if a candidate had a spouse or an aide listen to the rehearsal of a speech, or perhaps review drafts of a speech, in each instance making occasional suggestions to improve the language or organization. On the other end, most people might object to finding that speeches were written entirely by speechwriters who did not consult with the candidates, who in turn had no idea about what they were going to say until the moment they started to deliver the speeches that had been written for them. Where on this continuum does one draw the line between honest and dishonest borrowing and collaboration? This is an especially vexing question when speakers are using speeches to present themselves as competent to serve in a leadership position in their community, city, state, or nation.

Communication scholar Ernest Bormann finds that the point on the continuum where one must draw the line is

> where the speech changes character. The language becomes different from what it would have been had the speaker prepared the speech for himself with some aid in gathering information and some advice from friends and associates about parts that he should consider revising. At some point the ideas are different, the structure of the speech is different, the nuances of meaning change from what they would have been had this speech really been "his own." [19]

When this happens, the speech cannot achieve what should be one of its chief goals, portraying the speaker accurately to the audience, and the public clearly has reason to be troubled.

Thus voters accept the use of speechwriters. However, we remain vaguely troubled, because the speechwriter is a skilled artisan who produces a polished product, and this too causes the candidate to hire him. To the extent that the speech reflects the writer and not the speaker, the public has cause for concern.

The very nature of political speechwriting prevents us from knowing how often "the speech changes character," becoming more a creation of the speechwriter than of the candidate. However, an examination of the job demands imposed upon political speechwriters suggests that this is probably not a frequent occurrence. Fortunately for free societies, the demands of political speechwriting coincide with the needs of the public.

180

Job Demands

A veteran of over 25 years of political speechwriting for a wide variety of Democratic candidates, Josef Berger, claims that the most important part of a speechwriter's work is "to know his man, to know the man's ideas, not only his general philosophy and background but his thoughts on the issues that he's talking about if he's clear enough on them."[20] Similarly, virtually every political speechwriter who has commented on the job reaffirms the absolutely critical importance of knowing the candidate for whom they are writing because they seek to create a speech that is essentially that of the candidate, accurately portraying the candidate to the audience. Speechwriters must be thoroughly acquainted with the candidate's value system. For speechwriters must not present what they believe is the best justification for the candidate's policy but must present the candidate's justification for a policy. Moreover, speechwriters must do so using language with which the candidate will feel comfortable, language that is an accurate reflection of the candidate. Thus the primary demand placed on speechwriters is to gain an intimate familiarity with the candidate for whom they are working. That familiarity should include a thorough knowledge of the candidate's position on major questions, value systems, the way the candidate thinks through questions and makes decisions, as well as the candidate's manner of using language.

This information will enable the writer to produce a speech that accurately reflects the candidate. The speechwriter owes that to the public so that it might fairly judge the candidate. But what we often forget is that the speechwriter owes it to the candidate as well.

If the speechwriter does not accurately portray the candidate, the speech is likely to be a failure for several practical reasons. First, the candidate may choose to stray from the speech or ignore it altogether. In either case, the speechwriter will probably be fired for writing a speech with which the candidate felt uncomfortable or could not use. Second, if the candidate does choose to use a speech that is an inaccurate portrayal, there will likely be trouble in delivery. Unfamiliar with the basic lines of argument, the evidence, and the language, the candidate cannot be expected to do a good job in presenting the case. Third, candidates are likely to experience discomfort and nervousness in a public situation, where they are liable to make some type of error as a consequence of that discomfort. Fourth, they may repudiate parts of the speech in a question-and-answer session or in subsequent public appearances. This inconsistency could create an opening for criticism. Hence, the demands on the political speechwriter to produce a speech useful to the candidate creates a speech that is an accurate reflection of the candidate's policies, thought processes, values, and language. In so doing, the interests of the speechwriter and candidate coincide with the interests of the public in securing the accurate information about the candidate.

In addition to knowledge of the candidate, speechwriters need at least two other types of knowledge. First, they must know the subject. Occasionally, a political figure is concerned with a specific issue and calls on someone to help with speeches because of that individual's expertise on the issue. In 1980 Senator Sam Nunn of Georgia, for example, was concerned with U.S. military preparedness vis-à-vis the Soviet Union. Thus it was not surprising to find Dr. Jeffrey Record, an expert on U.S. and Soviet military affairs on Senator Nunn's staff. A U.S. senator, with a large staff, particularly concerned about one issue and perhaps having as many as six years before his next election can afford a subject-matter specialist. However, most political speechwriters are generalists because most candidates need generalists.

Campaign speechwriters must be versatile. The speechwriter for a Missouri congressional candidate in a recent election was asked to write speeches in a one-month period on such diverse topics as international terrorism, the importance of engineering technology to the St. Louis business community, abortion laws, Lock and Dam Project Twenty-Six on the Missouri River, Israel and Middle East affairs, and National Fire Prevention Week. Thus speechwriters invariably are widely read, often in literature as well as politics and current events. Moreover, they know how to do research. If they do not know about the topic, they know where to learn about it.

The final knowledge required by the good speechwriter is information regarding the audience and occasion. Speechwriters must know which audiences in the candidate's district are essential for victory. Moreover, they must know what message or impression the candidate wishes to leave with these target audiences. Is this speech being delivered exclusively to the audience in the room? If so, what is the nature of that audience? What are their interests? Is the immediate audience of secondary importance to the audience that will be reached by press accounts of this speech? How can the interests of those two audiences and the candidate be reconciled in an appropriate speech for this particular occasion? Answering these questions and then operationalizing the answers to produce a speech demands many kinds of information. It demands knowledge of the candidate's ideas, value system, reasoning process, and use of language. It demands knowledge of the subject matter, the audience(s), and the occasion.

A final demand placed on speechwriters is the trying circumstances in which their knowledge must be utilized. As one speechwriter expressed it when commenting about the type of person hired to help, "we looked for the capacity to work under harsh and often preposterous time pressures. When a speech for a particular evening calling for a ban on leaded gasolines has been co-opted by your opponent that morning, swiftness, along with eloquence, is routinely expected of the writer in coming up with a substitute."[21]

Speechwriting Teams

As the previous section has indicated, the job demands of political speechwriting are formidable. These demands grow in proportion to the office contested. While the types of knowledge we have discussed are required by every political speechwriter, they are normally felt to a greater degree by the speechwriter working for a major national candidate because of such factors as the need to coordinate the candidate's speaking with the radio and television messages of the campaign, the need to respond to an opponent who is also constantly speaking and using media, and the constant interjection into the campaign of new issues. Hence, speechwriting in most major campaigns is done by speechwriting teams characterized by a sharper division of labor than is found in the small campaign. Additionally, the team may perform functions that are not performed in smaller campaigns.

Firsthand accounts by members of the campaign staffs of Franklin Roosevelt, Harry Truman, Orville Freeman, Nelson Rockefeller, Richard Nixon, Gerald Ford, Ronald Reagan, Hubert Humphrey, George McGovern, Jimmy Carter, and a wide variety of other gubernatorial, senatorial, and congressional candidates suggest that speechwriting teams exhibit a similar division of labor in most larger campaigns. Craig Smith, who has been a part of several such teams and has studied many others, finds that typically speechwriting teams in larger campaigns are composed of three groups: the researchers, the stylists, and the media or public relations advisors.[22]

All these individuals should be familiar with the policies, values, and decision-making processes of the candidate. In practicality it may not be possible for each member of these teams to acquire that knowledge. Rather, key figures in each group acquire it.

The research group does basic library research. This is a group that frequently employs college students who are familiar with library research techniques. Pre-law students, college debaters, or other students interested in campaigns and with good research backgrounds may get their first experience in larger campaigns as part of the research force.

The second group, the stylists, is normally composed of

experienced speechwriters. They are often hired on the basis of recommendations and/or writing samples. These individuals must be able to write in any easy conversational style with which the candidate feels comfortable. They must be sensitive to the candidate's ability to tell a story, show righteous indignation, tell a joke, or use a particular jargon or group of metaphors. They use the materials presented by the researchers to produce a speech that meets high rhetorical standards and with which the candidate feels comfortable.

The final group, the media and public relations consultants, are particularly concerned with the audience. More than the other groups, they tend to be familiar with survey research techniques. Their suggestions are designed to make the speeches consistent with the other messages the audience is receiving from the campaign, and given their surveys of the audience/public, to make sure that the candidate's speeches are perceived favorably by the audience.

Thus the demands put on speechwriters in large campaigns do not differ greatly from the demands put on speechwriters in smaller campaigns. The basic differences are not so much in the demands of the task, but rather in the division of labor employed to accomplish the task. Additionally, since a larger campaign is providing the audience/public with a great number of messages, most larger campaigns involve media and public relations consultants who focus on the speech from an audience's perspective, seeking to make the speech consistent with other messages the audience is receiving from the campaign.

Methods of Political Speechwriting

The literature of speech communication, as well as an examination of newspaper reports, biographies of the principals, and similar material, indicate that most speechwriters and speechwriting teams operate in a similar manner.[23] In this section we will examine the basic steps involved in campaign speechwriting.

First, the speechwriter(s), the candidate, and in some instances subject matter experts will confer. In this initial conference, the purposes of the speech will be agreed upon. The candidate will indicate positions and rationales, "talking through" the speech. Many speechwriters have noted that often the conference would be taped, or a stenographer would be present. If not, the speechwriter would take copious notes. The record of the candidate's remarks would constitute a first rough draft. From the very inception, the ideas of the speech are those of the candidate. The justification and reasoning within the speech are those of the candidate. Often, some of the language used in these conferences by the candidate is worked into later drafts and remains intact in the final speech.

At this point the speechwriters, armed with a clear understanding of what the candidate wants, do their research. If the campaign has a research staff, it is brought into the development of the speech. If the campaign is small, the research is done by the speechwriter. One of the advantages of incumbency is that incumbent officeholders can often put the resources of government to work on their behalf. A speechwriter for the president might draw on the expertise of a cabinet member or someone in the appropriate department. Similarly, congressional speechwriters' efforts might be supplemented by the Legislative Reference Service of the Library of Congress, acting on a legislator's request.

At this point a draft is developed. In larger speechwriting teams, this draft is typically done by one staff member whose work may be reviewed by other speechwriters, and altered. In a small operation, an equivalent process takes place as the speechwriter prepares a draft and then revises it, perhaps drawing on the suggestions of staff members or advisors who know the candidate well but have no responsibilities for speechwriting. It is not uncommon that the original draft undergoes three or more revisions as speechwriters revise their own work and incorporate the suggestions of others. If it is possible, the candidate is shown successive drafts for input.

However, this is rarely possible with every draft in larger campaigns. Nevertheless, at some point the candidate is again brought back into the process.

Depending on the candidate's reaction, several actions can be taken with the version that the speechwriter believes to be close to final. Often the candidate accepts it as final, normally continuing to make minor changes, primarily stylistic, during free moments up until the time of delivery. If the speech is basically sound, but the candidate has more than stylistic concerns, these may be indicated in marginal notes or in a meeting. Subsequent drafts, better conforming to the candidate's wishes, can then be developed and resubmitted. The candidate may have an objection to one section of the speech or perhaps to some aspects of organization. Frequently when reading over the speech, the candidate may be concerned that the material will run too long or short for the allotted time. If the speech is to be delivered over radio or television, the media consultants will normally enter the speechwriting process during the final few drafts. Their suggestions will be geared to insuring that the speech is appropriate for the allotted time and contains portions that can be used for a 20-to-30-second spot on the news shows. These spots normally contain vivid and startling language that exemplify the point the candidate wishes to make. In smaller campaigns, media consultants will not be available, but a conscientious speechwriter will strive to include potential media "spots" in the speech in case of press coverage. Additionally, such spots, even in smaller campaigns, might be submitted to the media in the hope that they will be used.

With slight variations to accommodate their own circumstances, this process is an accurate characterization of speechwriting in the vast majority of political campaigns where speechwriters are employed.[24] Several key points result from this description.

First, throughout this process the candidate is a major writer/editor/collaborator in the creative process. The final speech is a clear reflection of the candidate. The candidate accepts responsibility for what is said. It is for this reason that, as one speechwriter has noted:

> I don't think it occurs to the general public that a speech is ghostwritten. Even if someone in the audience has read somewhere that Congressman X has a ghostwriter and he knows it as the man speaks, he forgets it. He's listening to the man, and he's holding him responsible, and he's responding to him for everything that is said.[25]

Second, though the speechwriter has also contributed to the final product, the speech belongs to the person who utters it. It is the candidate, not the speechwriter, who will receive praise or blame for the speech. Thus it is easy to understand why one experienced political speechwriter has commented that "if there is any prerequisite to ghostwriting for political figures, I suggest that it is a willingness to sublimate one's self to the figure for whom one works."[26]

Third, major campaign addresses undergo many drafts. A recent study of Congressmembers indicates that they typically draft major campaign speeches at least three times.[27] New York Governor Nelson Rockefeller's speeches typically underwent six drafts during his campaigns for office.[28] Florida Governor Ruben Askew's major speeches have been known to undergo at least nine drafts.[29] Senator Henry "Scoop" Jackson of Washington routinely delivers speeches that have been drafted and revised three or more times.[30] And though few presidents are as notorious for using the seven or more speech drafts that Franklin Roosevelt demanded for his major speeches, every president and presidential candidate of the last 50 years has made extensive use of speechwriters.

SURROGATE SPEAKERS

Even though most candidates make use of speech modules and speechwriters to help them meet the demands on their time, inevitably they find that they simply cannot be in two places at once. Hence, even in smaller campaigns, it is not unusual to see surrogate or substitute speakers filling in for an absent candidate. In large national campaigns, hundreds of people serve as surrogates for the candidate, many of whom have been trained by the campaign staff.

Selection of Surrogates

The selection of surrogate speakers is not left to chance. Candidates seek surrogates who meet these requirements. First, they should have a proven record of competence as a public speaker. In smaller campaigns, the skilled college debater, a lawyer, teacher, or anyone else with speaking experience may be called upon. In larger campaigns, public officials with extensive speaking experience might be used. In a governor's race, for example, members of the state legislature might serve as surrogates for their parties' nominee. At the presidential level, it is not uncommon to utilize cabinet members and members of Congress who are known for their ability as speakers.

Second, the surrogate should have some clearly identifiable connection to the candidate. It is for this reason that we so often see the relatives of candidates speaking. They are perceived as being close to the candidate, as are cabinet members and legislative allies.

If surrogate speakers do not have an obvious connection to the candidate, they should make their connection clear to the audience early in the speech. Perhaps they grew up with the candidate, previously worked with the candidate, or have simply been long-time supporters of the candidate. In 1976 Jimmy Carter made heavy use not only of his relatives, but of many other long-time supporters from Georgia, who became known as the "Peanut Brigade." In 1980 many of Carter's surrogates, members of his cabinet and Congress, could speak of their direct association with him as president and their opportunity to witness his conduct in office. Third, the surrogate should have

189

some clearly identifiable connection to the audience. Since the substitute is just that, a substitute, the candidate or the staff should select a substitute who is appropriate for the audience. In local campaigns, the surrogate may be a member of the organization sponsoring the speech or a native of the geographic area. In national campaigns, the surrogate may be the cabinet member with responsibilities for the area of government that most affects the sponsoring group, as when the secretary of labor represents the president at union affairs. Again, surrogates should make clear reference to this connection early in their speeches if it is not obvious.

Since the candidate is not present, it is clear that whomever is speaking on the candidate's behalf is not the audience's first choice. Hence, that individual may have to overcome the resentment of the audience. It is for this reason that the speaker should be able to stress a connection to the candidate. In effect, the surrogate is saying "I'm the next best thing" and reminding the audience that, like Hallmark cards, this candidate cares enough to send the very best.

Utilization of Surrogates

Surrogates should have attempted to familiarize themselves with the candidate's positions. Indeed, one reason that some candidates like to use their speechwriters for surrogates is that they are uniquely adept at putting themselves in the candidate's shoes. Nevertheless, two rules should govern every presentation. First, surrogates must acknowledge why the candidate is not there. Most people understand the demands placed on a candidate, and a frank statement of where the candidate is will be better received than an attempt to hide the fact that the candidate has chosen to speak elsewhere. Depending on the audience being faced, most surrogates can indicate why their principal is not present in a tactful or humorous way. One rather rotund surrogate we are acquainted with often opened his after-dinner or -luncheon addresses by saying that his candidate wanted to maintain his weight, and it was difficult to do so during the campaign when he was constantly attending breakfast meetings, luncheons, dinners, coffees, teas, beer busts, and the like.

> So he's out rounding up some votes tonight in _____ where they are not serving food. Since I am the one member of the staff who clearly does not have a weight problem, he sent me here to guarantee that your food would be appreciated. Well, I certainly appreciated this fine meal, and I hope that when I am finished this evening you will have a better appreciation of why _____ ought to be elected to the Congress.

An introduction like this one acknowledges that the candidate is campaigning elsewhere but does so in a humorous and tactful fashion, which reduces the audience's resentment.

Second, surrogates should not hesitate to remind the audience that they are not the candidate. Hence, they may not know all of the answers or precisely what the candidate thinks. If the surrogate is well prepared, there should not be many occasions for this to happen. However, the speaker may confront a difficult question. When this occurs the surrogate should simply acknowledge that to be the case rather than guess; arrangements should then be made for the candidate or staff to respond later.

Benefits of Surrogates

The use of surrogate speakers can provide a variety of benefits to campaigns. Martha Stout Kessler, who directed the Speakers Bureau of John Anderson's 1980 presidential race in New York, observed that in some instances surrogates may be more credible speakers for a given audience than the candidate. Moreover, she notes that surrogates also have the liberty to say things that the candidate might not wish to say, and they can also aid the candidate in fund raising.[31]

191

Surrogates who have a unique connection to the audience may, on occasion, be more effective with that audience than the candidate. For example, in recent presidential elections, well-known public officials of the Jewish faith were often used by the candidates to address predominately Jewish audiences. In a Missouri congressional election, the candidate's college-age children spoke on the campuses in the district. These surrogates were often exceptionally effective because of the common bonds of religion or age/occupation and because they were well prepared on the issues that most concerned the audiences they addressed.

Frequently, candidates may wish to say something but find that it is not politically expedient. A surrogate may be able to make the statements for the candidate. Kessler points out that in the 1980 presidential campaign the harshest criticism leveled at an opponent did not come from the candidate. Rather it was made by surrogates, such as Leon Jaworski and Coretta King.[32] Surrogates can deliver the candidate's message, but they are not the candidate. Hence, surrogates may be able to make remarks that are not politically expedient for the candidate to make.

Finally, surrogates are often able to help candidates raise money. Many candidates feel that is is unbecoming for them to personally ask for money. Surrogates are not embarrassed or compromised because the money is not for themselves.

In sum, the use of surrogate speakers can provide many benefits. Their primary function is to spread the candidate's messages to audiences that might otherwise not hear them. However, as Kessler stresses, this is by no means the only advantage to using surrogates. Indeed, the benefits of using surrogate speakers are so important in larger campaigns, where candidates cannot possibly address all the audiences that wish to hear them, that most national and many state and regional campaigns actively recruit surrogate speakers, provide them with training, and schedule them through a speaker's bureau.

CONCLUSIONS

Although, as we have seen in Chapter 4, the media have grown to play an increasingly important part in contemporary political campaigns, the public speaking of candidates and their surrogates nevertheless is at the core of any campaign. In small campaigns, public speaking may be virtually the only means of persuasion utilized. In this chapter, we have seen that the decisions to speak are not left to chance in well-managed campaigns. Rather, the campaign identifies the audiences to whom it wishes to speak and the messages it wishes to send and then arranges situations that conform to those wishes. Moreover, we have observed how candidates make use of speech modules to create a basic speech that can be used, with some variation, repeatedly during the campaign. Additionally, we have examined the reasons for the growing use of speechwriters, the demands placed on such individuals, and the methods they use to meet those demands. Finally, we have observed the use of surrogate speakers, focusing on the criteria for selecting such speakers, the techniques such speakers commonly employ, and the benefits surrogate speakers provide to a campaign. In spite of changes that have occurred in technology and in the way campaigns are managed, all candidates, whether they assume incumbency or challenger styles, whether they speak at a rally, a press conference, on television or radio, utilize the ideas we have discussed in this chapter. Clearly, public speaking remains a fundamental practice of political campaigns.

NOTES

1. Jacob Javits, "How I Used a Poll in Campaigning for Congress," *Public Opinion Quarterly* 11 (Summer 1947): 222–26.

2. See Martin Schramm, *Running for President: A Journal of the Carter Campaign* (New York: Pocket Books, 1977), pp. 428–31 for insight into a national campaign's targeting strategies.

3. Quoted in "Out of the Past," *People* 17 (February 16, 1981): 74.

4. Perry Sekus and Robert Friedenberg, "Public Speaking in the House of Representatives: The 97th Congress Speaks," unpublished study, Miami University, 1982), pp. 2–4.

5. Ibid.

6. *New York Times*, February 29, 1980.

7. Ibid.

8. Ibid.

9. Quoted in William Norwood Brigance, "Ghostwriting before Franklin D. Roosevelt and the Radio," *Today's Speech* 4 (September 1956): 11.

10. Robert Bishop, "Bruce Barton—Presidential Stage Manager," *Journalism Quarterly* 33 (Spring 1956); 85–89.

11. Irwin Ross, *The Loneliest Campaign* (New York: New American Library, 1968), p. 89.

12. Walter J. Stelkovis, "Ghostwriting: Ancient and Honorable," *Today's Speech* 2 (January 1954): 17.

13. John F. Kennedy, *The Speeches of Senator John F. Kennedy: Presidential Campaign of 1960* (Washington, D.C.: Government Printing Office, 1961), pp. 840–1267.

14. Jimmy Carter, *A Government As Good As Its People* (New York: Simon and Schuster, 1977), p. 7.

15. Donald K. Smith, "The Speech-Writing Team in a State Political Campaign," *Today's Speech* 4 (September 1956): 16.

16. Joseph Persico, "The Rockefeller Rhetoric: Writing Speeches for the 1970 Campaign," *Today's Speech* 20 (Spring 1972): 57.

17. Sekus and Friedenberg, "Public Speaking," p. 9.

18. Ernest Bormann, "Ethics of Ghostwritten Speeches," *Quarterly Journal of Speech* 47 (October 1961): 266.

19. Ibid., pp. 266–67.

20. Thomas Benson, "Conversations with a Ghost," *Today's Speech* 16 (November 1968): 73.

21. Persico, "Rockefeller Rhetoric," p. 58.

22. Craig R. Smith, "Contemporary Political Speech Writing," *Southern Speech Communication Journal* 42 (Fall 1976): 52–68; Craig R. Smith, "Addendum to Contemporary Political Speech Writing," *Southern Speech Communication Journal* 43 (Winter 1977): 191–94.

23. The speech communication literature utilized in this section includes Robert F. Ray, "Ghostwriting in Presidential Campaigns," *Central States Speech Journal* 8 (Fall 1956): 8–11; Benson, "Conversations with a Ghost," pp. 71–81; Persico, "Rockefeller Rhetoric," pp. 57–62; Howard Schwartz, "Senator 'Scoop' Jackson Speaks on Speaking," *Speaker and Gavel* 5 (November 1968): 21–31; Robert Friedenberg, "The Army of Invisible Men: Ghostwriting for Congressmen and Congressional Candidates," *The Forensic* 62 (May 1977): 4–8; Sara Arendall Newell and Thomas King, "The Keynote Address of the Democratic National Convention, 1972: The Evolution of a Speech," *Southern Speech Communication Journal* 39 (Summer 1974): 346–58; Smith "Political Speech Writing," pp. 52–68; Smith, "Addendum," pp. 191–94; Lois J. Einhorn, "The Ghosts Unmasked: A Review of Literature on Speechwriting," *Communication Quarterly* 30 (Winter 1981): 41–47.

24. An extremely brief description of the ghostwriting process, which coincides with this one, can be found in Einhorn, "Ghosts Unmasked," p. 42.

25. Benson, "Conversations with a Ghost," pp. 79–80.

26. Friedenberg, "Army of Invisible Men," p. 4.

27. Sekus and Friedenberg, "Public Speaking," p. 6.

28. Persico, "Rockefeller Rhetoric," pp. 59–60.

29. Newell and King, "Keynote Address," p. 357.

30. Schwartz, "Senator 'Scoop' Jackson," p. 22.

31. Martha Stout Kessler, "The Role of Surrogate Speakers in the 1980 Presidential Campaign," *Quarterly Journal of Speech* 67 (May 1981): 148–50.

32. Ibid., p. 148.

6

Recurring Forms of Political Campaign Communication

*I*N HIS CLASSIC ARTICLE, "THE RHETORICAL SITUATION," LLOYD BITZER DEFINED A RHETORICAL SITUATION AS "A COMPLEX OF PERSONS, EVENTS, OBJECTS AND RELATIONS presenting an actual or potential exigence which can be completely or partially removed if discourse, introduced into the situation, can so constrain human decision or action as to bring about the significant modification of the exigence."[1] Bitzer's work has served as the basis for much recent study of rhetoric based on the premise that comparable rhetorical situations produce comparable rhetorical responses.[2] While such studies have been subject to criticism, we find that the basic premise that some rhetorical situations are relatively analogous and hence produce relatively analogous discourse is a valuable premise for the study of much political campaign communication. In this chapter, we shall suggest that most political campaigns tend to produce several similar, comparable, or analogous situations. Moreover, these situations tend to produce similar, comparable, or analogous discourse. Four such comparable situations, found in most campaigns, are the rhetorical situations created by:

1) the need of candidates to announce formally their candidacies to the public
2) the need of candidates to accept publicly the nomination of their party
3) the need of candidates to seek media coverage of their views
4) the need of candidates to make public apologies for their statements or behavior.

In this chapter, we will examine the discourse to which these situations traditionally give rise; announcement speeches, acceptance addresses, press conferences, and political apologies. We will study these recurring forms first by describing the situations that create the need or exigence for their use. Second, we will discuss the purposes that these four recurring forms of political campaign communication traditionally serve. Third, we will discuss the strategies most frequently and successfully employed by candidates delivering these four recurring forms of political campaign communication.

ANNOUNCEMENT SPEECHES

Candidates normally announce that they are seeking public office through a formal address to the public.* However, this formal address is rarely the first act of the campaign. Rather, it has been preceded by considerable work. The effort that candidates and their associates have engaged in during the surfacing stage, helps to shape the rhetorical situation in which the announcement address is made.[3]

---

*On some occasions, as with President Gerald Ford and Governor Jerry Brown in 1976, preprimary efforts of the candidates have made their candidacies obvious, and they chose to deliver highly abbreviated speeches, little more than a minute in length, or they announced their candidacies through press releases.

Preannouncement Situation

At least three activities typically precede any announcement address, regardless of the office being sought or the candidate who is announcing. First, an assessment must be made of the likelihood of winning. This will include an assessment of the candidate's ability to attract sufficient voter support, sufficient financial support, and develop an organization capable of winning the office. The results of this analysis may enter into the announcement address itself. In any event, it gives the candidate a clearer understanding of the situation.

Second, most candidates tend to inform key individuals personally, prior to their public announcement. Typically, these are politically, financially, or personally significant individuals whom the candidate wishes to flatter. If the office being contested is statewide or national in scope, often the candidate may inform a small group of individuals personally and then send a personal letter of announcement, in advance of the candidate's public statement, to several dozen, hundred, or even thousands of others. The point is that these individuals are significant, and the candidate wishes to flatter them.[4]

However, the advance announcement in person to a few key figures fulfills a second purpose. It serves as a means of providing the candidate with feedback regarding the rhetorical situation to be faced. These key, well-placed individuals may be able to help shape strategy, better understand the concerns of the constituency, or identify possible obstacles. For example, a judge with a group of six family members and close friends decided to run for Congress. After having assessed his opportunity for winning, the judge personally set about contacting 25 key individuals whom he wanted to inform of his decision to run. He anticipated that all would be encouraging and would pledge their support. Among those contacted were three elected officials, several party leaders, five prospective financial contributors, the director of a prominent local political action committee, three journalists who were contacted entirely off the record, and officers of several organizations whose members the judge felt might be sympathetic to his candidacy. While those contacted pledged their support, over half indicated that they believed the incumbent would prove much more difficult to defeat than the judge's initial planning group had anticipated. Many pointed to aspects of the judge's record that might work against him in an election. Moreover, they pointed out characteristics of the incumbent that would make him much harder to defeat than he had been two years earlier, when he won election by under 5,000 votes. Thus through a tentative exploration of candidacy with key individuals, the judge became more aware of the situation that confronted him.

Finally, the announcement should conform to any preconceived expectations that the public might have about it. Hence, the third preliminary activity of the candidate is to determine public expectations about the announcement. For example, have prior candidates conditioned the public to expect that an announcement of candidacy for the office sought should be made from the state capital rather than from the candidate's home? Does the public have any expectations about who should be with the candidate when the announcement is made? Does the public have any expectations about what the candidate should say? Does the public have expectations about the qualifications necessary for this position, which might be mentioned in the announcement speech?

Clearly the rhetorical situation for every announcement address differs. Yet, typically, the candidate has first to analyze prospects for the campaign, second to share impending candidacy with a group of significant associates, and third to consider public expectations concerning the announcement address.

Purposes of Address

The announcement address should serve several purposes. Depending on the situation that the candidate confronts, one or more of the purposes discussed here may be minimized or underplayed, while others are stressed. Nevertheless, a sound announcement address may serve several purposes. First, it clearly signals the candidate's intention to run. Second, it may serve to discourage the competition. If the announcement address alludes to the candidate's strengths, such as the ability to articulate the issues, raise money, or wage an aggressive campaign, it may discourage other potential candidates from contesting for the party nomination or the office itself. As we will see in our discussion of strategies, typically the content of the address must be accompanied with actions that successfully discourage the competition. Nevertheless, one of the purposes of an announcement address, particularly if there is liable to be a primary, may be to discourage potential competition.

The third purpose announcement addresses often serve is to indicate why the candidate is running. Candidates may want to stress what they can bring to the office that others cannot—how they can uniquely serve the public.

A fourth purpose frequently served by the announcement address is to initiate the themes of the campaign. As the candidate's first major campaign address, it is appropriate to initiate any important themes that may run throughout the campaign. In sum, the announcement address may serve several purposes in addition to the obvious one of officially signaling the candidate's intent to run. It may serve to discourage possible competitors, indicate why the candidate has chosen to run, and initiate major campaign themes.

Strategies of Address

In preparing to announce their intention to run, a variety of choices confront candidates. They must consider the timing, location, who should be with them, speech content, and finally the means by which they follow up on their announcement.

Timing the announcement speech may be difficult. Often the first candidate to announce receives more coverage, and by

201

virtue of being first, may be perceived as being more serious, credible, or legitimate. Though an early announcement may attract media coverage, content of the coverage might well focus on the candidate's potential to win, the funds raised, and the staff that has been recruited. Obviously, by announcing early to gain coverage, the candidate runs the risk that the announcement will not be taken seriously because there are few other overt trappings of a campaign.

Timing is also vital because of the effect that it may have on others who are politically important, both other candidates and potential supporters. In 1976, for example, had either Governor Jerry Brown of California, the most populous state in the union, or Senator Frank Church of Idaho, chairman of the Senate Foreign Relations Committee, chosen to announce their campaigns much earlier, perhaps they would have attracted much of the early support that went to former Georgia Governor Jimmy Carter, the first Democratic candidate to announce his candidacy for president that year.[5]. In races for lesser offices, timing of the announcement can also be important. Obviously it may not receive the publicity that is associated with a presidential candidate's announcement, but it will be noticed and considered by other crucial decision makers in the constituency: potential opponents, potential contributors, volunteers, staff members, or supporters.

Where to deliver the announcement address is a second strategic consideration that candidates must confront. In so doing, they must also consider voter expectations and tradition. The location of the announcement speech may, in itself, be symbolic. In 1976 Jimmy Carter was advised to announce his candidacy in Washington D.C., preferably at the National Press Club. Such an announcement location would greatly facilitate extensive national media coverage. Moreover, it would link Carter to Washington and at least symbolically help overcome what he expected to be a major charge against him, his lack of Washington experience or exposure in dealing with national problems. The Carter campaign also recognized that much of his strength was as a Washington "outsider" who would bring a new perspective to the nation's problems. Hence, Carter's advisors also noted that though the Washington announcement was vital for coverage, later in the day or at the very latest, the next day, Carter should also reannounce his intention to run at a function in Georgia. Such an announcement would reinforce Carter's image as an "outsider" who could help clean up the mess in Washington and reassure his long-time Georgia supporters that he had not forgotten them.[6]

Similarly, the location of the announcement address is important in lesser campaigns. The candidate who is making improved road conditions a prominent issue might well deliver his announcement address from a major road repair site. Most communities have buildings and locations that have unique connotations. Candidates who announce their intentions to run at such locations are at least symbolically identifying themselves with the persons or events that have given this location its uniqueness. Additionally, if the site is visually attractive, the candidate may be increasing the limited likelihood of receiving television coverage of the announcement address.

A third question candidates consider when making their announcement addresses is with whom they might wish to share the spotlight. That is, who else should be present and in a prominent position? Traditionally, most candidates have announced their candidacies while surrounded by family, close friends, admirers, and supporters. However, exactly who should be invited, who should sit with the candidates, and who might also make a few brief remarks, are questions which must be answered by candidates as they plan their announcement event. Often the presence of prominent individuals in the community, city, or state, supportive remarks from party leaders, and similar visible signs of support for the candidate at the very outset of the campaign can help establish credibility and discourage potential competitors for the nomination or the office itself.

In 1960 the timing of John Kennedy's announcement of candidacy was in no small measure a function of the actions of Ohio Governor Michael DiSalle. The Kennedy announcement was not made until after DiSalle agreed to be the first governor to endorse Kennedy and bring the large Ohio delegation to the convention committed to him.[7] DiSalle's actions, immediately after the Kennedy announcement, made it clear to prospective challengers that the Kennedy campaign was not to be underestimated and may well, as the Kennedys hoped, have slowed down or discouraged the challenges of other possible contenders.

The announcement address itself is yet a fourth strategic consideration with which candidates must deal. The content of this speech is, in part, dictated by its purposes. Typically, two themes are present in most announcement addresses. Candidates announce that they are, in fact, running and offer an explanation of why.

Unless candidates can provide some cogent reasons for running, their candidacy may end very early. Senator Edward Kennedy experienced this difficulty in 1980 when he announced his intention to run for the presidency. In his announcement speech and in the speeches and interviews that followed, he had difficulty in offering cogent reasons for running. He chose to challenge an incumbent president of his own party. Yet, analysis of his positions on major issues, compared to those of President Carter, revealed very few significant differences at the outset of the campaign.[8] Kennedy's failure to offer a clear explanation of why he was running hurt his candidacy. The public expects candidates to have rational reasons for running and to share those reasons at the outset of the campaign. Candidates who fail to provide them in the announcement speech, or very shortly thereafter, tend to generate public distrust of their motives.

In announcing candidacy, most office seekers also stress the likelihood of their victory. In so doing, they often focus on their strengths and on the weaknesses of potential opponents. Implicit in this discussion is their fitness for the office. The candidate claims to be better able to manage the office, better able to represent the constituency, and of course better able to attract funds and wage an effective campaign than anyone else. In sum, the actual content of the candidate's announcement address varies with the situation. However, most candidates, perhaps conditioned in part by public expectations, will formally declare their candidacy, attempt to explain why they are running, and suggest that they will win.

The strategies involved in the announcement address must also include the immediate follow-up to the address. The candidate should not simply announce that he is running and then seemingly disappear from public view. Rather, the timing of the address, perhaps its location, the other people invited to the announcement, and the discourse itself, might all contribute to and be climaxed by the means by which the candidate follows up on the announcement. For example, in recent years many candidates have arranged their schedules so that immediately following their announcement they could start on a walking tour of the district or state. Such a method of following up may allow the candidate to stress key issues and begin to live up to announcement address promises. It enables the candidate to express concern for all constituencies within the district, evidencing ability to unify people. At various points in the walk, the candidate can be greeted by prominent supporters, discuss the campaign with them, and of course get extensive media coverage of all this. Regardless of the specific method used, a walk, the endorsement of prominent citizens, announcing staff appointments, or the like, it is sound strategy to coordinate the announcement address with some type of follow-up activity illustrating that the candidate is serious about seeking office and is already generating support for the candidacy.

In sum, the announcement address is not as simple as it may at first appear. Considerable thought must be given to the timing of the address, to its location, to the other parties who may share the spotlight with the candidate, to what the candidate will actually say, and to how the candidate will immediately follow up on the announcement. The announcement address is the centerpiece of a rhetorical situation created by the candidate's need for formally announcing candidacy to the public. Though the address may be the first public indication of candidacy, it should not be the first political activity the candidate attempts. Rather, the announcement speech should be preceded by considerable thought and preparation to ensure that the candidate's campaign is opened effectively.

ACCEPTANCE ADDRESSES

In the 1830s, national candidates nominated by the Democratic party began to respond to their nominations with letters of acceptance. By the 1850s, Democratic candidates began to respond to their nominations with informal speeches. In 1868 Horatio Seymour delivered the first formal nomination acceptance address, but like most such addresses in the latter portion of the nineteenth century, it was a perfunctory speech indicating gratitude at receiving the nomination and promising a full formal letter of acceptance. It was not until 1892, when Grover Cleveland accepted his nomination for the presidency by speaking at a large public meeting in Madison Square Garden, that acceptance addresses began to assume their current importance. Cleveland, William Jennings Bryan in 1896, and subsequent national candidates have used acceptance addresses as a means of thanking their supporters, seeking party unity, and dramatizing the issues. In 1932 Franklin Delano Roosevelt flew to the Democratic National Convention and became the first presidential candidate to accept personally his nomination at the convention.[9]

Situation during Address

The situations faced by candidates delivering acceptance addresses have often varied, but typically they share several key characteristics. Most importantly, candidates have successfully attained their party's nomination for office. This suc-

206

cess may be the consequence of running in dozens of primaries throughout the nation, as it is with current presidential candidates. It may be the consequence of persuading a majority of party voters in a statewide or local primary. It may be a consequence of persuading a majority of key party officials in a local, regional, or state party caucus or committee. It may even be a consequence of default, because no one else chooses to run. Regardless of how it was achieved, the important point is that candidates have obtained the nomination of their party and the legitimacy and attention accompanying that nomination.

Acceptance addresses are given to audiences as varied as the massive television audience that watches the major party presidential nomination conventions, or a small group of highly partisan political activists who form the Republican, Democratic, or third party central or executive committee for a small town. The acceptance address may be given after a long, exhausting, and bitter fight, or it may be given after a placid and uncontested nomination. Clearly the nature of the audience and the nature of the struggle preceding the nomination are situational factors that must be accounted for in the candidate's acceptance address.

A final situational factor that heavily affects acceptance addresses is the fact that they must be considered as part of what a variety of scholars have called "a legitimization ritual."[10] In full view of those who have nominated them, candidates lay claim to their nomination and attempt to justify their supporters' faith and belief. Both their nominators and the public have come to expect such a ritual. Both nominators and the public will judge the candidate's effort and begin to accord the nominee legitimacy in part based on their judgments of the candidate's success at fulfilling the demands of acceptance address ritual.

Purposes of Address

Acceptance addresses should satisfy four closely related purposes. First, the address is the means through which the

207

candidate publicly assumes the role of a candidate/leader of the party. Second, the address should generate a strong positive response from the immediate audience. Third, it should serve to unify the party. Finally, it is a partisan political address, which in some instances may be the most important such address the candidate makes throughout the campaign. Hence, it should also serve as a strong persuasive message.[11]

The candidate typically spends very little time formally assuming the role as a party leader. In their 1980 acceptance addresses to the Republican and Democratic National Conventions, Ronald Reagan and Jimmy Carter took 41 and 44 words respectively to acknowledge and accept their nominations. These perfunctory remarks, made at the outset of 4,000-word speeches, nevertheless, are vital.[12] The public has come to expect that candidates are grateful to be nominated and expects such ritualistic signs of that gratitude as acknowledgment and thanks. Convention delegates believe that they are doing an important job. They have come to expect that the candidate ritualistically acknowledge their efforts by formally accepting the fruit of their work, the nomination. Audiences would find something lacking, something incomplete, something unfulfilling if these rituals were not observed. The rhetorical situation demands that the candidate acknowledge obtaining the party's nomination.

The immediate audience for acceptance addresses is normally composed of those individuals who have affirmed the candidate's nomination. Hence, it is imperative that they respond positively to the candidate's remarks. These individuals, be they national, state, or local party officials, should constitute a nucleus of solid and vigorous support for the candidate in the forthcoming election. A second major purpose of the acceptance address is to arouse these individuals and properly motivate them for the responsibilities that will be falling upon them as the campaign progresses. This may be particularly difficult if large numbers of them have supported other candidates for the party nomination.

The third major purpose of acceptance addresses is to reaffirm, and if necessary reestablish, party unity. If the most active members of the party, its delegates to local, state, and national nominating conventions, leave the proceedings divided and with mixed attitudes toward the candidate, the base that most candidates count on for election—their party support—is of little value. In acceptance addresses that have been delivered by candidates who won bitterly contested nominations, it is not uncommon to see major segments of the acceptance address aimed at restoring party unity.

Finally, the acceptance address is a partisan political speech. David Valley has pointed out how each new advance in communications technology has brought national presidential acceptance addresses to larger and larger audiences.[13] Similarly, the acceptance address of state and local figures, delivered at state and local nominating proceedings, are often read or heard by a large portion of the public. Consequently, acceptance addresses present the candidate with a unique opportunity to speak not only to party partisans, but also to the general public. Valley concludes that as early as 1896, William Jennings Bryan was tailoring his acceptance address not to the immediate audience but to the hundreds of thousands of citizens who might read his speech.[14] Similarly, even state and local candidates must consider that their acceptance addresses may be carried in full, or quoted in part, by the newspapers. Moreover, segments of the address may be utilized in radio and television reports. Through such accounts and reports, even local acceptance addresses acquire broad audiences, while the audiences for the acceptance addresses of national figures number in the tens of millions. Hence, acceptance addresses serve partisan political purposes.

Strategies of Address

A variety of strategies have been utilized by campaigners to satisfy the purposes associated with acceptance addresses. Commonly, acceptance addresses are characterized by:

1) simplified partisan statements
2) laments about the present and celebrations about the future
3) stress on the crucial nature of this election
4) attempts to seek support from the entire constituency.

Which of these strategies will dominate an acceptance address is largely a function of the specific situation in which that address is being delivered. However, all four strategies are common in current acceptance addresses.

In an attempt to attain a strong positive response from the immediate audience, as well as deliver a frankly partisan political address to the large secondary audience, candidates often use simplified partisan statements. Such statements characteristically suggest that the nominees and their parties are necessary to solve any problems confronting the constituency and/or that opponents and their parties will exacerbate any problems confronting the constituency. Typically, in harsh and uncompromisingly partisan language, candidates suggest that there is no *real* choice in this election, that their position and party are clearly right, and their opponents are clearly wrong. In his 1980 acceptance address, Jimmy Carter examined Ronald Reagan's defense policies and claimed that "this radical and irresponsible course would threaten our security—and could put the whole world in peril. You and I must never let this come to pass."[15] In his 1980 acceptance address, Ronald Reagan examined Jimmy Carter's defense policies and found that they consisted essentially of four years of "weakness, indecision, mediocrity, and incompetence."[16] Each man used harsh and uncompromising language to suggest that there was no real choice. Simplified partisan statements are so characteristic of acceptance addresses that at least one scholar has characterized acceptance addresses as the "apotheosis of political oratory."[17]

A second strategy characteristic of acceptance addresses is that they tend to lament the present, while celebrating the future. As Kurt Ritter has illustrated in his examination of the acceptance addresses of presidential nominees, challengers lament the present, claiming that incumbents have abandoned the abiding principles of the American Dream, and hence, have contributed to the nation's problems. Challengers offer to lead the people back to fundamental American values, thereby resolving our problems, and thus giving rise to a bright future.[18] While this strategy seems uniquely suited to challenger nominees, Ritter points out that it is also used, with slight adaptation, by incumbents:

> The "in-party" version of the acceptance speech places the speaker at the later stages in the sequence of the rhetorical form. Instead of citing immediate difficulties, the incumbent cites the national decline immediately prior to his arrival at the White House. The incumbent typically describes the sorry state of America when he took office and then points out how he has brought the nation back to its historic purpose.... Each incumbent is quick to add that our work is not yet done. In fact, the opposing party threatens the restoration.[19]

Hence, this strategy of lamenting the past and celebrating the future is one that incumbents may also utilize in their acceptance addresses.

A third common strategy found in acceptance addresses is to stress the urgency and crucial nature of this election. Valley reports that 74 percent of all the words in the acceptance speeches of Democratic nominees he studied "have been used to discuss contemporary issues."[20] Ritter similarly concludes that "although incumbent and challenging candidates have found different lessons from the American past, they all find that their election represents a key moment in American history."[21] In his 1980 acceptance address, Ronald Reagan used the refrain "the time is now" five times in the peroration of his address, to stress the dramatic urgency of his election.[22] In his acceptance address, Jimmy Carter stressed the importance of the 1980 election, claiming that it would "shape the world of the year 2000."[23] Dramatizing the importance of this election, whether it be for county sheriff, state senator, Congressmember, or president, is an acceptance address strategy designed to mobilize support.

A fourth strategy characteristic of acceptance addresses is to call on all audience members, immediate and secondary, to unify behind the nominee to secure victory in the upcoming general election. Calls of this sort may be exceptionally important if the nomination has been bitterly contested. In 1980 because of the highly divisive primary campaign between Senator Edward Kennedy and President Carter, the latter made a special point of including a passage in his acceptance address in which he addressed Kennedy by name:

> Ted, your party needs—and I need—you and your idealism and dedication working for us. There is no doubt that even greater service lies ahead of you—and we are grateful to you and to have your strong partnership now in the larger cause to which your own life has been dedicated. I thank you for your support. We'll make great partners this fall in whipping the Republicans.[24]

Carter was trying to unify his party by beckoning to his Democratic opponent and inviting his support.

Candidates typically solicit not simply the support of their party colleagues, but also use their acceptance addresses to reach out beyond the immediate audience of party members, to solicit unity and support from others who might be listening, watching, or reading. Ronald Reagan implemented this strategy in his 1980 acceptance address when he stated:

> More than anything else, I want my candidacy to unify our country, to renew the American spirit and sense of purpose.
> I want to carry our message to every American, regardless of party affiliation, who is a member of this community of shared values.[25]

In passages like this, candidates seek to move beyond their own party, which has already granted them the nomination,

212

and establish identification and unity with other members of the village, city, state, or in the case of presidential candidates, nation.

In sum, acceptance addresses are often among the most important speeches of a campaign. They are responses to a unique rhetorical situation, which serve a variety of purposes beyond simply accepting a nomination, and which may utilize at least four common strategies to fulfill those purposes.

NEWS CONFERENCES

Candidates universally complain of their lack of media coverage. But some events or statements that occur during the campaign are perceived by candidates and their staffs as uniquely important and especially deserving of media coverage. Such occasions often cause the candidate to call a news conference.

Situation for News Conference

News conferences are normally occasioned by events or statements that the candidate feels warrant special attention. Ostensibly, they provide a means of making statements that will be passed on, through the media, to the public at large. Though the public is one audience in the news conference situation, we should not ignore the fact that at least four other audiences also exist: the candidates' rivals, their own staffs, political elites, and journalists. These five potential audiences exist for every news conference.[26] Moreover, on occasion, the candidate's remarks at a news conference are not meant primarily for the general public but for one or more of the other four audiences. It is through a news conference, ostensibly held for the public, that the candidate may also choose to address these other audiences.

News conferences are an exceptionally effective means of addressing an opponent. Candidates can exchange challenges,

213

promises, or threats in private and by using third parties. But, if such messages are conveyed through a news conference, they take on a different dimension. A message to one's rival, made publicly in the midst of a news conference, clearly implies a degree of commitment, which the same message conveyed privately, lacks. By deliberately going on public record and calling unusual attention to the message, the candidate is telling the opponent that this is no idle challenge, promise, or threat, but rather a deadly serious message. The use of a news conference, more than virtually any other form of communication, conveys that seriousness, and hence is occasionally used by candidates as a means of addressing one another.

Candidates may also use news conferences as a means of addressing their own staff. As political scientist Leon Sigal has observed, "campaign organizations tend to combine decentralization at the bottom with inaccessibility at the top."[27] The decentralized group of supporters at the bottom of the campaign have infrequent and short contact with the candidate. A news conference presents the candidate with a forum to which the campaign organization will no doubt be attentive. Hence, messages aimed primarily at the candidate's organization may be transmitted through the news conference.

News conferences also serve the candidate by providing a means of addressing political elites. In prior years, as discussed in Chapter 1, campaign decisions were often made by relatively few individuals, often in private meetings to which the public had little access. The decline of political parties and changes in campaign financing have tended to increase the number of politically elite. In the past, candidates might have used a few meetings and phone calls to put out the word that they needed money or had dramatically spurted in the last poll. Today, it would be difficult to contact all of those with whom a candidate might want to share this news. Hence, candidates may choose to use news conferences as a means of reaching political elites with information.

Finally, candidates use news conferences as a means of influencing journalists. Those journalists who attend the news conference comprise the immediate audience. The candidate clearly seeks to influence what they disseminate, and by so doing influence the many secondary audiences already discussed. Additionally, many news organizations may choose not to be represented at the news conference and fail to cover it. If candidates are newsworthy at the conference and if their remarks get good play in the media that is represented at the conference, the likelihood of increased media coverage of their campaign will be enhanced.

In sum, rhetorical situations in which candidates perceive the need to seek media coverage of their views for the purpose of better expressing them to the public, to rivals, to their own staffs, to political elites, and to journalists may frequently give rise to news conferences.

Purposes of News Conference

News conferences serve three basic purposes. First, they are an avenue by which the candidate can get the attention of a variety of audiences. News conferences often serve this purpose better than alternatives, such as news releases. However, they should not be abused. National candidates and major regional and state candidates can often be assured of reasonable media attendance at any news conference they call, simply because of the importance of any statement being made by a potential president, senator, or governor. Incumbents also have an advantage in attracting the media, simply because news organizations routinely assign someone to cover state senators, state representatives, members of city council, and administrative offices. Other candidates frequently have trouble getting media coverage of their campaigns. There are three reasons why properly used news conferences can increase coverage.

The first reason is novelty. The conference must be a reasonably unusual event. Candidates who are not overly newsworthy cannot expect the media to respond to daily announcements of press conferences. On the other hand, if

215

they call conferences only a few times during the campaign, the very novelty may cause some news organizations to send representatives. Second, the conference should be called with a clear newsworthy issue in mind. News organizations should be made aware of what the candidate will discuss. Unless the candidate has hard news and hopefully the data to support statements, news organizations may choose to ignore the conference. But if candidates are prepared to really make news that will be of interest to the readers, listeners, and viewers of the news organizations in their area, the news conference may be well covered.

For example, a recent congressional candidate, concerned about excessive government spending and what he believed to be unfair government intervention in strikes, linked these two issues together when a major employer in his district was struck during the campaign. He pointed out that federal government benefits would be given to these strikers. He noted that these men all had well-paying skilled labor jobs and that they had voluntarily, by their own vote, given up those jobs to strike. The candidate questioned whether people who were voluntarily unemployed should be subsidized by the government. He cited federal employees and federal laws to explain in detail the benefits that these strikers would receive from the federal government, noting that it could well approach half a million dollars. This portion of his presentation was made with visually interesting aids for the benefit of television. He contrasted the government help that these strikers were receiving with the benefits received by people in his district who were physically disabled, could not work, and hence also received government aid. He claimed that the physically disabled should receive more money since they clearly needed it, while those who had voted to strike should not receive any government subsidy. Unlike the physically handicapped, they had well-paying jobs to which they could return at a moment's notice. He concluded by criticizing his opponent who had voted for much of the legislation that provided help to strikers.

This news conference was one of only three that the candidate called throughout the campaign. It was directly related to an important news story, a large strike that affected thousands of families in the district. It related this strike to a major difference in the position of the two candidates. Moreover, the candidate provided hard information by way of facts and figures on government programs, quotes from government officials, and the voting record of his opponent. The material was presented orally but also with an awareness of the needs of television. The novelty and newsworthiness of this conference resulted in extensive coverage for the candidate.

A final reason why news conferences can effectively serve to focus widespread attention on the candidate's message is that reporters consider them reliable. Reporters often express doubts about the reliability of press releases. But the reliability of news conferences, witnessed by many reporters, with the candidate's statements captured on both audio and video tape, cannot be doubted.

Thus the news conference can serve as an avenue through which the candidate is able to reach many audiences. Even candidates whom news-gathering organizations judge to be unworthy of much attention can gain some attention if they use news conferences properly.

A second important purpose served by news conferences is to allow the candidate to focus attention on one issue or a limited number of issues. As we discussed in Chapter 2, a major function of the press is to help set the campaign agenda. But the candidate also wants to help shape the agenda. By focusing remarks on one issue, the candidate is able to influence strongly what issue the media will cover. Using a press conference, but focusing the issues treated and stressed in that conference, is an effective means utilized by many candidates to help set the campaign agenda.

A final purpose served by news conferences is to establish and improve relationships between the candidate and individual members of the media. The more efficiently run the conference is, the more prepared and responsive the candidate is, the easier the job of the reporter becomes. Press conferences are one means by which candidates can make the job of reporters easier and in so doing improve relationships between themselves and the media. The chief purpose of news conferences—to allow candidates to bring their views to the attention of many audiences—may be readily apparent, but we should not ignore the other purposes served by press conferences: to allow the candidate to focus attention on one or a limited number of issues, presumably selected by the candidate to be of advantage to the candidate, and to enhance candidate-press relationships.

Strategies of News Conference

Candidates attempt to use news conferences to their own advantage. One of the reasons they are used is to foster the illusion that the candidate is not in control. C. Jack Orr has suggested that presidential news conferences can be thought of as "counterpoised situations" in which the reporters have competing obligations. They must both confront the president, and they must give deference to him.[28] To a lesser extent, the same counterpoised situation exists when reporters interview any office seeker. The candidate must be shown some deference as a responsible individual running for a responsible job. Moreover, the conference is, after all, the candidate's proceeding. Yet, reporters also may seek to confront, challenge, and criticize.

The candidate's control extends beyond the deference that may be extended by reporters. The control is real. The candidate decides when and where to hold a news conference. The candidate decides what format will be used. The candidate decides who will ask questions, and of course the candidate provides the answers. Most scholars who have examined news conferences have concluded that while the situation may appear to be one in which the press has considerable control, ultimately it is the skilled respondent who controls the news conference.[29] Candidates exercise their control by utilizing one or more of at least eight common strategies.

Since it is the candidates who call news conferences, they will do so to suit their own needs. Decisions by the candidate about the timing of news conferences are important, and determining when to call a conference is the candidate's first strategic decision. As indicated earlier, typically the fewer conferences called, the more attention the press will extend to those that are called. Calling a news conference to deal with a topic is a clear means of signaling not only that the candidate attaches major importance to this topic, but of also increasing the treatment it receives in the media.

In addition, the candidate must consider the media that will attend and the deadlines with which they operate. Typically, candidates vary the time of day that they hold press conferences, so that they are not slighting any of the media organizations serving their constituency. However, this too is a strategic decision. The candidate, by determining the time of day to hold the conference, can play favorites with the media.

A second consideration is where to hold it. Candidates may make their conferences visually interesting to audiences and hence especially appealing to television news organizations by holding them in visually appealing settings. The candidate who has promised to repair the roads and eliminate dangerous potholes might choose to hold the conference at the site of a recent fatal accident caused by poor roads. This site selection might be highly advantageous for television news. However, it might be difficult and time consuming to reach and cause radio and print media representatives to feel that it is hardly worth the effort. Typically, candidates seek to balance their news conference site selections. Some are held with television in mind, while others are held in the campaign headquarters or some highly accessible central location. Whatever decision is made, the candidate can use the selection of a news conference site strategically, to help fulfill overall purposes.

These first two strategic concerns involving news conferences, where and when to hold them, relate primarily to the candidate's goal of increasing news coverage. The second group of strategies can help focus the topic of the conference on the areas that the candidate wants covered and stressed in the media.

Candidates utilize at least four strategies to guarantee that the agenda-setting function of the media works in their favor when news organizations cover their press conferences. Perhaps the most commonly used of these strategies is to make an opening statement at the outset of the conference. Though this tactic seems commonplace today, as recently as 30 years ago it was not frequently used. Dwight Eisenhower was the first president who regularly made opening statements at his news conferences.[30] The opening statement should, in itself, be newsworthy. If it is, it will generally prompt questions on the issue it treats and be the focus of most reports of the news conference. Moreover, as Catherine Collins has illustrated in her examination of Henry Kissinger's press conferences, if the interviewee assumes the role of the expert, defines the topic of immediate concern, develops a perspective from which events should be viewed, utilizes data to depict the event, and warns the media that other perspectives will not be considered acceptable, the chances are greatly increased that the interviewee's perspective will be reflected clearly in media accounts of the conference.[31]

Similarly, candidates may not only present opening statements, but they may also restructure questions. In restructuring a question, candidates are again generally attempting to focus attention onto key issues, from certain perspectives, in order to make their points better.

A third strategy utilized to make sure candidates are able to focus the conference on their topics and from their perspective is to plant questions. This tactic was commonplace in the presidential press conferences of Eisenhower and Johnson.[32] It has been used by many candidates for public office. Typically, a staff member approaches a reporter and suggests a question that might be asked, noting that it will no doubt produce a newsworthy response. Obviously, many reporters may not choose to be used in this fashion. But others will, perceiving the suggested question as a means of drawing attention to something that is newsworthy, which is just what the candidate also wants. The ethics of restructuring questions and planting questions is certainly open for debate. But clearly they are strategies that are utilized by many interviewees, including political candidates, who wish to limit the focus of news conferences.

The final strategy, utilized primarily to focus the news conference, is selective recognition of reporters. Candidates recognize those who question them, but they can fail to recognize those who wish to question them. Most of the time, recognition is haphazard. But it can also be done in a deliberate fashion. A survey of the White House press corps found that "the random selection of questioners by the President" was among the most serious problems associated with White House news conferences.[33] News conferences held by candidates for lesser office will not draw the massive number of reporters that a White House news conference attracts. But any conference that draws a reasonable sample of the media is one in which a candidate might selectively recognize reporters.

Candidates normally hold news conferences when they seek extensive coverage of their views. Typically, they have a limited number of issues on which they wish to focus in the news conference and that they hope the public will learn of through the efforts of the journalists in attendance. To insure that these topics are clearly the centerpieces of the news conference, candidates often assume the role of the expert, utilizing an opening statement that spells out their position on issues, and indicates the perspective on the issue that they find satisfactory. They may also choose to restructure questions, plant questions, and selectively recognize reporters. All these strategies are done primarily to enable candidates to stress their issues and prevent the conference from dealing with other issues.

221

Two final strategies can be utilized by most candidates in news conferences. First is to prepare. Candidates differ in the manner of their preparation for news conferences. However, most attempt to anticipate questions that might be asked and prepare responses. Presidents, such as Truman and Kennedy, typically rehearsed for news conferences by reviewing 40 to 75 possible questions that might arise in their press conferences.[34] Most candidates follow similar procedures. They rely on their staffs to generate possible questions and then prepare responses.

Given the many controls and strategies available to candidates who utilize news conferences, it may be easy to forget that there are other actors in this situation. President Carter's television advisor noted that even though the news conference was in effect a theatre in which the president called upon reporters to play their supporting roles, "it is important that the President appear vulnerable."[35] Similarly, most candidates wish to appear vulnerable in news conference situations. The desire to appear vulnerable often motivates the use of the news conference. It is one of the reasons why candidates will utilize "risky" news conferences, rather than safer press releases, audios, or other forms of communication with the public. The appearance that the candidate is taking a chance and is vulnerable is one that most candidates believe the public admires. The news conference situation suggests openness and honesty, as well as confidence in one's ability, that candidates are rarely able to attain through the use of other forms of communication.

The symbiotic relationship that exists between candidates and journalists is, perhaps, nowhere more evident than in the news conference. News conferences are called by candidates seeking widespread coverage of their views. They are attended by representatives of news organizations who sense that the conference may produce newsworthy material. Both the candidate and the reporter have an interest in aiding one another. But candidates are not only desirous of creating news, they are also desirous of influencing and persuading. Hence, most candidates utilize a variety of strategies attempting to insure that their conferences are indeed covered and that the conferences focus on those issues that the candidates wish to focus upon. Moreover, though they prepare in order not to be vulnerable and weak, they recognize that a format that suggests their vulnerability may be desirable.

APOLOGIAS

An increasingly recurring form of speech that many candidates have recently found necessary to deliver is the apologia. In this section, we will examine the situations that create apologias and in so doing perhaps also gain an understanding of why they have been on the increase in recent years. We will also examine the major purposes of such speeches and the strategies utilized to attain those purposes.

Situation for Apologia

Apologias are speeches made by candidates who find it necessary to apologize for some statement or behavior. Typically, the statement or behavior implies a serious flaw in the candidate's character, one that if widely accepted by the public would prevent the candidate from ever winning office. For example, in 1976, Jimmy Carter gave an interview in which he used the term "ethnic purity." This statement was taken by many as a code word for segregation, and suggested that Carter, a former Georgia governor, might be a racist. In the 1982 Ohio gubernatorial primary, it became common knowledge that years earlier, one of the candidates, Cincinnati City Councilman Gerald Springer, had visited a prostitute. This action was taken by many to suggest that Springer did not have the qualities of character and morality desired of a governor.

Apologias have become an increasingly more common feature of recent campaigns for two reasons. First, the news media seem more prone then ever before to report on the candidate's weaknesses and flaws. Gone are the days when

Franklin Delano Roosevelt could dictate that he never be photographed in leg braces or being carried by his aides. Gone are the days when the candidate's private life was not discussed. The press is far more unsparing of candidates today.[36] Additionally, one of the effects of Watergate has apparently been to sensitize the public to the personal integrity of candidates. More than ever before, candidates are finding the media inspecting their character closely, and the public is concerned about the candidates' personal integrity and morality.

Purposes of Apologia

Apologias serve to enable the candidate to explain some statement or behavior that casts doubt on the candidate's suitability for office. To accomplish this explanation, with the least amount of damage to their image, candidates often have three purposes in mind when they deliver apologias.

First, they hope to explain the behavior or statement in a positive light. In so doing, they hope to minimize damage to their character and image. If the incident that triggered the need for the apologia cannot be explained positively, the second purpose of the apologia may be considered. The candidate can at least justify behavior. Again, by so doing, the candidate hopes to minimize damage to character and image.

The final purpose of an apologia is to remove the topic from public discussion. Ellen Reid Gold has pointed out that, at least with major national figures, frequently reporters repeat the charges against a candidate so often that it is difficult for the candidate not to appear guilty.[37] Day after day, the candidate is seen denying the charge. To the extent that an apologia can put an end to questioning and allow the campaign to move on to other issues, it has served a vital purpose.[38]

Strategies of Apologia

Rhetoricians have identified five strategies commonly utilized by speakers delivering apologias. Not every strategy can

224

be used in every apologia, but all five have been used frequently. First, apologias are often best delivered in settings where individuals other than the candidate seem in control.[39] Many early apologias were delivered in settings where the candidate seemed to be in complete control. For example, Richard Nixon's 1952 Checkers address and Ted Kennedy's 1969 Address to the People of Massachusetts, following the incident at Chappaquiddick, were both made by men who had purchased air time and were in complete control of what was said. However, as Sherry Butler points out in contrasting these two addresses, by 1969 mass media viewers were "more sophisticated, less likely to place automatic belief in magic power of the television tube, more likely to question."[40] Additionally, the legacies of Vietnam and Watergate include voter disenchantment with less than honest officials. Both of these facts, growing voter sophistication in using media and growing voter disenchantment with public figures, have contributed to changes in the early apologia, typified by Richard Nixon's Checkers address.

Rather than an address such as Nixon's, in which the candidate is in complete control of the setting, candidates today often deliver their apologias in settings that appear to be controlled by others. For example, in 1980 President Carter found it necessary to apologize for the meanness he had exhibited in his criticisms of Ronald Reagan. Carter's image and character as a good, moral, nice man were called into question by his seemingly intemperate remarks that Ronald Reagan would divide the nation along economic, racial, and religious lines.[41] Rather than address this issue of meanness himself, Carter agreed to an interview with Barbara Walters. That Carter had deliberately chosen to make his apologia in a setting that he did not fully control was evident from Walters's first comment. "Mr. President, in recent days you have been characterized as mean, vindictive, hysterical, and on the point of desperation."[42] As Walters's interview with Carter illustrates,[43] the strategy of appearing in a setting where one does not have complete control involves risk. However, many contemporary candidates choose to take this risk, believing that public

225

sophistication with media and alienation from leaders make this an acceptable risk that must be taken if their message is to be appreciated.

A second strategy utilized by candidates delivering apologias is to simply deny the "alleged facts, sentiments, objects, or relationships," that give rise to the charge.[44] If the candidate cannot deny the substance of the charge, one can deny the intent, arguing that the statement or action has been misunderstood.[45] In 1980 Jimmy Carter tried both approaches. In response to one question Walters asked, Carter noted that "I don't think I'm mean, Barbara." Moments, later, asked how he could allow himself to engage in mudslinging, Carter noted that "It's not a deliberate thing."[46]

A third strategy frequently used in apologias is what B. L. Ware and Wil Linkugel characterize as "bolstering strategies." Bolstering strategies are attempts by the candidate to identify "with something viewed favorably by the audience."[47] In his Address to the People of Massachusetts, Senator Edward Kennedy repeatedly reminded his audience that he was a Kennedy, continually referring not simply to himself but to his family. Such remarks are meant to remind the audience that prior to the current accusations they once viewed the candidate in a favorable light and that the dramatic change in character implied by the accusation is unlikely.[48]

A fourth strategy frequently used in political apologias is differentiation. Ware and Linkugel define differentiation strategies as "separating some fact, sentiment, object, or relationship from some larger context within which the audience presently views that attribute."[49] As Gold notes, "in political campaigns, the candidate may try not only to redefine the larger context for the audience, but to separate himself symbolically from the accusation by attacking the source."[50] In responding to Walters, Carter finds that his meanness should not be perceived simply as an aspect of his overall campaign style, as it was viewed. Rather, he finds that his meanness is in part a function of the failure of the press to treat substantive issues between the candidates but to focus instead on personal characteristics.[51]

The fifth type of strategy found in political apologias is what Ware and Linkugel have called the transcendental strategy. This kind of strategy "cognitively joins some fact, sentiment, object, or relationship with some larger context within which the audience does not presently view that attribute."[52] Such strategies "psychologically move the audience away from the particulars of the charge at hand in a direction toward some more abstract, general view of his character."[53] In 1980 Jimmy Carter engaged in this strategy when he attempted to move the audience away from the charge of meanness toward an understanding of his intensity over the issues. Twice in his interview with Barbara Walters, he linked his harsh attacks on Reagan with his own intense feelings about arms control, national defense, and the SALT talks.

In sum, apologias seem to be characterized by the use of one or more of five strategies. Increasingly, candidates are making their apologias in situations over which they do not have full control. Moreover, they are using denial, bolstering, differentiation, and transcendental strategies to carry out their apologias.

Apologias do not seem to have been a common form of political speech until relatively recently. Contemporary stress on the character of candidates and the aggressiveness of contemporary journalists seems, in recent years, to have created far more situations calling for apologias than ever before. Most scholars anticipate that apologias will be a feature of U.S. political rhetoric for years to come.[54]

CONCLUSIONS

In this chapter, we have observed that most campaigns are marked by similar, comparable, or analogous situations that require a rhetorical response. The responses to four such situations take the form of announcement of candidacy speeches, nomination acceptance addresses, news conferences, and apologias. We have examined the situations that give rise to these types of presentations, the purposes of such presentations, and the major strategies employed in each type of presentation.

NOTES

1. Lloyd Bitzer, "The Rhetorical Situation," *Philosophy and Rhetoric* 1 (January 1968): 6.

2. Karlyn Kohrs Campbell and Kathleen Hall Jamieson, "Form and Genre in Rhetorical Criticism: An Introduction," in *Form and Genre: Shaping Rhetorical Action*, eds. Karlyn Kohrs Campbell and Kathleen Hall Jamieson (Falls Church, Va.: Speech Communication Association, 1977), p. 15.

3. Judith S. Trent, "Presidential Surfacing: The Ritualistic and Crucial First Act," *Communication Monographs* 45 (November 1978): 281–92.

4. See for example, Hamilton Jordan, "Memo of August 4, 1974 to Jimmy Carter," in *Running for President: A Journal of the Carter Campaign*, ed. Martin Schram (New York: Pocket Books, 1977), p. 416.

5. Trent, "Presidential Surfacing," p. 284.

6. Jordan, "Memo to Jimmy Carter," p. 418.

7. Kenneth P. O'Donnell and David F. Powers, *Johnny, We Hardly Knew Ye* (New York: Pocket Books, 1973), pp. 169–74.

8. See Kennedy and Carter responses in *The Candidates 1980: Where They Stand* (Washington, D.C.: American Enterprise Institute, 1980). Also see Robert V. Friedenberg, "Why Teddy Wasn't Ready: An Examination of the Speaking of Senator Edward Moore Kennedy during the 1980 Presidential Primaries," paper presented at the Ohio Speech Association, October 1980, pp. 3–4.

9. For a concise history of acceptance addresses, see David B. Valley, "Significant Characteristics of Democratic Presidential Nomination Acceptance Speeches," *Central States Speech Journal* 25 (Spring 1974): 56–60.

10. Thomas B. Farrell, "Political Conventions as Legitimation Ritual," *Communication Monographs* 45 (November 1978): 293–305; and Kurt W. Ritter, "American Political Rhetoric and the Jeremiad Tradition: Presidential Nomination Acceptance Addresses, 1960–1976," *Central States Speech Journal* 31 (Fall 1980): 153–71.

11. For discussions of these purposes, see Robert O. Nordvold, "Rhetoric as Ritual: Hubert H. Humphrey's Acceptance Address at the 1968 Democratic National Convention," *Today's Speech* 18 (Winter 1970): 34; Valley, "Nomination Acceptance Speeches," p. 60; and Ritter, "American Political Rhetoric," p. 155.

12. Jimmy Carter, "Acceptance Speech, Democratic National Convention, August 14, 1980," and Ronald Reagan, "Acceptance Speech, Republican National Convention, July 17, 1980," both in *The Pursuit of the Presidency 1980*, ed. Richard Harwood (New York: Berkley Books, 1980), pp. 401–27.

13. Valley, "Nomination Acceptance Speeches" p. 61.

14. Ibid.

15. Carter, "Acceptance Speech," p. 406
16. Reagan, "Acceptance Speech," p. 424.
17. Nordvold, "Rhetoric as Ritual," p. 34
18. Ritter, "American Political Rhetoric," pp. 157–64.
19. Ibid., pp. 161–62.
20. Valley, "Nomination Acceptance Speeches," p. 60.
21. Ritter, "American Political Rhetoric," p. 162.
22. Reagan, "Acceptance Speech," p. 426.
23. Carter, "Acceptance Speech," p. 404.
24. Ibid., p. 402.
25. Reagan, "Acceptance Speech," p. 416.
26. This analysis of news conference audiences is adapted from Leon V. Sigal, "Newsmen and Campaigners: Organization Men Make the News," *Political Science Quarterly* 93 (Fall 1978): 466–67.
27. Ibid., p. 466.
28. C. Jack Orr, "Reporters Confront the President: Sustaining a Counterpoised Situation," *Quarterly Journal of Speech* 66 (February 1980): 17–21.
29. Most such examinations have focused on presidential news conferences, but the rationales for the conclusions, as well as the conclusions themselves, seem appropriate for most political candidates. See Michael Grossman and Martha Kumar, *Portraying the President: The White House and the News Media* (Baltimore: Johns Hopkins University Press, 1981), pp. 243–44; Orr, "Reporters Confront President," pp. 31–32; Delbert McQuire, "Democracy's Confrontation: The Presidential Press Conference," *Journalism Quarterly* 44 (Winter 1967): 638–44.
30. Peter M. Sandman, David M. Rubin, and David B. Sachsman, *Media: An Introductory Analysis of American Mass Communications* (Englewood Cliffs, N.J.: Prentice-Hall, 1972), p. 344.
31. Catherine Ann Collins, "Kissinger's Press Conferences, 1972–1974: An Exploration of Form and Role Relationship on News Management," *Central States Speech Journal* 28 (Fall 1977): 190–93.
32. Grossman and Kumar, *Portraying the President,* p. 248.
33. McQuire, "Democracy's Confrontation," p. 640.
34. A. L. Lorenze, Jr., "Truman and the Press Conference," *Journalism Quarterly* 43 (Winter 1966): 673–75; and Harry P. Kerr, "The President and the Press," *Western Speech* 27 (Fall 1963): 220–21.
35. Barry Jogoda quoted in Grossman and Kumar, *Portraying the President,* p. 243.
36. For a good sense of the irreverent attitude of reporters toward candidates, see Timothy Crouse, *The Boys on the Bus* (New York: Ballatine Books, 1974).
37. Ellen Reid Gold, "Political Apologia: The Ritual of Self Defense," *Communication Monographs* 45 (November 1978): 311–12.

38. Lawrence W. Rosenfeld, "A Case Study in Speech Criticism: The Nixon-Truman Analog" *Speech Monographs* 35 (November 1968): 438–39; and Sherry Devereaux Butler, "The Apologia, 1971 Genre," *Southern Speech Communication Journal* 37 (Spring 1972): 283.

39. Gold, "Political Apologia," p. 311.

40. Butler, "Apologia," p. 287.

41. Jack W. Germond and Jules Witcover, *Blue Smoke and Mirrors: How Reagan Won and Why Carter Lost the Election of 1980* (New York: Viking Press, 1981), pp. 255–60.

42. Ibid., p. 262.

43. See Germond and Witcover, *Blue Smoke and Mirrors*, pp. 262–65 for an analysis of the negative effects of Walters's interview with Carter.

44. B. L. Ware and Wil A. Linkugel, "They Spoke in Defense of Themselves: On the General Criticism of Apologia," *Quarterly Journal of Speech* 59 (October 1973): 275.

45. Gold, "Political Apologia," p. 308.

46. Germond and Witcover, *Blue Smoke and Mirrors*, p. 256.

47. Ware and Linkugel, "General Criticism of Apologias," p. 277.

48. Gold, "Political Apologia," p. 308.

49. Ware and Linkugel, "General Criticism of Apologias," p. 278.

50. Gold, "Political Apologia," p. 308.

51. Germond and Witcover, *Blue Smoke and Mirrors*, p. 262–63.

52. Ware and Linkugel, "General Criticism of Apologias," p. 280.

53. Ibid.

54. Gold, "Political Apologia," p. 316; and Butler, "Apologia," pp. 288–89.

7

Debates in Political Campaigns

*I*N THE SUMMER OF 1858, ONE OF THE MOST RE-
MARKABLE LOCAL POLITICAL CAMPAIGNS IN
U.S. HISTORY WAS BEING WAGED ON THE
PLAINS OF ILLINOIS. THE 1858 ILLINOIS SEN-
ate race was remarkable for many reasons. Few races, regardless of office, bring together two such outstanding public
servants as those competing for the senate seat from Illinois in
1858. Few races, regardless of office, have had as profound an
impact on our national history as did the race for the Illinois
Senate seat in 1858. Few races have produced such master-
pieces of campaign oratory as those produced on the plains of
Illinois in the summer of 1858. For in that year, Abraham Lincoln and Stephen Douglas vied for the senate seat from Illinois.

On July 24, Lincoln challenged Douglas to a series of debates. Douglas accepted. As the front runner in what was anticipated to be a close election, Douglas dictated the terms. He
suggested seven debates and demanded the opportunity to
both open and close four of the debates. Lincoln would open
and close only three. Lincoln accepted, and thus ensued what
the *New York Tribune* called "a mode of discussing political
questions which might well be more generally adopted."[1]

233

The Lincoln-Douglas debates were the first significant political campaign debates in U.S. history. Moreover, unlike their successors, they were real debates rather than joint speeches or joint press conferences. Most authorities would agree with J. Jeffery Auer when he argues that there are five essential elements for a true debate. "A debate," claims Auer, "is (1) a confrontation, (2) in equal and adequate time, (3) of matched contestants, (4) on a stated proposition, (5) to gain an audience decision."[2] Auer points out that "each of these elements is essential if we are to have true debate. Insistence upon their recognition is more than mere pedantry, for each one has contributed to the vitality of the debate tradition."[3]

The Lincoln-Douglas debates were not followed by many other debates. It was not until a century later, in 1960, that we next had "Great Debates" of comparable significance. However, the 1960 presidential debates between Senator John F. Kennedy and Vice-President Richard M. Nixon made political debating popular. In two of the five presidential elections that have followed, we have had presidential debates. Debates are now a common feature of political campaigns for virtually any office.

Yet most contemporary political debaters, including Presidents Ford, Carter, and Reagan, have not engaged in political debates. Based primarily on the Kennedy-Nixon model of 1960, most contemporary political debates can be characterized as "counterfeit debates."[4] This is not to say that contemporary political debating is, like a counterfeit bill, of little value. As we will see later, contemporary political debates are extremely valuable. But in large part because of the influence of media, they involve different formats and strategies than those of the Lincoln-Douglas era.

Perhaps the counterfeit nature of contemporary political debates can best be understood by using Auer's five essentials of debate to compare the Lincoln-Douglas debate with the prototypic contemporary media political debate, that of Kennedy and Nixon in 1960.

234

First, the Kennedy-Nixon debate and most political debates since do not involve direct confrontation. Lincoln and Douglas confronted one another. They met on the same platform, questioned one another, and refuted one another. Indeed, the highlight of the seven debates came in the second debate, at Freeport, when Lincoln confronted Douglas with a series of four questions to set up what became known as "The Freeport Dilemma."

Lincoln claimed that Douglas had to repudiate the Supreme Court's Dred Scott decision (which made it illegal for voters to prohibit slavery in the territories and hence was enormously popular in the South) or repudiate his own program of popular sovereignty. As chairman of the Senate Committee on Territories, Douglas had argued that each of the Western territories should be allowed to choose by popular vote if it would enter the Union free or slave. Repeatedly in the debates after Freeport, Lincoln confronted Douglas with this dilemma. Lincoln demanded that Douglas choose between a fundamental tenet of U.S. democracy—the sanctity of Supreme Court decisions—or his own proposal. If Douglas supported the Dred Scott decision, he was admitting that he had labored in the Senate on behalf of a policy that was illegal. If he supported popular sovereignty, he was admitting that Supreme Court decisions were not the highest law of the land and was isolating himself from the Southern wing of the Democratic party. Lincoln confronted, questioned, followed up, and harangued Douglas. Douglas responded, claimed the dilemma was false and argued that Lincoln ignored a third alternative.

In contrast, it was not Richard Nixon but a journalist who suggested to John Kennedy that "you are naive and at times immature." Nor was it John Kennedy but rather a journalist who suggested to Richard Nixon that his experience as vice-president was as an observer not as a participant or initiator of policy.[5] Kennedy and Nixon did not talk to each other, as did Lincoln and Douglas. Kennedy and Nixon did not question and pursue one another, nor did they respond to one another.

Rather, if Kennedy, Nixon and most political debaters since are confronted at all, it is by the media not by one another.[6]

Second, the Kennedy-Nixon debate, and most political debates since, did not involve equal and adequate time. The key, of course, is adequate time. Lincoln and Douglas dealt almost exclusively with one issue, the future of slavery in the territories. Each man spoke for 1.5 hours in each of seven debates. Kennedy and Nixon each spoke half an hour in each of four debates. The subject matter for the first Kennedy-Nixon debate was domestic affairs, for the last foreign affairs, and no restrictions whatsoever existed for the middle two debates. It is entirely fair to say that Lincoln and Douglas spent up to 21 hours debating one issue, while Kennedy and Nixon spent eight minutes on any one issue. Formats like the Kennedy-Nixon format typically allow candidates three to five minutes to deal with an issue.[7] Kennedy and Nixon, and most political debaters since, did not have adequate time to deal with major public issues.

Political debates do typically meet the third criteria for debates. The contestants are closely matched. If one contestant is vastly brighter, more fluent, more poised, more knowledgeable, and better prepared, no real debate can take place. Typically, this is not the case in political debates, where both candidates must agree to debate and hence are probably able debaters, having merit enough to secure major party nominations to the office.

However, political debates frequently do not meet the fourth criteria of debates. The Kennedy-Nixon debate and most political debates since did not involve one stated proposition. Rather, depending on format, ten or more topics are discussed in a single debate. In the first Kennedy-Nixon debate, the two men dealt with such diverse questions as who was most fit and prepared to lead the country, how would each man handle the farm subsidy programs, what policies each would advocate for reducing the federal debt, what would each man do about improving the nation's schools, what policies would each pursue with respect to medical aid to the aged and with respect to a comprehensive minimum hourly wage program. Moreover, each was asked how serious a threat to national security he believed communist subversive activity in the United States was and how he would finance public school construction. In sum, Kennedy and Nixon had under an hour to deal with nine totally diverse topic areas.

Finally, the Kennedy-Nixon debates did not really gain an audience decision of the issues. Debates, as Auer suggests, are "clashes of ideas, assumptions, evidence, and argument."[8] They secure from audiences a decision on the issues. In 1858 the Lincoln-Douglas debates revealed the inadequacies of Douglas's program of popular sovereignty for the territories and the inconsistency of that program with existing institutions. It was because he illustrated the inadequacies and inconsistencies of Douglas's position, while justifying and defending his own belief in restricting slavery's spread into the territories, that Lincoln emerged from the debates a national figure, and Douglas' national aspirations were shattered. Those debates were a true clash of ideas, assumptions, evidence, and argument. In 1960 the Kennedy and Nixon debates did not facilitate the audience's making a decision about the issues. Contemporary political debates that are heavily oriented toward the broadcast media audience are not in the tradition of issue-oriented debates.

Political debating is widespread in this country. It is almost a ritualistic aspect of campaigns for one candidate to challenge the other to a debate. Yet, as we have seen, contemporary media-oriented debates, regardless of what office is sought, are vastly different from the first political debates in our nation's history. Though they typically involve matched candidates, they rarely if ever entail direct confrontation, equal and adequate time, one stated proposition, and a clear decision on the issues. In the next section, we will trace how political debates evolved from the Lincoln-Douglas debates to the media-oriented debates we have today.

HISTORY OF POLITICAL DEBATES

During the latter half of the nineteenth century, following the Lincoln-Douglas confrontations, there was relatively little political debating in the United States. However, a few debates of local or statewide interest did take place.[9] Although Lincoln and Douglas had gained national attention, figures of comparable stature did not engage in campaign debates in the years that followed. Hence, few debates received attention beyond their own constituencies, and none attained national prominence.[10]

By the mid-1920s, due to the growth of radio, national debates began to seem feasible. In 1924 testifying before a congressional committee investigating broadcast regulations, William Harkness, an executive of the American Telephone and Telegraph Company, made what is generally believed to be the first suggestion for broadcasting political debates.[11] At the time of Harkness's suggestion, such a broadcast would have probably been local or regional in scope, but within two years, with the birth of the National Broadcasting Company in 1926, nationwide political broadcasts became feasible. NBC's first programs were carried over a 24-station hookup serving 21 cities from the East Coast as far west as Kansas City. Other networks soon followed.

The implication of national radio networks for political campaigns was not lost on Congress. In 1927 Congress included a section in its radio broadcast regulations dealing with political broadcasts. Those regulations were modified in 1934, and section 315 of the Communications Act of 1934 affected political broadcasts for years. This "equal time" provision required that if any licensed radio or television station allows a legally qualified candidate for any public office to use its station, it must "afford equal opportunities to all other such candidates for that office in the use of such broadcasting station."[12] This provision, designed to provide equal access to the public's airwaves to all candidates, tended to inhibit political debates. It required that if major party candidates received airtime from a station, that station would have to provide airtime to every other candidate, regardless of the extent of their following. Few broadcasters were willing to make time for the many minor party candidates, and hence little time went to any campaign activities. Although this act was modified in 1959 to insure that broadcasters could cover the normal newsworthy activities of political candidates without being subject to harassment by other candidates,[13] throughout the period 1934–76 section 315 inhibited political debates in any race where more than two candidates were involved.

Nevertheless, political debating did not come to a complete standstill during this period. On October 17, 1936, during the presidential election between Governor Alfred Landon and President Franklin Roosevelt, Republican Senator Arthur Vandenberg of Michigan produced a "fake" debate over the CBS network by editing recordings of Roosevelt's speeches. The live Vandenberg naturally bested the edited Roosevelt. The nature of this debate was not made clear to stations until shortly before the broadcast. Of the 66 stations scheduled to broadcast the debate, 23 did so without interruption. Clearly Vandenberg had edited Roosevelt's speeches to produce a partisan one-sided program. However, perhaps more than anything that had preceded it, this program focused attention on the possibilities of nationally broadcast political debates between major figures.[14]

Four years later, in 1940, Republican Wendell Wilkie opened his campaign by challenging President Roosevelt to debate. Polls found the public almost evenly divided in their response to Wilkie's challenge; 49 percent opposed.[15] Apparently much of the opposition stemmed from the public's perceptions of the risks that might be involved in having an incumbent president debate. Roosevelt suffered no significant political consequences in declining to debate.

In 1948 the first broadcast debate between two major presidential candidates took place. The candidates were Governor Harold Stassen of Minnesota and Governor Thomas Dewey of New York. They were seeking the Republican nomination to challenge President Harry S. Truman. In the midst of the Oregon primary, Stassen challenged Dewey to debate. Dewey accepted but specified the terms. As Dewey wished, the debate would be held in private, with only a small audience of journalists. Stassen had suggested that it might be held in a ballpark with a large public audience. Dewey spoke last as he wanted. Dewey selected the topic: that the Communist party should be outlawed in the United States. Moreover, Dewey chose to defend the negative. The debate was broadcast nationally by all four major radio networks and was well received by audiences and political observers.[16]

The first suggestion that 1952 presidential candidates General Dwight David Eisenhower and Illinois Governor Adlai Stevenson engage in a televised debate was made by Michigan Senator Blair Moody.[17] Both NBC and CBS immediately offered to provide the airtime, if Congress would suspend or revoke the equal time provision. However, nothing came of the network's offer, since both Eisenhower and Stevenson were reluctant to debate.[18] Not so reluctant were the two Massachusetts senatorial candidates, Henry Cabot Lodge and John F. Kennedy, who debated in Waltham, Massachusetts.

By 1956 virtually the entire country had access to television. Televised political programs of every sort were commonplace. Candidates at all levels—presidential, senatorial, congressional, as well as scores of local candidates—were routinely appearing on television. But with one significant exception, broadcast debates between political candidates were not seen on the nation's television screens.

In 1956 the contest for the Democratic presidential nomination became a fight between Tennessee Senator Estes Kefauver and Adlai Stevenson. Kefauver had become a well-known political figure in 1951 when, as chairman of the Senate Crime Investigating Committee, he had presided over nationally televised hearings investigating organized crime. Kefauver challenged Stevenson to debate during the primaries. Stevenson, reluctant to debate Eisenhower in 1952, was again reluctant. However, after losing the Minnesota primary, Stevenson agreed to debate Kefauver in the Florida primary. The debate was nationally televised, and though it apparently helped Stevenson he came away unimpressed with political debates.[19] As in 1952, in 1956 neither Stevenson nor Eisenhower wished to be involved in broadcast debates during the general election.

In 1960 John Kennedy was challenged to debate in the primaries by Senator Hubert Humphrey. During the West Virginia primary, both men agreed to a televised debate. Observers agreed that Kennedy did well in the debate, which was televised throughout the East Coast as well as throughout West Virginia. Perhaps this experience and his 1952 debate with Lodge contributed to Kennedy's acceptance of an NBC offer for free time during the general election if he would agree to a series of joint appearances with the Republican nominee. This offer had been made feasible by a joint resolution of Congress suspending the equal time law until after the election. Like Kennedy, Richard Nixon quickly accepted the NBC offer but noted that since the other networks had issued similar invitations the networks should coordinate their proposals. The networks had lobbied earlier in the year to suspend the equal time law for just this opportunity. They perceived televised presidential debates as providing them with enhanced credibility as a news medium. As we will see in more detail in the next section, 1960 was one of those rare years where the selfish interests of both candidates seemed best served by involvement in political debates. Hence, in 1960, for the first time since 1858, the United States was absorbed by a political debate or at least a joint appearance, national in scope and significance.

Political debates at the presidential level were not held for the 16 years following the Kennedy-Nixon debate, for reasons that will be discussed in the next section. However, they became commonplace in campaigns for almost all other offices. In the years immediately following the Kennedy-Nixon debate, there were political debates between candidates for statewide offices in Michigan, Massachusetts, Connecticut, Pennsylvania, and California. Races for lesser offices frequently included debates. In 1962 debates were held between the candidates for all six congressional seats in Connecticut.[20] Although presidential candidates frequently utilized debates during the primaries that were held after 1960, it was not until 1976 that presidential debates were held during the general election. However, unlike their presidential counterparts, local, regional, and statewide candidates made increasing use of debates during the 1960s and 1970s. One such debate, which took place between the two candidates for governor of Tennessee in 1970, indirectly led to the 1976 presidential debate between Governor Jimmy Carter and President Gerald Ford and resolution of the impediment to political debates caused by the equal time provision.

In 1970 Winfield Dunn, Republican, and John J. Hooker, Jr., his Democratic opponent for the governorship of Tennessee, decided to debate. Aiding Dunn was a University of Virginia law student, Stephen A. Sharp, who found several Tennessee stations reluctant to carry the debates for fear that they would have to provide equal time to all other minor candidates for the governorship. Sharp's involvement in the Tennessee race caused him to prepare a law school paper on the history and interpretation of section 315. He found that political debates between major candidates might well be considered "bona fide" news events under the 1959 changes to section 315. If so, they could be reported on by stations as normal newsworthy activities, and those stations would not be subjected to providing equal time to all other candidates.

Sharp was subsequently hired by the Federal Communications Commission (FCC) where his work with section 315 became known. The FCC had previously ruled that candidate appearances not "incidental to" other news events were not newsworthy and hence not exempt from the equal opportunities requirement. Political debates by major candidates that were not incidental to any other activity were not exempt. But a political speech incidental to a rally or a dinner was exempt.

After considerable legal maneuvering by a variety of interested parties including the Aspen Program for Media and Society, the Columbia Broadcasting System, and others, the FCC ruled in 1975 that debates that were covered live and in their entirety and not sponsored by broadcasters (and hence presumably legitimate news events that would take place with or without the press) could be covered without fear of having to provide time to all minor candidates.[21]

This 1975 FCC ruling, known as the Aspen decision, made nationally televised presidential debates feasible from the network's standpoint. But debates do not take place without willing debaters. In 1960 Kennedy and Nixon had both been willing to debate for reasons that will become evident in the next section. Republicans and Democrats in Congress, following the lead indicated by their presidential candidates, had suspended section 315. After the Aspen decision, an act of Congress was no longer necessary for presidential debates, but willing debaters were.

The League of Women Voters, responding to the Aspen decision, took it upon itself to become the sponsoring organization for presidential debates in 1976. In 1976 both major candidates perceived that their own self-interest might be well served by political debates. We will examine in detail what motivates candidates to accept or reject an invitation to debate in the next section. However, in 1976 and again in 1980, both major presidential candidates were willing to debate. The Carter-

Ford debate of 1976 and the Reagan-Anderson and Reagan-Carter debates of 1980, like the Kennedy-Nixon debates of 1960, have given rise to countless other political debates. Today, political debates are widespread at all levels. Although no data exist to indicate how many campaigns involve debates of some sort, a survey of the members of Congress indicated that fully 75 percent of them report that they engaged in a political debate in the 1980 congressional elections.[22] The League of Women Voters and the Speech Communication Association have projects established to encourage and support political debating throughout the country. In 1978 these projects resulted in political debates for statewide offices in New York, California, Minnesota, Missouri, Illinois, and Massachusetts, as well as debates in scores of lesser campaigns.[23] In sum, it would appear that in the approximately 130 years since Lincoln and Douglas first met at Ottawa, Illinois, political debating has become a firmly established feature of political campaigning.

DECIDING WHETHER TO DEBATE

At every level of politics, candidates and their advisors strategically address themselves to six questions in determining whether to engage in political debates.[24]

1. *Is this likely to be a close election?*
Expectations about the outcome of the election are vital to the decision to engage in debates. If the election seems as though it will be close and both candidates are in doubt about the outcome, the likelihood of political debates is greatly increased. If either candidate has a strong conviction that they can win the election without engaging in debates, the likelihood of debates taking place is dramatically reduced.

2. *Are advantages likely to accrue to me if I debate?*
No candidate willingly engages in counterproductive activity.

244

Consequently, both candidates must have good reason to expect that the debates will be advantageous to them. As we will see in the next sections, the advantages a candidate perceives may come as much from the act of debating as from the actual debates themselves. Nevertheless, unless both candidates can anticipate advantages, political debates are unlikely to be held.

3. Am I a good debater?
No candidates willingly put themselves in a position where their foe will clearly appear to be stronger. Consequently, when measuring themselves against their opponent, each candidate must be confident about being a good debater.

4. Are there only two major candidates running for the office?
Typically, our political system produces two serious candidates for each office. On those occasions where a third candidate seems to have a possibility of drawing a respectable share of the vote, it is highly unlikely that political debates will take place. Third party candidates are not predictable. They are not bound by the same "rules" as candidates who anticipate election. Often they speak to make a point, to dramatize an issue, rather than to win an election. Moreover, the presence of a third candidate provides the possibility that two candidates may "gang up" on one. These variables make it highly unlikely that political debates will take place in races where a third candidate is on the ballot and appears to have a possibility of drawing a respectable share of the vote.

5. Do I have control of all the important variables in the debate situation?
Candidates cannot be expected to place themselves in positions where they cannot reasonably anticipate what will happen. Consequently, each candidate must feel comfortable with all the major variables in the debate situation: the dates, location, formats, topics, and other participants (moderators and

questioners). Unless every candidate feels in control of all the major variables in the debate, they are unlikely to consent to debating.

6. *Is the field clear of incumbents?*

If either candidate is an incumbent seeking reelection, the probability of debate taking place is sharply reduced. Most incumbents reason that their credibility is unquestioned by virtue of prior service. The credibility of their opponents is often an issue in the campaign. Moreover, incumbent officeholders are frequently able to make their views known to the public. Hence, they are reluctant to provide their opponents with a platform from which to be heard. Additionally, almost any incumbent will necessarily be placed on the defensive in a political debate. The incumbent's record will probably be a major topic of discussion. Typically, no incumbent will hand an opponent the opportunity to attack vigorously, much less in a well-publicized situation.

APPLYING THE CONDITIONS
REQUISITE FOR POLITICAL DEBATES

Regardless of the office sought, few political debates will occur unless the conditions implicit in these questions exist to the satisfaction of both candidates. The importance of these conditions can be illustrated by analyzing virtually any campaign. However, in the next few pages we will examine two presidential campaigns to better illustrate the ways in which candidates and their managers determine whether they should debate. We have chosen to focus on these two campaigns first because they are especially instructive and also because readers are probably more acquainted with the circumstances and events of presidential campaigns than with those of any other campaigns. However, keep in mind that these same principles are used by all candidates. Candidates do not choose to debate by chance; rather, their decisions are based on self-interest.

1960: Kennedy-Nixon Debates

From the outset, most observers anticipated a close election.[25] As the campaign progressed, public opinion polls confirmed expectations. Neither candidate ever led by more than six points in the major polls. Clearly, both camps anticipated a close election.

In 1952 vice-presidential candidate Richard Nixon gave one of the most successful political speeches in U.S. history. Using the new medium of television, he had saved his position on the ballot as Dwight Eisenhower's running mate with his Checkers speech. His 1960 advisors considered him a "master" of television.

His own extensive background as a college debater and his recent "kitchen" debates with Soviet Premier Khrushchev also contributed to Nixon's confidence in his ability to debate Kennedy. Nixon's strategists were so confident that their candidate would gain in the debates that they initially argued for only one debate. They believed that Nixon could virtually eliminate Kennedy in one debate and that it would be disadvantageous to give Kennedy any opportunity to recover. Clearly, Nixon's camp believed that advantages would accrue to him from debating and that he was a good debater.

Few 1960 observers recalled what most of Kennedy's inner circle best remembered about 1952. John Kennedy ran for the Senate against a heavily favored, vastly more experienced, incumbent Republican, Senator Henry Cabot Lodge. Kennedy debated Lodge at Waltham, Massachusetts. From that point forward, Lodge's assertions about his superior experience, maturity and judgment—the same issues Nixon was using in 1960—were no longer viable. At least two of Kennedy's inner circle, his brother Robert and close advisor Kenneth O'Donnell, anticipated that the Kennedy-Nixon debates might well be a "rerun" of the Lodge debate. Clearly, Kennedy's strategists felt that their man was an able speaker and that his presence on the same platform as Nixon, as well as what he said, would prove advantageous.

Kennedy and Nixon were the only major candidates for the presidency. After 15 negotiating sessions, which included discussions of virtually every detail of television production—camera angles, staging, lighting, and backdrops—both camps felt that no unexpected variable would confound the situation.

Thus Nixon and Kennedy had every reason to debate. It was no accident that they became the first presidential candidates to engage in an extensive series of public debates. It was at their bidding that both Republican and Democratic members of Congress voted to suspend section 315 of the Communications Law to allow national coverage of the debates.

1980: Reagan-Carter-Anderson Debates

From the outset, the presence of Congressman John Anderson of Illinois as a major third-party candidate distinguished the 1980 election.[26] Anderson's presence clearly inhibited political debates and almost entirely prevented debate between the two major candidates. The presence of a third-party candidate, combined with the presence of an incumbent, makes the 1980 presidential election an unusually instructive one for examining how candidates determine whether they should debate.

As the general election opened, Congressman Anderson was the favored presidential candidate of approximately 15 to 20 percent of the nation's prospective voters. Moreover, the vast majority of the public seemed disturbed with the two traditional choices. An exceptionally high percentage of voters were undecided.

Faced with this situation, the League of Women Voters had two choices. First, it could invite only the two major party can-

248

didates to debate. In 1976 the League had done just this, ignoring Governor Lester Maddox and Senator Eugene McCarthy among others, while extending its invitation to debate only to President Gerald Ford and Governor Jimmy Carter. Second, the League could invite all three candidates. In doing so, the League would imply that it felt Anderson's candidacy was credible and that in fact there really were three major candidates. The League invited Anderson to debate.

By extending an invitation to Anderson, the League sharply diminished the prospects of a debate involving Carter and Reagan. Major party nominees cannot be expected to readily agree to participate when a third nominee is involved. President Carter immediately refused to debate. Patrick Caddell, the Carter campaign pollster, explained:

> We just assume Anderson's presence helps him, makes him more legitimate, establishes him. Such added strength hurts Carter far more than Reagan since Anderson has been getting most of his strength from disgruntled Democrats and this could give key states and the election to Reagan.[27]

By early September, based on Caddell's polls, the White House had concluded that Anderson's candidacy was going downhill and if left alone would soon be of little consequence. But the League would not leave it alone. Unwittingly or otherwise, by inviting Anderson the League had increased his legitimacy, thereby preserving his slim opportunity for victory and perhaps enhancing the likelihood of a Reagan victory.

Carter cited additional reasons for not appearing with Anderson and Reagan. The president noted that Anderson "ran as a Republican and he's still a Republican." The president constantly called the upcoming event "a Republican debate." Surrogates for President Carter repeated this theme, claiming that the two Republicans would gang up unfairly on the president in a debate. For highly predictable reasons, the president refused to participate in any debate with both Anderson and Reagan.

Similarly, for highly predictable reasons, Reagan accepted the League's invitation to join both John Anderson and Jimmy Carter in a debate. Reagan saw several advantages to debating. First, all the polls suggested that any improvement in Anderson's vote would hurt Carter more than Reagan. Second, the debate itself had become an issue. During the Iowa primary, Reagan had failed to appear in the Republican forum. This decision was subsequently believed to have hurt his Iowa campaign. By agreeing to appear with Anderson, Reagan was focusing attention on Carter's refusal. This strategy quickly proved effective against Carter, as it had in Iowa when other Republicans used it against Reagan. The Harris poll found that 69 percent of the public wanted Carter to debate. Finally, the debate with Anderson gave Reagan an opportunity to attack Carter in front of a large audience at no expense.

President Carter's refusal to participate in the September 22 debate between Anderson and Reagan reduced that event to little more than another Republican candidates' forum. One of the three major networks did not even bother televising the event, accurately anticipating that millions of voters would prefer to watch "Midnight Express," a recent movie chronicling the adventures of a U.S. citizen convicted of drug dealing in Turkey. Newspapers the next morning also characterized the event as little more than another Republican candidates' forum.

Having effectively minimized the possibility of presidential debates by inviting John Anderson to their first debate, the League of Women Voters in mid-September sought a rationale for not inviting him to subsequent debates. Three weeks after finding him a viable choice for the presidency, league President Ruth Hinderfeld claimed that Anderson was "no longer the significant candidate he was." Anderson had fallen from the favorite of a "significant" 15 percent of the voters to the favorite of an "insignificant" 10 percent of the voters. Thus in mid-October the League of Women Voters issued an invitation to Carter and Reagan, but not to Anderson, to appear jointly in Cleveland for a presidential debate.

With only three weeks left in the campaign, and the League not having invited John Anderson, the conditions requisite for political debates now existed. In deciding to accept the League's invitation to debate without John Anderson, both Carter and Reagan had to evaluate the remaining conditions presented earlier.

First, each man had to conclude that this was likely to be a close election. Neither candidate could feel that he would be a sure winner without debating. Reagan had been consistently ahead of President Carter in virtually every poll taken since the general election campaign opened on Labor Day. However, by the last weeks of October, Carter had closed to within a few points of Reagan in most polls. Coupled with the large undecided vote, and the fading Anderson vote, which might not hold firm for the congressman, Carter's October surge had placed the election in doubt.

Second, each man perceived advantages likely to accrue to him if he debated. The *Cincinnati Enquirer* accurately summarized the situation confronting Reagan in mid-October. "There is widespread agreement among pollsters such as George Gallup and political operatives in both campaigns that the issue that is hurting Reagan most among women voters is the fear—hammered on constantly by the Carter campaign that he might embroil the country in war." The *Enquirer* pointed out that among women voters Reagan was trailing Carter badly and that the vast preponderance of undecided voters were women. Reagan himself acknowledged that Carter's use of the war issue "has been effective in creating a stereotype of me." Reagan's pro-debate advisors perceived the debate as a means of dispelling fears of Reagan as a warmonger. James Baker spoke for many of Reagan's advisors when he commented about the Californian, "Is he dangerous? Any time anybody's exposed to him we dispell those doubts."

Moreover, Reagan was evidently concerned that Carter's use of foreign policy in the final days of the campaign was shifting voters. Indeed, as speculation concerning release of the hostages in Iran mounted in late October, the Reagan cam-

251

paign was frustrated by its inability to respond or to even command press attention. Fear of an "October surprise" in the form of an administration foreign policy breakthrough clearly motivated Reagan's decision to debate.

Additionally, Reagan's advisors felt that by mid-October the campaign might have gotten almost all it could get from attacking Carter. The Reagan campaign was stagnating. Undecided voters, the Reagan team felt, were already disenchanted with Carter. That case had been made, but undecided voters were remaining undecided because they saw no reason to vote for Reagan. Observing Reagan side by side with President Carter would provide them with reasons to vote for Ronald Reagan and hence resolve their indecision.

President Carter also perceived advantages accruing to him from a debate. Carter the president, Carter the engineer, Carter the technician, Carter the manager might well overwhelm Reagan in a debate, thought many of his advisors. Carter's staff was reported to be "confident he can crush Reagan." A resounding debate victory late in the campaign might be just the impetus the fast closing campaign needed.

Moreover, as the election grew closer, many traditional Democratic voter blocs that had been displeased by Carter, particularly black, Hispanic, Jewish, and labor voters, seemed on the verge of returning to the president. A debate would give the president a huge audience at no cost. He could remind Democratic voters that he was an incumbent Democratic president in the tradition of Roosevelt, Truman, Kennedy, and Johnson. This ploy had been effective in 1976. It might be even more effective in 1980 against an opponent who could be portrayed as the very antithesis of the Democratic tradition.

Finally, Carter had avoided debates with Ted Kennedy and Jerry Brown during the primaries. He had avoided debating with John Anderson earlier. He had defended these decisions, but the cumulative effect of his repeated refusals to debate, particularly in light of his eagerness to debate four years earlier, might well be to signal the public that Carter was afraid to defend himself.

The third factor both candidates evaluated was their ability to debate. The Carter campaign seemed to perceive the president as far brighter, quicker, and better prepared than his opponent. In a remarkable speech delivered at Miami's Edison Senior High School, Carter spoke about his abilities vis-à-vis Reagan's to fulfill the demands of the presidency. He might equally have been speaking about the demands of a political debate. "Ronald Reagan is better at making speeches than I am . . . but in the oval office you can't rely on 3 by 5 cards and you can't rely on a teleprompter." Carter went on to claim that he was "prepared to deal with issues, think on my feet, and respond to questions," while Reagan was not.

Ronald Reagan was also confident of his ability. Reagan had been widely reported to favor debating Carter early in the campaign but to have acceded to the advice of his strategists who saw little point to debating. Many observers felt that Reagan's greatest attribute as a politician was his ability to communicate. His political career had begun with an impressive television address to the nation on behalf of Barry Goldwater in 1964. By late October, he too had endured repeated political debates and forums. Throughout 1980, including his most recent encounter with John Anderson, he had done well. A professional actor, Reagan seemed relaxed and poised in debate situations. Asked earlier in the year whether he ever got butterflies before debates, Reagan laughingly responded, "Debate butterflies? I've been on the same stage as John Wayne."

The fourth factor that both candidates had to evaluate was the variables associated with the debate situation: format, date, location, time limits, and similar questions. In 1960 representatives of Kennedy and Nixon discussed virtually every detail of their debates in 15 negotiating sessions. In 1980 almost all of the details were resolved in six hours of discussion, which stretched over two days.

Thus by late October of 1980, five of the six conditions normally associated with fostering political debates were in place. The League of Women Voters had not invited John Anderson, and thus only two major candidates were involved. Second, the election appeared to be close. Third, both candidates could perceive advantages accruing to them from debate. Fourth, both candidates believed themselves to be good debaters. And fifth, both candidates were satisfied with the important variables in the debate situation.

The 1980 presidential debate may prove significant not simply because of any impact it may prove to have had on the election itself, but also because it may prove to have "institutionalized" political debates as a part of future presidential campaigns. For the reasons we have examined, incumbents typically shy away from debates. In 1980 an incumbent chose to debate. This was the second consecutive presidential election in which this anomaly took place. Public expectations may have been conditioned by the last two presidential elections. Though incumbents may have good reasons for wishing not to debate, public expectations may make it politically costly for future presidents to refuse. Nevertheless, in races other than presidential, it is still probable that the presence of an incumbent inhibits the likelihood of debates.

POLITICAL DEBATE STRATEGIES

Political debate strategies can best be understood if we recognize that they involve three stages. First are those strategies that take place prior to the debate itself. Second are those the candidate attempts to implement during the debate. Finally are those following the debate. Each is important. A political debate can be won or lost before it takes place, as it takes place, or after it is held. In this section, we will examine political debating strategies.

Predebate Strategies

The candidate who is perceived to have won the debate is often a function of what people expected. Hence, many candidates seek to lower public expectations of their performance. If prior expectations are low, then it may not take a strong effort on the part of the candidate to appear to have done well. Moreover, if a candidate is expected to be outclassed but does well, it may be perceived as a major victory.

Goodwin F. Berquist and James L. Golden have noted that the media tend to establish public expectations regarding the probable outcome of political debates.[28] Observing the 1980 Reagan-Carter debate, Berquist and Golden point out that prior to the debate the media alerted the public to what might take place by discussing expected candidate strategies, interviewing campaign staff, and presenting guidelines for successful debating to which the candidates might adhere.[29]

The interaction between the candidate and campaign staff on the one hand, and the media on the other, can be crucial during the predebate period. As the media go about their job, they will seek comments from the campaigners. Campaigners will normally tend to downplay the potential outcome of the debate. By minimizing expectations, campaigners feel they are putting themselves in the best possible position to capitalize on a strong performance and to rationalize for a weak one.

Typically, it is easier for a challenger to minimize expectations than it is for an incumbent. For this reason, Patrick H. Caddell, President Carter's political aide, in a private memo to the president cautioned him that "debates are the vehicles of challengers." Caddell explained that the incumbent is already well known, experienced, and relatively safe, thus making it difficult to minimize expectations.[30] It is far easier for unknown, inexperienced candidates to assert that they may not do well and successfully minimize public expectations. Caddell wrote about the problem Carter faced in 1980 this way:

> We can think of our debate as a football game with each team having one chance to move the ball and score. However, we get the ball on our five yard line. Reagan starts with the ball on *our* 40 yard line—already in near field goal range. Mild success can put Reagan in certain field goal range. A moderate sustained drive can give him a touchdown. The President must move 95 yards for a touchdown without losing possession. He must move 70 yards or more to get a field goal. He can easily gain more total yards and yet lose the real score.[31]

Minimizing public expectations allows the candidate to start on his opponent's 40-yard line. But, for an incumbent, this is difficult to do. In elections where debates take place, incumbency may not be as advantageous as was once believed. As Berquist and Golden point out, there is a widely held assumption that a president running for reelection must always appear to be a winner. Therefore, any debate that is judged even "is in fact a perceived victory for the lesser known challenger."[32] Hence, the first predebate strategy is to minimize public expectations. Regardless of the office being contested, the size of the constituency, or the extensiveness of media coverage, the lower the expectation, the more likely the candidate will appear to do well.

Closely related to this first predebate strategy is the second—preparing the press and through them the public for the opponent. Typically, candidates will stress the anticipated shortcomings of their opponents, so that the press and public will be especially attentive. In predebate interviews, candidates will ask if they might finally hear their opponent's plan to revitalize the economy, or conserve natural resources. Candidates continually remind audiences prior to the debate of their opponent's penchant for talking in simple terms, or flip-flopping on issues, or failing to be specific. All of these remarks are meant to attract the public's attention to an opponent's anticipated weaknesses. Thus the second predebate strategy is to heighten expectations of an opponent, by alerting the press and public to expected shortcomings and demanding that the opponent be held accountable.

The third predebate strategy is to determine clearly the target audience. Political debates, as will be illustrated in the next section, typically draw the largest audiences of any single communicative event of the campaign. The candidates must determine who their target audiences are for the debate. Typically, they will be the same as the normal campaign target audiences. However, due to the unusual size of the audience, it is possible that the candidate may choose to go after a new target group of voters during a debate. The debate may be the first time that this group has been exposed to the candidate. Most practitioners would not suggest using the debate to attract massive numbers of new and different voters to the candidate. But the unusual nature of debate audiences—their size, the presence of many adherents of the opponent, the propensity of both the college educated and women to attend debates— means that the candidates must clearly determine whether they wish to maintain their campaigns' targeted audiences for the debate or whether they wish to make some changes, normally in the form of adding a targeted group.

Finally, with a clear conception of targeted audiences in mind, candidates must work out answers to possible questions and practice them. This is the fourth predebate strategy. The firsthand reports of many participants in political debates suggest several successful approaches to practice.[33] First, in a relaxed atmosphere the candidate and a limited number of aides should work through possible questions and answers, consistently keeping in mind overall themes and target audiences. Second, the candidate should practice the answers in a situation as similar to the real one as possible. For nationally televised debates, such as the presidential debates of 1960, 1976, and 1980, this has meant simulating the television studio or auditorium to be used. This also means, if possible, utilizing a stand-in for the opponent. Some candidates have reviewed the speeches and tapes of their opponent's past performances. In the case of opponents who have debated in the past, an examination of their past debates has proven helpful.[34] Preparing for a debate may well mean curtailing other campaign activity for several days, but given the attention normally focused on debates, this sacrifice would seem worthwhile.

Debate Strategies

As the debate progresses, candidates must constantly respond to specific questions on the issues of the day. While those issues vary from campaign to campaign, most successful political debaters have been able to integrate the specific issues into an overall framework. For example, when Senators John Kennedy and Hubert Humphrey debated in West Virginia, Kennedy developed the overall thesis, just as he did months later when debating Nixon, that while the United States was a great nation, it could and should be greater. As he dealt with specific issues concerning West Virginia and the nation, he integrated many of them into his overall thesis, that the United States could do better.[35] Similarly, in 1980 Ronald Reagan's overall thesis was that President Carter had failed to provide adequate leadership and that Reagan was a reasonable alternative. Repeatedly, his answers returned to this theme. Hence, the first debate strategy is to utilize issues by relating them to an overall theme.

Issues serve skilled debaters by allowing them to develop an overall thesis. We know that most people forget 70 percent or more of what they hear in as little as 24 hours. Any response to an opponent or a panelist on a specific issue is liable to be forgotten by most of the audience. But by making the response to a specific issue part of a theme that is consistently repeated, issues can be used to best advantage. Strategies on specific issues, of course, cannot be generalized. They vary depending on the candidate and the situation. But developing an overall thesis, which can be reinforced by the responses to many specific issues, is a highly effective strategy employed by many political debaters.

Issues are one of the two major concerns of the candidate during the debate. The other is image. As Robert O. Weiss has argued, in political debates "issues and images are in practical fact overlooked and . . . they intertwine in all manner of convolutions and mutually affect one another in countless ways."[36] Weiss calls this relationship the "issue-image interface."[37] Though issues and images are closely intertwined, there are several image strategies that can be employed in political debates.

The principal image strategies that can be utilized in political debating include the development of a leadership style, personification, and identification.[38] As Dan Nimmo points out, political figures can develop an activist leadership style or a passive leadership style. The activist is just that. In a debate, activists consistently refer to their actions, their initiatives, their effect on events. Passive leaders are cautious. They do not speak of their initiatives, but rather portray themselves as reacting to events.

Both Carter and Reagan seemed to be seeking an activist image in 1980. Carter noted of himself or his administration that "I've made thousands of decisions. . . . I'll always remember. . . We initiated . . . We are now planning . . ."[39] He continually spoke of his as an activist administration, which was tackling the hard problems that the United States confronted. Similarly, Reagan told the audience that he was an activist. "I have submitted . . . I have opposed . . . I stood . . . As Governor when I . . ." Like Carter, Reagan's language was that of the activist, focusing attention upon himself and his actions.

The second image strategy that lends itself to political debating is personification, the effort of the candidate to play a definite role. For example, the candidate may work to be perceived as a nice guy or an efficient manager. In 1980 concerned about President Carter's attempts to characterize him as a

warmonger who might have an itchy trigger finger on the nuclear button, Ronald Reagan worked to counter that image in
the debate. He did so in part by personifying a kind, statesmanlike, religious family man, seeking peace. For example, at
various points in the debate he observed that "I believe with all
my heart that our first priority must be world peace. . . . I am a
father of sons; I have a grandson. . . . I'm going to continue
praying that they'll come home [the Iranian hostages]." In sum
Reagan was attempting to personify himself, to play a role, as a
kindly, statesmanlike, religious family man. This personification would be most distant from the image of warmonger.

The final image strategy is identification. Debaters attempt to symbolize what they believe are the principal aspirations of their audience. Reagan was exceptionally effective at
this throughout the campaign, as he attacked the economic
shortcomings of the administration and attempted to present
himself as the candidate who could provide economic leadership, thus meeting the aspirations of his audience. At the end of
the 1980 presidential debate, he attempted to summarize the
nation's frustrations with the economy and present himself as
a means of improving it.

> Next Tuesday is election day. Next Tuesday all of you will go
> to the polls, will stand there in the polling place, and make a
> decision. I think when you make that decision it might be
> well if you would ask yourself, are you better off than you
> were four years ago? Is it easier for you to go and buy things
> in the stores than it was four years ago? Is there more or
> less unemployment in the country than there was four
> years ago? . . . And if you answer all of those questions
> "yes" why then I think your choice is very obvious as to
> whom you will vote for. If you don't agree, if you don't think
> that this course that we've been on for the last four years is
> what you would like to see us follow for the next four, then I
> could suggest another choice that you have.[40]

In this passage, Reagan is identifying himself with all the frustrations the public has experienced in the past four years and

attempting to offer himself as the means of fulfilling their aspirations.

As these examples make clear, there is a close relationship between a candidate's response to specific issues and the image that the candidate projects. Nevertheless, as the debate is in progress, the candidate should have a clear idea of an overall issue strategy or thesis to which specific answers can be related. Moreover, candidates should be cognizant of the image they may be projecting and develop appropriate strategies, such as a leadership style, personification, and identification, to create the persona they want.

Postdebate Strategies

Political debates are not over when the last word is uttered. Who won? Who made a grievous error? Who seemed best in control? Questions like these immediately follow the debate, and their answers are often as important as the debate itself. After all, it is what the audience perceives to have happened in the debate that is of consequence. Therefore, the well-prepared campaign will be ready to try to influence audience perceptions of the debate as soon as it concludes.

The importance of postdebate strategies was dramatized in the second Ford-Carter debate of 1976, perhaps best remembered because President Ford seemed to be unaware of the Soviet domination of Eastern Europe. Yet, at the time that Ford made his unfortunate statement, it was barely noticed. It was not until the next day, after continual publicity of his remark, that Ford was perceived as having erred badly. Frederick T. Steeper studied this debate and concluded:

> The volunteered descriptions of the debate by the voters surveyed immediately after the debate included no mentions of Ford's statement on Eastern Europe. Not until the afternoon of the next day did such references appear, and by Thursday night they were the most frequent criticism given of Ford's performance. Similarly, the panelists monitored during the debate gave no indication of an unfavor-

able reaction at the time they heard Ford's Eastern European remarks. The conclusion is that the preponderance of viewers of the second debate most likely were not certain of the true status of Eastern Europe, or less likely, did not consider Ford's error important. Given the amount of publicity given to Ford's East European statements the next day by the news media and the concomitant change that took place it is concluded that this publicity caused the change.[41]

Most students of political debate believe that the effects often lag behind the debate itself. Often, audience members do not reach final judgment until they have discussed the debate with others and have observed the media reaction.[42] It is during these hours, when interpersonal influence and media influence are often operating, that the campaign engages in the postdebate strategy of favorably influencing perceptions of the debate.

The principal postdebate strategy is to provide a massive and well-coordinated surrogate effort. Spokespersons for the candidate are made readily accessible to the media. Not only do they suggest that their candidate won, but they stress issues and responses the campaign wants emphasized. Often, to the extent it is possible, these spokespersons are briefed prior to the debate, so that they will be sensitive to the issues and responses their candidate seeks to stress.

A massive and coordinated surrogate effort means that in the crucial postdebate hours, viewers and media representatives are hearing many respected figures present a cogent rationale of why their candidate did well in the debate. Often these interviews are widely reprinted and broadcast and may serve to influence audience perception of the debate. Learning from Ford's problem after the second debate in 1976, both the Carter and Reagan camps made prominent spokespersons available to the media following their debate.

The use of prominent spokespersons to present a positive view of the debate is the most common postdebate strategy. It is used in all levels of campaigns. Other strategies are less common and often depend on the circumstances and formats of the specific debate. Often, if an audience is present, campaign staff members will work to "load" the audience with partisans. Not only will they provide positive responses during the debate, but as they are interviewed later, they may well do the same thing. Community leaders, known to be sympathetic to the candidate, can be urged to write letters to the editors of local papers, commenting favorably upon the candidate's performance. In every instance, postdebate strategies such as the use of surrogates, audience members, and letters are designed to influence public perception in the crucial hours and days that immediately follow.

EFFECTS OF POLITICAL DEBATES

Any discussion of the effects of political debates must be tempered with an awareness that it is difficult to draw strong conclusions about them. This difficulty arises for several reasons. First, each debate is different. It involves different candidates, different offices, different issues, different audiences, different press coverage, different formats, and a host of other differences. Hence, to talk about the specific effects of debates is virtually impossible, for no two will be identical, nor will their effects be identical.

Second, debate effects cannot be isolated from the effects of all the other communication that voters receive during the campaign. Individuals may be exposed to a dozen messages about the candidates on the very day of the debate. Distinguishing the effects of the debate from all the others is difficult.

While there have been scores of political debates in the last 20 years, researchers have only studied the presidential debates of 1960, 1976, and 1980 in detail. Hence, our discussion of effects must necessarily be limited to a consideration of the effects of presidential debates. We cannot be certain that the effects of nationally televised political debates are similar to those of the vast majority of political debates held in campaigns for lesser offices. Most debates are not nationally televised. They are not well publicized in advance. They are not subjected to endless speculation, examination, and evaluation for days afterward. However, while findings concerning the effects of presidential debate are not necessarily valid for other debates, there is reason to suspect a broad similarity in the pattern of effects produced by political debates. But, we cannot be absolutely certain.

Finally, unlike laboratory experiments, scientists cannot control political debates. Hence, those debates that have been examined are often subject to studies that, of necessity, are prepared under less than ideal conditions, including little advance planning and an inability to control fully all of the variables in the study.

Despite each of the above problems, at this time there appear to be some striking findings about the effects of political debates, which are subject to revision as debating becomes an even more widely studied communication event.

Effect 1: Increased Audiences

Political debates, even at the local or state level, attract large audiences. Debates create conflict, the essence of drama. Hence, it should not surprise us that presidential debates attract huge audiences. Similarly, we might well hypothesize that debates attract larger audiences than virtually any other activity that takes place during the typical campaign. While research on audiences for nonpresidential debates is not yet widely available, the basic element of conflict exists and might operate as it evidently does in presidential debates—to attract a large audience.

In 1960 CBS estimated that over 100 million people in the United States watched at least part of the Kennedy-Nixon debates.[43] Numerous other surveys also suggested that the

Kennedy-Nixon debates drew an immense national audience. In fact, the debates drew the largest audience for any speaking event in history, up to that time.[44] Similarly, every measure of audience size conducted in connection with the 1976 debates also suggests a massive audience. Most measures of the 1976 debates claim that over 70 percent of the nation watched at least part of the first Carter-Ford debate. While viewing fell off somewhat as the series of debates progressed, it never fell below 60 percent.[45] The 1980 Reagan-Carter debate also drew an immense audience, generally estimated at about 120 million people.[46] Clearly, the first effect of political debates seems to be that they generate audiences far larger than those that are generated by any other communication activity during the campaign.

Effect 2: Audiences Reinforced

Studies that have attempted to determine what audiences learn from political debates have yielded varying findings. Patterns seem to be emerging that suggest that debates often tend to reinforce the positions of a candidate's partisans. After the 1960 debates, most researchers did not find substantial shifts of voter opinion. Rather, they found that Kennedy and Nixon partisans became more strongly committed to their candidate. As *Newsweek* reported, the debates "merely stiffened attitudes."[47]

Research since the 1960 debates tends to confirm these early findings. According to Sears and Chaffee, "the information flow stimulated by debates tends to be translated by voters into evaluations that coincide with prior political dispositions. They perceive their party's candidate as having 'won' and they discuss the outcome with like-minded people." Sears and Chaffee continue, noting that since the Democratic party is substantially larger than the Republican, the net effect of the cumulative reinforcement stimulated by the debates probably benefits Democratic candidates.[48] Sears and Chaffee's discussion is based on national audiences for presidential debates. The logical outgrowth of these conclusions, applied to local campaigns, would be that debates, because they tend to reinforce prior political dispositions, generally work to the advantage of the party that is dominant in the district, city, or state.[49]

Effect 3: Shifting Limited Numbers of Voters

Political debates do not normally result in massive shifts of votes. As indicated above, most audience members have their existing predispositions reinforced by the debate. However, some voters may shift. In a close election, the number who shift as a consequence of debates might be decisive.

The Kennedy-Nixon debates were widely perceived at the time as having affected massive numbers of voters. President Kennedy helped foster this impression by attributing his election to the debates. Yet evidence on this point suggests that while they may have been decisive due to the extremely close nature of the election, the debates did not shift massive numbers of votes. The highest estimate of voter shift is pollster Elmo Roper's guess that 4 million voters, about 6 percent of the vote, changed as a consequence of the debates.[50] However, most researchers are far more cautious. Katz and Feldman, after examining 31 studies of the 1960 debates, typify the conclusions of most when they write, "did the debates really affect the final outcome? Apart from strengthening Democratic convictions about their candidate, it is very difficult to tell."[51]

McLeod and his associates found very little vote shifting as a result of the 1976 debates.[52] Similarly, writing about the Carter-Ford debates, Hagner and Rieselbach concluded that "for the large question of the debates' overall impact, we conclude that the debates reinforced existing predispositions considerably, but actually changed them very little."[53] This limited effects paradigm also seems to have operated in 1980. In their study of the 1980 debates, Leuthold and Valentine first examined the results of earlier presidential debates and concluded that "viewing presidential debates tends to maintain or reinforce previous positive or negative attitudes toward the candidates." Then, examining the data from their study of the 1980 debate, they found that "these patterns were repeated in 1980."[54] In sum, debates seem to shift a very limited number of voters.

Effect 4: Debates Help Set Voters' Agenda

As we have discussed in Chapter 4, much recent research has stressed the importance of the agenda-setting function of mass communication. In essence, this research holds that "we judge as important what the media judge as important. Media priorities become our own."[55] If the considerable body of evidence that supports the agenda-setting function of mass media is correct, then it would stand to reason that those issues stressed in mass media political debates, and mass media coverage of those debates, should also become issues of high priority for voters who watch the debates and attend to the media coverage of them. Swanson and Swanson offer strong evidence in support of the agenda-setting function of political debates.[56] They attempted to determine whether those issues of primary concern to voters changed as a consequence of watching political debates. Based on research done at the University of Illinois during the 1976 campaign, they concluded that "the first Ford-Carter debate exerted an agenda-setting effect on our subjects who viewed it, although that effect was tempered by enduring personal priorities of subjects."[57] As Swanson and Swanson subsequently observed, "to the extent that citizens base their voting choices on their assessment of campaign issues, this is surely an effect of some political importance."[58]

Effect 5: Debates Increase the Voters' Knowledge of Issues

A wide variety of studies have attempted to determine whether political debates increase the voters' knowledge of the issues. These studies seem to point to two conclusions. First, voters do seem more knowledgeable as a consequence of watching political debates. Tempering this conclusion is the second: often voters do not learn about the very issues that most concern them.

That voters do learn about the issues as a consequence of watching debates seems to have been well established by research. A study by Becker and his colleagues concerning the results of the 1976 Ford-Carter debates in Onondaga County, a metropolitan area located near the center of New York State, seems to typify the results of most researchers who have attempted to establish what voters actually learn from political debates. Becker and his associates found that "the debates did in fact increase voters' understanding of the candidates and the issues in 1976." On the basis of their work, these researchers maintain that "the debates made some voters better able to describe the candidates and better informed on the candidates' stands on some of the issues. In that sense, at least, the debates were successful in doing what their sponsors had intended: to produce a better informed electorate."[59]

Stephen Chaffee's 1976 study of Wisconsin voters similarly suggests that debates do facilitate political learning. Chaffee finds that "it seems safe to conclude that there was substantial political learning as a consequence of holding the debates in 1976."[60] Chaffee also notes that, although few studies of the 1960 debates attempted to measure their effect on political learning, it is likely that the Kennedy-Nixon debates did contribute to political learning.[61]

As noted above, although voters apparently learn about issues by watching debates, often they do not learn about the issues that most concern them. Michael Pfau has cogently argued that "a political debate ought to match—to the extent possible—the agendas of the candidates and the public." However, as he and many others have concluded, "the journalists' questions have virtually ignored the public's agenda (at least in

1960 and 1976)."[62] Moreover, Pfau's complaint about the presidential debates of 1960 and 1976 seems to have also been at least partly true in 1980. Indeed, one of the journalists who helped to set the agenda of the 1980 debates with her questions wrote that she "felt under enormous pressure to try forming a single question that would somehow catch the well-briefed candidates by surprise on a subject of importance."[63] More appropriately for the public, she might have attempted to ask a question dealing with those issues that were of greatest public concern. But far too often, the public's concerns are not reflected in the journalists' questions. Obviously, if they are not reflected in the questions, they can scarcely be reflected in the candidates' answers.[64] Thus because of problems with formats that allow journalists to set the debate agenda and secondarily because of formats that may allow candidates to avoid answering questions, the public often seems ill-served. The issues of chief importance to the public simply may not be developed in political debates.

However, this difficulty with political debates may be on the wane. Many local political debates, such as those held in the campaigns for South Dakota's first and second congressional districts and its Senate seat during 1980, are using formats that require the candidates to focus on issues of high public concern.[65] The League of Women Voters changed the format of the Reagan-Carter debate from that used earlier in the Reagan-Anderson debate. The second half of the Reagan-Carter debate minimized the role of reporters. Prentice, Larson, and Sobnosky compared the two formats utilized in the Reagan-Carter debate and concluded that the second format, which eliminated reporters' follow-up questions and increased the opportunity for rebuttals by the candidates, was "more conducive to meeting the League's goal of clarifying positions between the candidates and allowing voters to make comparisons."[66] Clearly, the format will affect the issues covered in the debate. It would appear that criticism of presidential debate formats is slowly resulting in a variety of format shifts that may gradually cause debates to focus more directly on issues of highest public concern.

Effect 6: Debates Modify Candidate Images

Debates apparently affect the images of candidates. In their evaluation of the impact of the 1976 debates, Hagner and Reiselbach suggest that debates affect candidate images primarily when the candidate is not well known and hence the candidate's public image is not well developed.[67] When the public is unfamiliar with the candidate, perception of the candidate's general character, personality attributes, and general competency seems to be affected by political debates and their subsequent media coverage.

Most accounts of the 1960 debates note that Kennedy, the comparative unknown, improved his image as a consequence of the debates. He was able to convey a sense of competency and familiarity with major issues, as well as a charming personality. Similarly, Sears and Chaffee summarize a number of studies of the 1976 debates and conclude that the public's image of the candidates was affected by the debates.[68] Particularly noteworthy is their conclusion that Democratic vice-presidential candidate Walter Mondale's popularity, competence, and trait evaluation all improved following his debate with his counterpart, Republican Robert Dole.[69] Those who seek lesser offices, such as Mondale, tend to be less well known. We might anticipate political debates having a great effect on their image.

Most accounts of the 1980 campaign stress that the lesser-known Ronald Reagan was perceived, as a consequence of his debate with President Carter, as possessing an "easygoing manner," "warmth and compassion," but indignation and sternness when appropriate.[70] It was the improvement in his image, not the substance of the issue differences between the two men, that caused most observers to consider Reagan the winner of the debate.

In sum, debates can affect public perception of a candidate's image—general competency, personality attributes, and character traits. The potential for affecting image seems to be inversely related to public knowledge of the candidate. The better known the candidate, the less likely the debate will greatly affect that candidate's image. Hence, the potential for improving one's image is generally greater for the lesser-known candidate. Moreover, it is likely that in races for lesser offices, among lesser-known candidates, the impact of a debate on the image of the candidates is potentially great.

Effect 7: Debates Build
Confidence in U.S. Democracy

A wide variety of studies have attempted to evaluate the effects of political debates on U.S. institutions. Do debates result in greater confidence and support of political institutions and office holders? Do debates facilitate political socialization? While individual studies differ, and continued research will no doubt shed greater light on questions such as these, current research does offer some tentative answers.

First, as Kraus and Davis argue, debates are consistent with democratic theory, which stresses the importance of rational decision making by an informed electorate.[71] Second, as Becker, Pepper, Weiner, and Kim point out, debates provide voters with greater exposure to information about candidates, which "probably resulted in a certain degree of commitment to the election process and to the candidate selected through that process."[72] Third, as Chaffee illustrates, debates apparently have a positive impact on people's confidence in government institutions and play a positive role in political socialization or the recruitment of new members into the body politic.[73]

In sum, it appears as though political debates contribute to voters' satisfaction with the democratic process. Though much has been written about growing voter apathy, growing voter disenchantment with the political process, and growing voter skepticism of politicians, it would appear that this over-all trend of disaffection with the political process is not fostered by debates. Rather, current research suggests that political debates might be a step in the direction of remedying current disaffection.

CONCLUSIONS

In sum, it would appear that political debates have at least seven distinct effects. Typically, they attract large audiences. Second, they seem to reinforce many of the preexisting attitudes and beliefs of audience members. Third, they seem to shift a limited number of voters. Though the number of voters whose opinions are shifted by the debates is limited, it should be kept in mind that, as discussed earlier in this chapter, debates are much more likely to be held in close elections, where the shift of a limited number of voters might well prove crucial to the outcome. Fourth, debates help to set the political agenda. Fifth, debates contribute to the education of audience members. Voters who watch the debates apparently are more knowledgeable as a consequence of their watching. This educational benefit of debates must be tempered somewhat by the recognition that current debate formats often preclude the viewers really learning about the issues that most concern them. Sixth, debates seem to affect the images of candidates. The image of the lesser-known participant is normally affected more by a political debate. Finally, debates seem to contribute to the public's confidence in government institutions and leaders.

This discussion of the effects of political debates also, by implication, suggests one final observation. Since they tend to reinforce existing attitudes and shift only a limited number of votes, debates typically do not provide a "crushing" blow. One candidate is not likely to break the election wide open as a consequence of participation in a debate, but in close elections debating may prove decisive.

NOTES

1. Quoted in *The Lincoln-Douglas Debates,* ed. Robert W. Johannsen (New York: Oxford University Press, 1965), p. 3

2. J. Jeffery Auer, "The Counterfeit Debates," in *The Great Debates: Kennedy vs. Nixon, 1960,* ed. Sidney Kraus (Bloomington: Indiana University Press, 1962), p. 146.

3. Ibid.

4. This term was first used by Auer in his essay, "The Counterfeit Debates," to describe the 1960 debates. It has since been used to describe many political debates, most notably by Lloyd Bitzer and Theodore Rueter in their work *Carter vs. Ford: The Counterfeit Debates of 1976* (Madison: University of Wisconsin Press, 1980).

5. The statements in this paragraph were made by panelists Robert Flemming and Stuart Novins during the opening minutes of the first Kennedy-Nixon debate. See *The Joint Appearances of Senator John F. Kennedy and Vice-President Richard M. Nixon: Presidential Campaign of 1960* (Washington, D.C.: Government Printing Office, 1961), p. 78

6. See Bitzer and Rueter, *Carter vs. Ford,* especially Chapter 3, for an excellent analysis of the adversary nature of the press in the 1976 debates.

7. Formats of the presidential debates are fairly well known. For an examination of the formats used in recent presidential primary debates, see Susan A. Hellwig and Steven L. Phillips, "Form and Substance: A Comparative Analysis of Five Formats Used in the 1980 Presidential Debates," *Speaker and Gavel* 18 (Winter 1981): 67–76. Examinations of debate formats at the nonpresidential level can be found in Jack Kay, "Campaign Debate Formats: The Non-Presidential Level," paper presented at the Speech Communication Association Convention, Anaheim, California November 1981; and Michael Pfau, "Criteria and Format to Optimize Political Debates: An Analysis of South Dakota's 'Election 80' Series," paper presented at the Speech Communication Association Convention, Anaheim, California November 1981. Ironically, Patrick Caddell noted that the 1980 presidential debate format used by Reagan and Carter, which allowed for nine to ten minutes of discussion on a single topic, was "exhaustive." See his "Memo of October 21, 1980," reprinted in Elizabeth Drew, *Portrait of an Election: The 1980 Presidential Campaign* (New York: Simon and Schuster, 1981), p. 426.

8. Auer, "Counterfeit Debates," p. 148.

9. Perhaps the debate with the most significance for the subsequent development of political debating was the one held between the Tennessee gubernatorial candidates in 1886. For an explanation of the subsequent impact of this debate, see Herbert A. Terry and Sidney Kraus, "Legal and Political Aspects: Was Section 315 Circumvented?," in *The Great Debates: Carter vs.*

Ford, 1976, ed. Sidney Kraus (Bloomington: Indiana University Press, 1979), pp. 44–45.

10. When debates were held, they were frequently the centerpieces of the campaigns. For an especially informative example of this, see Cal M. Logue, "Gubernatorial Campaign in Georgia in 1880," *Southern Speech Communication Journal* 40 (Fall 1974), 12–32.

11. Samuel L. Becker and Elmer W. Lower, "Broadcasting in Presidential Campaigns," in *The Great Debates: Kennedy vs. Nixon, 1960,* ed. Sidney Kraus (Bloomington: Indiana University Press, 1962). p. 29.

12. Quoted in Sidney Head, *Broadcasting in America* (Boston: Houghton Mifflin, 1976), p. 331.

13. For a full discussion of these changes, see Edward W. Chester, *Radio, Television and American Politics* (New York: Sheed and Ward, 1969), pp. 247–65. Also see Head, *Broadcasting in America,* pp. 330–32.

14. Chester, *Radio, Television and American Politics,* p. 37. Also see Becker and Lower, "Broadcasting in Presidential Campaigns," p. 35.

15. Chester, *Radio, Television and American Politics,* p. 42

16. An excellent description of this debate can be found in Robert F. Ray, "Thomas E. Dewey: The Great Oregon Debate of 1948," in *American Public Address: Studies in Honor of Albert Craig Baird,* ed. Loren Reid (Columbia: University of Missouri Press, 1961), pp. 245–70.

17. Lee M. Mitchell, *With the Nation Watching* (Lexington, Mass.: D. C. Heath, 1979), p. 28.

18. In 1952 neither man felt comfortable with the idea of televised debates. Both candidates were also advised not to debate.

19. Mitchell, *With the Nation Watching,* p. 30.

20. Chester, *Radio, Television and American Politics,* pp. 133–35 provides a brief account of the stimulus that the 1960 presidential debates had on political debating.

21. For a complete and far more thorough account of this change in the equal time provisions, see Terry and Kraus, "Legal and Political Aspects," pp. 41–49.

22. Perry Seekus and Robert Friedenberg, "A Survey of the Public Speaking Practices of the Members of Congress," unpublished Miami University Undergraduate Research Fund Project, 1981, p. 7

23. See the account of the League of Women Voters activities found in the Speech Communication Association, Taskforce on Political Debates, *Newsletter* 1 (April 1980).

24. This section is based primarily on two articles by Robert Friedenberg. Full citations for all quoted material and fuller explanations of all major points can be found in those two articles. See Robert V. Friedenberg, " 'We Are Present Here Today for the Purpose of Having a Joint Discussion':

275

The Conditions Requisite for Political Debates," *Journal of the American Forensic Association* 16 (Summer 1979): 1–9; Robert V. Friedenberg, " 'Selfish Interests,' or the Prerequisites for Political Debate: An Analysis of the 1980 Presidential Debate and Its Implications for Future Campaigns," *Journal of the American Forensic Association* 18 (Fall 1981): 91–98. The authors wish to thank the American Forensic Association for permission to use those articles.

25. The following account of the 1960 debates is based primarily on Theodore White, *The Making of the President 1960* (New York: Pocket Books, 1961); Kenneth P. O'Donnell and David F. Powers, *Johnny, We Hardly Knew Ye* (New York: Pocket Books, 1973); and Friedenberg, "Conditions for Political Debates."

26. The following account of the 1980 debates is based primarily on *Time*, September 15 to November 3, 1980 and *Cincinnati Enquirer*, September 11 to October 27, 1980. Also see Friedenberg, "Prerequisites for Political Debates."

27. Quoted in *Time*, September 22, 1980, p. 9

28. Goodwin F. Berquist and James L. Golden, "Media Rhetoric, Criticism, and the Public Perception of the 1980 Presidential Debates," *Quarterly Journal of Speech* 67 (May 1981): 125–26.

29. Ibid., pp. 127–28.

30. Patrick Caddell, "Memo of October 21, 1980," p. 412

31. Ibid.

32. Berquist and Golden, "Media Rhetoric," p. 135.

33. See for examples Myles Martel, "Debate Preparations in the Reagan Camp: An Insider's View," *Speaker and Gavel* 18 (Winter 1981): 34–46; Martin Schram, *Running for President* (New York: Pocket Books, 1977), pp. 326–31, 348–64, 370–89; Caddell, "Memo of October 21, 1980," pp. 410–39; White, *Making of The President 1960*, 335–55. Robert Friedenberg has also been involved in a wide variety of political debates.

34. By all accounts, Ronald Reagan's preparation for his 1980 debates with John Anderson and Jimmy Carter was the most thorough in this regard. Reagan practiced in a garage converted to resemble the actual television studios used in the debates. His staff went to great lengths to simulate and anticipate his opponents. Eventually David Stockman, a former administrative assistant to John Anderson, played both Anderson and Carter in Reagan's practices.

35. An informative account of this frequently overlooked precursor to the 1960 general election debates can be found in Goodwin F. Berquist, "The Kennedy-Humphrey Debate," *Today's Speech* 7 (September 1960): 2–3.

36. Robert O. Weiss, "The Presidential Debates in Their Political Context: The Issue-Image Interface in the 1980 Campaign," *Speaker and Gavel* 18 (Winter 1981): 22–27.

37. Ibid., p. 22

38. This threefold analysis of image strategies is based on Dan Nimmo's discussion of the image techniques that can be used by a political figure. The terminology and definitions are Nimmo's. See Dan Nimmo, *Popular Images of Politics* (Englewood Cliffs, N.J.: Prentice-Hall, 1974), pp. 100–2.

39. Quoted passages from the Reagan-Carter debate cited in this and the following paragraphs are from the NBC-verified transcript record of the debate found in Richard Harwood, ed. *The Pursuit of the Presidency 1980* (New York: Berkley Books, 1980), pp. 359–400.

40. Ibid., pp. 398–99.

41. Frederick T. Steeper, "Public Response to Gerald Ford's Statements on Eastern Europe in the Second Debate," in *The Presidential Debates: Media, Electoral, and Policy Perspectives,* eds. George F. Bishop, Robert G. Meadow, and Marilyn Jackson-Beeck (New York: Praeger, 1978), p. 101.

42. Ibid. Also see Roger Desmond and Thomas Donohue, "The Role of the 1976 Televised Presidential Debates in the Political Socialization of Adolescents," *Communication Quarterly* 29 (Fall 1981): 306–8; and George A. Barnett, "A Multidimensional Analysis of the 1976 Presidential Campaign," *Communication Quarterly* 29 (Summer 1981): 156–65.

43. Cited in Harry P. Kerr, "The Great Debates in a New Perspective," *Today's Speech* 9 (November 1961): 11.

44. Susan A. Hellweg and Steven L. Phillips, "A Verbal and Visual Analysis of the 1980 Houston Republican Presidential Primary Debate," *Southern Speech Communication Journal* 47 (Fall 1981): 24.

45. John P. Robinson, "The Polls," in *The Great Debates: Carter vs. Ford, 1976,* ed. Sidney Kraus (Bloomington: Indiana University Press, 1979), pp. 262–63.

46. *TV Guide,* November 8, 1980, p. A1.

47. *Newsweek,* October 17, 1960, p. 27

48. David O. Sears and Steven H. Chaffee, "Uses and Effects of the 1976 Debates: An Overview of Empirical Studies," in *The Great Debates: Carter vs. Ford, 1976,* ed. Sidney Kraus (Bloomington: Indiana University Press, 1979), p. 255.

49. For a study of the 1980 debates that clearly supports these implications, see David Leuthold and David Valentine, "How Reagan Won the Cleveland Debate: Audience Predispositions and Presidential Debate Winners," *Speaker and Gavel* 18 (Winter 1981): 60–66, esp. pp. 65–66.

50. Elmo Roper, "Polling Post-Mortem," *Saturday Review,* November, 1960, pp. 10–13.

51. Elihu Katz and Jacob Feldman, "The Debates in Light of Research: A Survey of Surveys," in *The Great Debates: Kennedy vs. Nixon, 1960,* ed. Sidney Kraus (Bloomington: Indiana University Press, 1962), p. 211

52. Jack M. McLeod et al., "Reactions of Young and Older Voters: Ex-

POLITICAL CAMPAIGN COMMUNICATION

panding the Context of Effects," in *The Great Debates: Carter vs. Ford, 1976,* ed. Sidney Kraus (Bloomington: Indiana University Press, 1979), pp. 365–66.

53. Paul R. Hagner and Leroy N. Rieselbach, "The Impact of the 1976 Presidential Debates: Conversion or Reinforcement?," in *The Presidential Debates: Media, Electoral, and Policy Perspectives,* eds. George F. Bishop, Robert G. Meadow, and Marilyn Jackson-Beeck (New York: Praeger, 1978), p. 178.

54. Leuthold and Valentine, "How Reagan Won," p. 62.

55. Maxwell McCombs, "Agenda Setting Research: A Bibliographic Essay," *Political Communication Review* 1 (Summer 1976): 3.

56. Linda L. Swanson and David L. Swanson, "The Agenda Setting Function of the First Ford-Carter Debate," *Communication Monographs* 45 (November 1978): 347–53.

57. Ibid., p. 353.

58. Ibid.

59. Lee B. Becker et al., "Debates' Effects on Voter Understanding of Candidates and Issues," in *The Presidential Debates: Media, Electoral, and Policy Perspectives,* eds. George F. Bishop, Robert G. Meadow, and Marilyn Jackson-Beeck (New York: Praeger, 1978), pp. 137–38.

60. Steven H. Chaffee, "Presidential Debates—Are They Helpful to Voters?," *Communication Monographs* 45 (November 1978): 336.

61. Ibid.

62. Pfau, "Criteria and Format," pp. 5–6.

63. Soma Golden, "Inside the Debate," *New York Times,* September 24, 1980, p. A30.

64. For an examination of the differing agenda of voters, reporters, and candidates, see Marilyn Jackson-Beeck and Robert Meadow, "The Triple Agenda of Presidential Debates," *Public Opinion Quarterly* 42 (Summer 1979): 173–80.

65. Pfau, "Criteria and Format," p. 6

66. Diana B. Prentice, Janet K. Larson, and Matthew J. Sobnosky, "The Carter-Reagan Debate: A Comparison of Clash in the Dual Format," paper presented at the Speech Communication Association National Convention, Anaheim, California November 1981, pp. 10–11.

67. Hagner and Rieselbach, "Impact of 1976 Presidential Debates," p. 172.

68. Sears and Chaffee, "Uses and Effects of 1976 Debates," pp. 246–47.

69. Ibid.

70. See, for example, Jack Germond and Jules Witcover, *Blue Smoke and Mirrors: How Reagan Won and Why Carter Lost the Election of 1980* (New York: Viking Press, 1981), p. 281–84; and Drew, *Portrait of an Election,* pp. 325–26.

71. Sidney Kraus and Dennis Davis, "Political Debates," in *Handbook of Political Communication,* eds. Dan Nimmo and Keith Sanders (Beverly Hills: Sage, 1981), pp. 273–98.

72. Samuel L. Becker et al., "Information Flow and the Shaping of Meanings," in *The Great Debates: Carter vs. Ford, 1976,* ed. Sidney Kraus (Bloomington: Indiana University Press, 1979), p. 396.

73. Chaffee, "Presidential Debates," pp. 343–45.

Interpersonal
Communication
in Political
Campaigns

*T*HIS CHAPTER EXAMINES THE PLACE OF INTERPERSONAL COMMUNICATION IN POLITICAL CAMPAIGNS. WE PERCEIVE IN- TERPERSONAL COMMUNICATION TO BE transactional. When people communicate they define them- selves and simultaneously respond to their perceptions of the definitions being offered by others. This transactional per- spective, which we share with most communication scholars, has several implications that have unusual importance for po- litical communication.

First, interpersonal communication is contextual. Part of the context in which any communication takes place is the other person. You behave differently when you are with your children than when you are with your boss. Each participant affects the other. Similarly, candidates behave differently when they visit with a small group of bowlers in neighborhood bowling alleys than when they visit with a few large financial contributors in someone's home. The physical setting of the two transactions, the differences in background music and noise, the differences in clothing worn by the bowlers and the

281

contributors, the differences in the language used by the two groups, and countless other stimuli help define the bowlers and the contributors to the candidate. Simultaneously, the presence of the candidate in the bowling alley or at a contributor's home, the clothing and language of the candidate, and countless other stimuli that the candidate emits enable the bowlers and the contributors to define the candidate. As each party to the transaction shapes and refines definitions of the other, their own behavior will be affected, thus continually changing the communication context.

Second, this perspective suggests that each party to the transaction is simultaneously both a sender and a receiver of verbal and nonverbal messages. When you meet the candidate at a neighborhood coffee and criticize a local bond issue that the candidate supports, you are simultaneously watching facial expressions, observing the tightening of the candidate's fist, and noting that the candidate's face is becoming flush. As candidates emit these communicative stimuli, they are defining themselves to you. You better sense the candidate's support for this bond issue and the irritation your criticism provokes, even though the candidate may have said nothing.

Clearly, as you observe candidates listening to your criticism, they appear affected by your statements. Similarly, as you see the candidate's face flush and fist tighten, you begin to temper your criticism. You gradually lower your voice and use more moderate language. You have been affected by this communication transaction, and so has the candidate. This is the third major implication that the transactional perspective has for political communication; each participant affects and is affected by the other.

As we discuss interpersonal communication in political campaigns, we will frequently note the importance of our transactional perspective. However, before beginning the discussion, we want to note two other characteristics of the interpersonal communication to be studied in this chapter. They deliberately narrow the expanse of interpersonal communication, limiting it to interpersonal communication utilized in political campaigns. First, one party to the interpersonal transactions discussed in this chapter is either a candidate or the surrogate/advocate of a candidate. The surrogate/advocate may be a formal representative of the candidate, such as a member of the campaign staff, or an informal representative, such as a voter who is not in any way affiliated with the candidate but nevertheless discusses the candidate. The final characteristic of the interpersonal transactions examined is that the overt, normally verbal, messages either directly or indirectly involve a campaign for public office.

In this chapter, we will discuss three crucial areas of interpersonal communication in political campaigns: interpersonal communication between the candidate and voters, interpersonal communication between the candidate and potential financial contributors, and interpersonal communication between voters.[1]

INTERPERSONAL COMMUNICATION BETWEEN CANDIDATES AND VOTERS

As indicated in Chapter 5, no resource is more vital to the campaign than the candidate's time. This is a finite resource. Once the time is lost, it cannot be replaced. Consequently, if candidates are spending time meeting individuals or small groups of individuals, they must be sure that there is an unusually high chance that these meetings will be productive. For candidates to spend three hours with two, four, or ten people and come away with nothing is a loss that cannot be recovered. More money cannot buy lost time, nor can more volunteers produce it. Hence, decisions on where the candidates should spend time and with whom they should meet are critical.

The use of the candidate's time is especially critical in local campaigns. Over 500,000 public offices in the United States, from president to the infamous dog catcher are filled by election.[2] Lynda Lee Kaid points out that the tendency of researchers to study highly visible national and statewide campaigns has caused us often to neglect what is the most effective channel of political persuasion in vast numbers of races—the interpersonal communication of the candidate.[3] As Kaid notes, the channels of communication available to candidates in thousands of campaigns below the national and statewide levels are often severely limited.

In many campaigns, the geographic makeup of the district precludes the effective use of mass media such as radio and television. For example, the eighth congressional district of Ohio, located between Cincinnati and Dayton, includes about 60,000 residents of suburban Cincinnati. It also includes Hamilton (a town of 80,000), Middletown (a town of 50,000), all of Preble County (a prosperous agricultural county with no town over 7,000) and parts of Darke, Green, and Montgomery counties, including portions of suburban Dayton. To use television effectively in this district, the candidate would have to purchase time on both Dayton and Cincinnati stations. Yet the approximately 70 percent of the district receiving Cincinnati television constitutes less than 20 percent of the Cincinnati media market. The remaining 30 percent of this district, within the Dayton media market, constitutes less than 10 percent of the Dayton media market. To cover this district adequately with television, candidates would have to pay for an audience approximately 10 times larger than the one they want.

Moreover, within this single congressional district, there are at least 500 other elected public officials; county commissioners in Butler, Preble, Darke, Green, and Montgomery counties, county prosecutors, treasurers, sheriffs, and the like in each county, city council members, mayors, and a variety of other officials in at least 15 communities. The point should be abundantly clear. Geographic and financial considerations make television, radio, and other mass media impractical for hundreds of races in this area alone and for hundreds of thousands of races nationally. Additionally, messages on behalf of most local candidates, delivered through the mass media, are liable to be ignored or ineffective when those media are saturated with information concerning the major contests for president, governor, or senator. As Kaid concludes, "the interplay of some or all of these limitations may create an environment in which interpersonal communication, particularly communication between the candidate and the voters, may be a crucial factor in the outcome of an election."[4]

Given the importance of the candidate's time and given that in many races its waste cannot be offset by purchasing media time, it is essential that the candidate's interpersonal communication be utilized effectively.[5] This means that candidates must know where to campaign. Consequently, in local races especially, the most valuable materials that a campaign can have are often the precinct analysis of recent voter statistics, such as those illustrated in Chapter 5. The thoroughness of such analysis is a direct function of the amounts of money spent on obtaining them. In most states, local party organizations will prepare voter statistics for candidates. Hence, even in areas where the local organization is weak, candidates should not have trouble obtaining a complete analysis of prior voting statistics for their district. Moreover, if the various party organizations do not provide adequate statistics, candidates can obtain them themselves, since all vote totals are a matter of public record and kept on file by the appropriate election boards.

Once they have access to prior election results, particularly a precinct-by-precinct analysis, candidates can determine which precincts are essentially Republican, Democratic, or marked by a high incidence of ticket-splitting. As we observed in Chapter 5, the candidate should direct the campaign primarily at those precincts where the party traditionally runs well and those precincts where ticket-splitting commonly takes place. It is in these precincts that most of the candidate's interpersonal communication should take place.

Far more than national figures, local candidates must know precisely where to spend their time. Because their constituencies are smaller, in many instances local candidates can knock on every door in their district or at least on every door in those precincts that are deemed most important. The door-to-door campaigning of candidates for major offices is most often done for media coverage, rather than for any direct impact. It allows the major candidate to appear in the media while walking through a ghetto, or a cornfield, presumably illustrating concern for blacks or farmers. Vice President Agnew's widely repeated 1968 remark, "when you've seen one ghetto you've seen them all," while callous and insensitive, is nevertheless not far from the truth in describing the function that door-to-door campaigning serves for major figures. Perhaps Agnew might have said, "when you've been seen in one ghetto, it serves as though you've been seen in them all."

Local candidates will not receive media exposure of their door-to-door campaigning. Rather, their efforts will put them face-to-face with a large percentage of their constituency. Interpersonal campaigning is not symbolic for the local candidate, as it is for the major candidate. Rather, it is often the major thrust of the campaign, an essential means of compensating for the lack of media exposure.

Though major candidates do not rely as extensively on interpersonal campaigning as do local candidates, it does often serve an important place in their campaigns. Clearly, because of the size of the constituency, the major candidate, as well as many local candidates, will utilize surrogate advocates to represent him in door-to-door canvasses of a community. The door-to-door canvass is often especially effective in the primary campaigns of major candidates. Such races typically involve substantially fewer voters than the general election. Candidates and their representatives can often reach a high percentage of those voters who are eligible to vote in the primary. George McGovern's effective use of the principles of interpersonal communication in door-to-door canvassing in small states such as New Hampshire, Massachusetts, and Rhode Island, whose primaries occurred early in 1972, played a substantial role in his success that year.[6]

The most typical methods of interpersonal campaigning by candidates or their representatives are coffees and door-to-door canvasses. Each method allows the candidates or their representatives to interact for brief periods of time with a small number of voters. Done repeatedly, they may serve as an effective means of supplementing media campaigning or, as in the case of many local candidates, almost entirely replace it.

The Coffee

Keeping in mind the precinct analysis of voters, the campaign organization will arrange a schedule of coffees (in some areas, tea or beer might be the preferred beverage) for the candidate. The organization should arrange the coffees so that the candidate is able to meet with two groups. First, "those people residing in areas which generally are independent. . . . Second, coffees should be scheduled in areas where the candidate and his party can be expected to run well."[7] In these areas, coffees give "the candidate an opportunity to pay personal attention to those who are working for him. It gives the campaign organization an opportunity to recruit new workers."

Keeping in mind our transactional viewpoint of interpersonal communication, we can readily see why campaigners seek to hold coffees and similar events that promote interpersonal transactions with neutral and friendly voters. Such events provide the candidate with much more than the opportunity simply to meet voters. They provide the candidate with the opportunity to establish a relationship, to affect the other parties in the transaction.

During the surfacing stage of his 1976 campaign, Jimmy Carter met with groups of voters in countless small social gatherings, especially in the early primary states. He followed up on the relationships initiated at these meetings by remaining in contact with short notes, letters, and calls. He affected these people, and they subsequently helped him.

Conversely, candidates are also affected by interpersonal transactions such as coffees. As we have seen in Chapter 2, promises made during the surfacing and primary stages of a campaign tend to be kept more than those made later. Part of the reason for this seems to be that promises made early in the campaign are frequently made in small interpersonal contexts, where the candidate is more prone to be affected by voters. Later in the campaign, crowded candidate schedules often prohibit the types of interpersonal transactions that frequently take place early in the campaign.

The candidate "should never attend the coffee by himself. He should always have with him another man (or woman if the candidate is a woman)." The function of this other individual is to get the candidate away from the coffee gracefully if the hostess fails to do so. The candidate's associate, not the candidate or the hostess, can take the blame for rushing the candidate away if that becomes necessary. The candidate should avoid making speeches at coffees. "He need give only brief informal remarks." After the candidate's brief remarks, a short question-and-answer period is appropriate.

Four rules should govern every coffee. First, "optimum size of the gathering is twenty to thirty people." This includes the hostess, candidate, and those traveling with the candidate. Second, name tags should be provided for each guest. The affair is essentially social, and the candidate wants to establish a first name relationship with the guests, if possible. Third, the host or hostess should "never permit a guest to buttonhole the candidate or enter into arguments." Finally, it should always be remembered that the coffee "is an excuse for getting together, and the stress should be on easy informality and comfort."

This description of an ideal coffee clearly indicates that the simple act of being present and interacting with a number of voters is as important, if not more so, than what the candidate actually says. A well-run coffee maximizes the opportunities for fruitful interpersonal transactions. Time is devoted to establishing personal friendships. The group is small enough for the candidate to interact with everyone, and the candidate's aide as well as the host or hostess of the coffee facilitate the candidate's interaction with everyone.

Local candidates often run for administrative positions that do not involve issues of policy. The county recorder, engineer, or sheriff, for example, provide administrative services, but they do not set policy. Hence, interpersonal communication opportunities, where candidates can establish relationships illustrating their concern, personality, and character, are vital. Given that many local races lack real issues between the candidates and that the candidates are relatively unknown, often the candidates who have met the most people, who are best known in the district, who have visited the neighborhood, who seem to make themselves available and accessible, and who have worked at establishing relationships are the candidates who most appeal to the voter.

Good campaigns can effectively arrange three coffees an evening for their candidates, several evenings a week, through the last months of the campaign. Such programs, particularly in local races, enable candidates to interact with a significant percentage of their constituency. Moreover, the candidate's presence in the neighborhood will be rapidly reported the next day over backyard fences, in beauty and barber shops, gas stations, and stores, as those invited to the coffee discuss their experience.

The Door-to-Door Canvass

The use of small social gatherings such as coffees serves primarily to foster interaction between the candidate and voters. A second major form of interpersonal communication between the candidate and voters, the door-to-door canvass, typically serves several additional purposes. Like the coffees, it should provide candidates and their representatives with an opportunity to deal personally with a large number of voters. Hopefully, as with the coffees, candidates will be perceived as accessible and concerned, leaving a positive image with the voters they meet. Presumably, the same impressions should be left with voters who meet the candidates' representatives.

The canvass can serve additional functions and is often utilized in major races, where coffees play a lesser role. When utilized in major races, most of the canvassing is done by representatives of the candidate. Regardless of who is canvassing, the canvass can identify voters who are favorable, neutral, or hostile to the candidate. Depending on their attitudes, these voters can subsequently be contacted. The canvass also is an excellent means of distributing information about the candidate. A conversation between the canvasser and the voter can provide information about the candidate. Additionally, the canvasser can leave materials and if the voter has a specific concern, the canvasser can arrange to have additional information sent later.[8]

Important principles of interpersonal communication should be implemented by canvassers if they are doing their jobs well. Representatives of George McGovern, canvassing during the 1972 presidential primaries, were given instructions that, as Patrick Devlin illustrates, "exhibited a sensitivity to psychological principles so important to effective interpersonal communication."[9] Instructions such as those issued by the McGovern staff are now commonplace in door-to-door canvassing. They include:

1) Speak enthusiastically and sincerely about the candidate.
2) Be a good listener. Let the voters speak; do not interrupt them.
3) Be open-minded. Whenever possible, express your agreement with the voter.

Canvassers who follow instructions such as these can accomplish much. They can leave literature, determine voting intentions, or question for other information that the campaign desires.[10] Additionally, when done by well-prepared canvassers, the door-to-door canvass leaves voters with a positive feeling about the candidate that will not be readily forgotten. Devlin describes the effect of the McGovern canvasses by noting:

> The canvass left voters with the impression that McGovern was a candidate someone else felt so strongly about that he or she would take the time to speak with them about him. That impression was important. Respondents might not be able to remember all the specifics of the conversation and the follow-up letters or calls. But they were able to remember that the McGovern campaign had made the effort and many voters voted for McGovern because of this effective effort at interpersonal communication.[11]

In sum, interpersonal communication between the candidate and the voter is, for most people, a unique event. The details of the coffee or the canvass meeting will no doubt fade from an individual's memory. But the fact that the candidate cared enough to come to the neighborhood or send a representative and followed up the initial coffee or canvass will often remain and loom far larger in the voter's mind than the specifics of what may have been said.

INTERPERSONAL COMMUNICATION BETWEEN THE CANDIDATE AND PROSPECTIVE FINANCIAL CONTRIBUTORS

Before examining interpersonal communication designed to solicit campaign contributions, we must first answer two fundamental questions about fundraising. First, who currently contributes to political campaigns? Second, who is likely to contribute in the future?

In recent years, federal laws on campaign contributions have encouraged candidates for federal office to solicit relatively small contributions from large numbers of voters. As mentioned earlier, federal laws today place a $1,000 ceiling on the amount of money that a single individual can contribute to a candidate, and a $5,000 ceiling on the contributions of political action committees. Twenty-five states have also imposed ceilings on the amounts that can be given to candidates for state and local office.[12] Restrictions on state and local candidates are generally not as tight as those placed on candidates for federal office. Nonetheless, the effect of the campaign spending reforms has been to reduce the number of large contributors and the size of their contributions, while increasing the total number of campaign contributors.

Consequently, the largest single source of political contributions is the individual citizen donor. In recent years, a pattern of campaign giving seems to have emerged. Though this pattern varies for any individual campaign, generally speaking about 30 to 35 percent of the money raised for political campaigns comes from individual citizens contributing $100 or less. This percentage tends to be a little higher for lesser races and a little lower for major races. About 35 to 40 percent of the money raised for political campaigns comes from individual citizens contributing $100 to $1,000. Hence, approximately 65 to 75 percent of all contributed money comes in the form of individual citizen donations in relatively small amounts. The remaining money comes in the form of aid from political and special interest groups as well as loans.[13]

It is likely that the current pattern of campaign contributions will continue in the future. Surveys taken repeatedly over the last two decades indicate that in major election years 15 to 20 percent of the population is solicited for a political contribution. Of those solicited, slightly more than 40 percent make some type of contribution.[14] Currently, it is estimated that over 12 million U.S. citizens contribute to political campaigns.[15] Moreover, Gallup Poll figures suggest that about 40 percent of those not solicited for a political contribution would have made at least a $5 contribution to a political candidate if they had been asked.[16] The widespread success of direct mail, since 1972 when computer technology was brought to direct mail political solicitations, further suggests that in the future most money raised for political purposes will be raised through the relatively modest contributions of large numbers of individual citizens. Robert Agranoff summarizes the situation facing most political candidates when he concludes:

> The campaigner is faced with having to raise most funds from individual contributions within a relatively narrow base of contributors that include family, friends, and associates of the candidate, plus other committed supporters, particularly partisans. On the other hand, there is a hint that the potential exists to broaden the financial base. The evidence also suggests that campaigners should not be deluded into expecting generous party and group financial support.[17]

People do not contribute to a political campaign unless they are attracted to the candidate. Political fund raising is largely interpersonal in nature. Typically, the candidate, finance director, and members of the finance committee seek contributions from individuals they believe would be receptive to such an appeal. Similar in conception, though obviously less personal in execution, is direct mail fund raising. Here again, the campaign seeks contributions from individuals believed to be receptive to the candidate. Invariably, the key is to determine who would be attracted to the candidate and thus receptive to financial appeals.

Students of interpersonal communication identify at least five principles of human attraction.[18] First, we are attracted to people who are in close physical proximity to us. Second, we are attracted to people who are similar to us. Third, we are attracted to people who provide us with positive feedback. Additionally, at least two situational factors tend to heighten the likelihood of our being attracted to other people. Fourth, if we find ouselves in an anxiety-producing situation, we tend to have a greater need for human interaction and hence are more prone to be attracted to other people. Fifth, if we have already extended some type of supportive behavior to an individual, we are more likely to be attracted to that individual than if we had never provided such behavior. Each of these five principles of human attraction has major implications for conducting political fund raising.

The first determinant of attraction is proximity. That is, all things being equal, the more closely two people are located the more likely they are to be attracted to one another. Far too often, campaigns tend to neglect this simple fact. Rather than seek fiscal support from the most likely sources, people within the district, they seek financial support out of the district. Doing so creates two potential problems. First, and most serious, it rarely works. Just as charity begins at home, just as most of us contribute to our own United Way, our own church, our own civic groups, few of us will contribute to political campaigns outside our own districts.

In 1978 a congressional candidate who was a Christian Scientist and a graduate of Principia College, the only Christian Science institution of higher education in the country, made an extensive fund-raising effort among Principia alumni. But he was running in Missouri and Principia is in Iowa. Additionally, as the only Christian Science school in the nation, it has a national flavor, attracting students from throughout the country, and its alumni have settled throughout the country. However, his effort failed to produce any significant results because so few of those he contacted were located in close proximity to him and his district. Indeed, he received a number of responses indicating that some people were annoyed by his soliciting them, since they did not live in his district.

Similarly, it is revealing to note that both the Republican and Democratic national committees have similar guidelines to determine which candidates will receive financial support.

One of those guidelines is that candidates must demonstrate fund-raising ability *within* their district. The assumption is that if they cannot raise money among people in close proximity, they cannot raise money from anyone.[19]

The second determinant of human attraction that is of exceptional importance for political fund raising is similarity. We are attracted to people who are similar to us. Potential donors should always be approached by people who are highly similar to them. A carefully selected and highly motivated fund-raising committee, working through their own social networks or precincts, the people with whom they are most similar, and drawing on the candidate's presence when necessary is perhaps the most effective means of utilizing the concept of similarity. And for that reason, it is the most successful means of raising funds in most campaigns.

The third principle of attraction that has import for political fund raising is that we are attracted to, and respond favorably to, people who like us and validate us with positive feedback. Candidates and their surrogates must keep this fact uppermost in their minds as they seek funds. This does not mean the fund raiser must be overly compliant. If fund raisers feel compelled to do that, then they are not dealing with equals. They should not be attempting to get donations from persons with whom they do not feel similar and equal. Rather, it means that fund raisers must do their research. They should be able, if the situation arises, to make reference to the potential contributors' family by name, to make reference to recent accomplishments of the potential contributors' businesses, etc. In many fund-raising meetings, it is fair to say that topics such as politics, current events, and making a political contribution do not take up more than 3 minutes of a 30-minute conversation. Fund-raising situations are so patently obvious that they do not need any belaboring. Rather, the meetings stress the similarities between the candidates, their supporters, and the prospective contributors, as the candidates or their supporters attempt to provide positive feedback to the prospective contributors. Often this is done by focusing comments on the contributors' role in mutual projects of a nonpolitical nature, such as charitable, social, educational, or civic programs.

A fourth principle of human attraction enters into political fund raising. Research suggests that we experience a heightened need for human attraction during moments of anxiety.[20] This point should be noted by the competent political fund raiser. As events develop, the good fund raiser will keep in mind who might be made anxious by the events. As opponents make statements and develop their campaigns, the good fund raiser will follow them closely, seeking to determine who might be made anxious by the opponents' statements and positions. And as these events take place and receive publicity, the well-run campaign will have the appropriate person seeking funds from the individuals most likely to be made highly anxious by these events, at the very moment that they may be causing anxiety. For example, in a recent St. Louis area congressional race, one candidate announced that he was in favor of a controversial Army Corps of Engineers construction project that involved erecting several dams and flooding thousands of acres of lowland to create a large lake and recreational area to be utilized primarily by St. Louis residents. His opponent opposed this project as an unnecessarily wasteful and extravagant use of federal funds that would prove utterly disruptive to much of the Missouri environment and wildlife. Within three days of the first candidate's announcement, the second candidate or his representatives had contacted over 120 members of the St. Louis chapter of the Sierra Club, as well as similar environmental organizations. Within three days, this effort produced almost $8,000 of unexpected contributions and many new enthusiastic workers for the campaign.

The final basis of human attraction that warrants the attention of the political fund raiser is the concept of supportive behavior. Research suggests that our own behavior greatly influences our perception of other people. If, for example, you perform a favor for another person, you tend to like that person better as a consequence.[21] Hence, good fund raisers, if un-

296

successful in getting what they want, large contributions, should always have backup requests. If the car dealer will not contribute $500, $100, or $25, maybe the dealer will let candidate Smith use that beautiful yellow car in the showroom for three hours during the Labor Day parade. If worse comes to worse, at least the car dealer can look over some of Smith's campaign literature.

The practice of consistently seeking some type of supportive behavior, minimal as it may be, has at least two beneficial effects. First, the tangible benefit requested will be honored. Candidate Smith does ride in the most attractive car in the parade. Second, now that the car dealer has provided some sort of supportive behavior to the candidate, the dealer is more likely to respond favorably to a second fund-raising appeal. Importantly, once people have made an initial contribution to the candidate, they are prone to make a second or third contribution. Effective fund raisers are aware of the positive effect that supportive behavior has on subsequent behavior and consistently strive to obtain some type of supportive behavior from everyone they approach.

These principles of interpersonal communication should guide candidates and fund raisers as they seek contributions. Moreover, they clearly have implications for other forms of fund raising. They can help determine, for example, both the mailing list and the message content of direct mail solicitation on behalf of the candidate. In sum, candidates and fund raisers who are skillful interpersonal communicators, clearly sensitive to and aware of the determinants of human attraction, are far more prone to achieve success than those who ignore these important variables of interpersonal communication.

INTERPERSONAL COMMUNICATION BETWEEN VOTERS

Voters talk among themselves about politics, campaigns, and candidates. Interpersonal communication between voters

297

is an important aspect of virtually every campaign. In this section, we will try to answer three questions about interpersonal communication between voters. First, in what campaigns is it likely to be of unusually high importance? Second, what do voters typically discuss? Third, what is the relationship between interpersonal communication and mass media in political campaigns?

Importance

Interpersonal communication between voters is normally of greatest importance in those campaigns that receive little media attention. When information about the campaign and the candidates is lacking in the media, voters rely more heavily on interpersonal communication. Consequently, several types of campaigns, characteristically lacking in media coverage, often must rely heavily on interpersonal communication. First are campaigns for lesser offices or local offices, discussed earlier in this chapter; second are primary campaigns. Atwood and Sanders have found that communication with other people was the most credible source of information for 32 percent of the voters in a primary election, but that it was the most credible source of information for only 12 percent of the voters in a general election.[22] Often, as when three or more candidates seek a single office in a primary, the media coverage received by any single candidate tends to be more limited than in a general election. Moreover, the media budgets of most primary campaigns are lower than those of general elections. The reduced media coverage of individual candidates and campaigns in some primaries causes voters to rely much more heavily on interpersonal communication in these elections than in general elections.

The third group of campaigns where interpersonal communication between voters seems to play an unusually important role are those campaigns in which the constituency has a relatively high educational level. Research on this point is limited, and much of it has been done primarily on school-age populations. Nevertheless, it does tend to suggest that voters with good educational backgrounds are less affected by the media, more prone to discuss current events, and more prone to be influenced by those discussions.[23]

Discussion Topics

Voters discuss virtually everything that is pertinent to a campaign. However, three subjects tend to dominate their conversations. First, interpersonal communication is often the means by which people initially learn of a newsworthy development in the campaign. In a study of the 1956 presidential campaign, Wayne Danielson found that knowledge of news events was most rapidly spread throughout the population by radio and interpersonal communication. Television and newspapers, according to Danielson, did not transmit knowledge of news events as rapidly.[24] Though Danielson's findings may have since been altered by the widespread growth of television, it nevertheless seems safe to conclude that people do frequently discuss and often first learn of news events through interaction with one another.*

Second, Kimsey and Atwood found that voters tend to "talk most about the things they like least about candidates."[25] Conversations between voters are not subject to libel laws, equal time laws, and the other legal constraints that may effect the various mass media. Media coverage of the negative aspects of a candidate may be tempered by considerations such as these, but interpersonal communication is not.

Additionally, Kimsey and Atwood found that voters tend to use interpersonal communication selectively to reinforce their

---

*Although general acceptance of the social influence model has declined, it remains true that interaction regarding political campaigns takes place. For example, cocktail party talk throughout Ohio during the 1982 primaries often centered around gubernatorial candidate Jerry Springer's advertisements that dealt with his visit to a prostitute.

vote decisions.[26] This finding makes good sense because of our tendency to be attracted and communicate primarily with those who are similar to us. Hence, we are prone to be exposed to messages congruent with our own ideas. Moreover, we do not equally attend to all the messages we receive. We tend to selectively attend to those messages that conform to our existing attitudes and beliefs. Kimsey and Atwood's findings, that we use interpersonal communication selectively to reinforce prior decisions, seems to be very much in accord with our existing knowledge of interpersonal communication.*

In sum, interpersonal communication is used by voters to deal with virtually everything that happens in a campaign. However, in contrast to other forms of campaign communication, it may be especially important as a medium of news transmission, as a medium by which negative information about a candidate is transmitted, and as a medium that serves to reinforce attitudes and beliefs.

Interpersonal Communication Between Voters, Mass Media, and Voting Behavior

As early as 1948, students of mass media realized the relationship and importance of interpersonal communication. Currently, John P. Robinson provides us with a critique of the relationships between voting behavior, mass media, and interpersonal communication.[27] Robinson, like prior researchers, finds that when interpersonal communication is in conflict with media information "interpersonal sources wield greater influence."[28] The explanation for this no doubt rests in large part on the feedback and adaptation that one voter can provide to another as they discuss politics. Mass media messages can-

*The importance of selective exposure in affecting a voter's use of mass media and interpersonal communication seems to differ. See Chapter 4 for a discussion of selective exposure in the mass media literature.

not adapt and react to feedback, as can interpersonal communication. However, Robinson also finds that interpersonal influence attempts are not that pervasive in elections. More people seem to be exposed to media attempts to influence their votes than to interpersonal attempts to influence their votes.[29] Those people who receive media messages attempting to influence their votes, but no interpersonal messages, seem much more receptive to direct influence from the media.[30]

Robinson does find one situation in which the basic two-step flow scenario of a downward communication flow still takes place: when an individual attentive to the media exerts interpersonal influence on persons less attentive to the media. This pattern still seems to be common in nuclear families. Robinson found that husband-wife discussions are different from most other discussions. Husbands and wives seem to have more influence on each other's votes than do other conversational partners. Moreover, Robinson reports that generally the husband is more attentive to politics and plays the influential role in deliberations with his wife.[31]

Though most candidates make special efforts to facilitate interpersonal communication between themselves and voters, and between themselves and financial contributors, few candidates make concrete efforts to facilitate interpersonal communication between voters that might have a favorable impact on their candidacy. However, at least one nationally prominent political consultant has long attempted to stimulate interpersonal communication among voters to benefit his clients. Stephan Shadegg advises candidates to develop "social precincts" as crucial elements of their campaigns.[32] Social precincts, as Shadegg employs them, are simply enthusiastic and knowledgeable supporters of the candidate. They are not members of special organizations or groups, nor are they in any way prominent in their communities. Initially, members of social precincts are recruited from among friends and associates of the candidate, and gradually the number of members is increased. Many of these people may not even know the candidate well.

Members of social precincts are provided "inside" information. As the campaign progresses, they get key press releases a day in advance, and their opinion is solicited before the candidate makes a key speech. They are made to feel that they are insiders whose opinions and advice are valued by the candidate. And indeed, they are just that. By using the mail, the candidate is able to develop a large group of people who look upon the candidate as someone with whom they have a special relationship. Based on extensive experience with social precincts, Shadegg claims that if he can enlist 3 to 5 percent of the constituency in these social precincts, he will win the election. For if 3 to 5 percent of the constituency believe they have a special interest in a candidate, Shadegg feels that in their normal day-to-day social interactions they will prove influential.

Shadegg's approach is one of the few clear attempts to mobilize interpersonal communication among voters on behalf of a candidate. His success with social precincts, as well as research evidence on the relationship between voting behavior, mass communication, and interpersonal communication, speaks to the importance of interpersonal communication between voters.

CONCLUSIONS

In this chapter, we have examined interpersonal communication in political campaigns. We have found that interpersonal communication between the candidate and voters is exceptionally important in local campaigns, in campaigns where the use of media may not be feasible, and in primary campaigns. In such campaigns, the interpersonal communication between the candidate and voters, through programs of informal coffees and canvasses, can be extremely valuable.

Moreover, we have found that political fund raising lends itself to interpersonal communication and that current interpersonal communication research on attraction has major implications for interpersonal fund raising by political candidates and their advocates. Finally, we have examined the often neglected interpersonal communication between voters. We have seen in which campaigns such communication is most important, what voters tend to discuss among themselves, and the relationship between voting behavior, media, and interpersonal communication.

NOTES

1. For a discussion of some of the mechanics involved in implementing the first two of these types of interpersonal communication, see Robert Agranoff, *The Management of Election Campaigns* (Boston: Holbrook Press, 1976), pp. 411–54.

2. Herbert E. Alexander, *Financing Politics: Money, Elections and Political Reform* (Washington, D.C.: Congressional Quarterly Press, 1980), p. 1.

3. Lynda Lee Kaid, "The Neglected Candidate: Interpersonal Communication in Political Campaigns," *Western Journal of Speech Communication* 41 (Fall 1977): 245.

4. Ibid.

5. The following analysis of the importance of interpersonal campaigning in local political campaigns is based heavily on Robert V. Friedenberg, "Interpersonal Communication in Local Political Campaigns," *Ohio Speech Journal* 12 (1974): 19–27.

6. L. Patrick Devlin, "The McGovern Canvass: A Study in Interpersonal Political Campaign Communication," *Central States Speech Journal* 24 (Summer 1973): 83–90.

7. This statement and all quotations in this section are drawn from "Coffee: The Campaign Beverage," a pamphlet issued by the Republican State Central and Executive Committee of Ohio to candidates for state and local offices. No date or place of publication.

8. See Devlin, "McGovern Canvass," for an excellent description of a highly effective canvassing operation that served all of the functions described in these paragraphs.

9. Ibid., p. 84

10. See Agranoff, *Management of Election Campaigns*, pp. 411–54 for a discussion of the many purposes of canvasses as well as illustrations of the materials used in canvasses.

11. Devlin, "McGovern Canvass," p. 89.

12. Alexander, *Financing Politics*, pp. 130–32.

13. These figures are similar to those reported by Agranoff, *Management of Election Campaigns*, pp. 232–34 in his account of 1972 congressional races. See also Alexander, *Financing Politics*, pp. 45–67 for a discussion of individual donors. Candidates for federal offices tend to raise a higher percentage of their funds from special interest groups. Female candidates, regardless of office, have much more difficulty raising money from special interest groups, according to Ruth B. Mandel, *In the Running: The New Woman Candidate* (New Haven: Ticknor and Fields, 1981), pp. 191–94.

14. The best brief examinations of political campaign contributors can be found in Agranoff, *Management of Election Campaigns*, pp. 230–34 and Alexander, *Financing Politics*, pp. 62–64.

15. Alexander, *Financing Politics*, p. 64.

16. Ibid., p. 63.

17. Agranoff, *Management of Election Campaigns*, p. 234.

18. Many researchers have attempted to establish the major determinants of human attraction. Two of the best summaries of current research, upon which this analysis is based, are Stewart L. Tubbs and Sylvia Moss, *Interpersonal Communication* (New York: Random House, 1978), pp. 97–114; and William Wilmot, *Dyadic Communication: A Transactional Perspective* (Reading, Mass.: Addison-Wesley, 1975), pp. 68–74.

19. This guideline is a longstanding one, used by Republican and Democratic national committee field staff, to help determine which of their candidates are the most viable and hence warrant aid from their respective national committees.

20. Tubbs and Moss, *Interpersonal Communication*, p. 112.

21. Wilmot, *Dyadic Communication*, pp. 73–74.

22. L. Erwin Atwood and Keith R. Sanders, "Information Sources and Voting in a Primary and General Election," *Journal of Broadcasting* 20 (Summer 1976): 298.

23. John P. Robinson, "Interpersonal Influence in Election Campaigns: Two-Step Flow Hypotheses," *Public Opinion Quarterly* 40 (Fall 1976): 312; and Marilyn Jackson-Beeck, "Interpersonal and Mass Communication in Children's Political Socialization," *Journalism Quarterly* 56 (Spring 1979): 53.

24. Wayne A. Danielson, "Eisenhower's February Decision: A Study of News Impact," *Journalism Quarterly* 33 (Fall 1956): 437.

25. William D. Kimsey and L. Erwin Atwood, "A Path Model of Political Cognitions and Attitudes, Communication and Voting Behavior in a Congressional Election," *Communication Monographs* 46 (August 1979): 429.

26. Ibid., p. 430.

27. Robinson, "Interpersonal Influence in Election Campaigns," pp. 304–19.

28. Ibid., p. 315.

29. Ibid.

30. Ibid., p. 316.

31. Ibid., p. 318.

32. This discussion of social precincts is based on Stephen C. Shadegg, *The New How to Win an Election* (New York: Tapplinger, 1976), pp. 103–19.

9

Political
Campaign
Communication:
An Epilogue

THE CENTRAL THESIS OF THIS BOOK HAS
BEEN THAT COMMUNICATION IS THE HEART
OF THE MODERN POLITICAL CAMPAIGN. IT
IS, AS WE ARGUED IN CHAPTER I, THE EPIS-
temological base. Without it, there would be no campaign.
With this as our premise, we explored many principles of contemporary political campaigning including the communicative functions, styles, and media channels. We have also
examined a number of the communicative practices in the contemporary campaign including speechmaking, debating, and
interpersonal communication. Moreover, as we analyzed the
technological advancements or changes in the modern campaign, we were talking about techniques of communication.
Media, computers, videodisc systems, push button phones, microelectronic chips, polls and surveys are all communication
techniques. And each has, in relatively few years, not only
changed the nature of the practice but made communication the preeminent factor. While we have not denied the
importance of such variables as political parties, voter demo-
graphics, philosophical questions, or even economic prag-

matics, we have consistently maintained that understanding the principles and practices of campaign communication is the only way to come to grips with the reality of the modern campaign.

We have striven to present a realistic picture of the way in which candidates and their consultants go about their tasks, implementing the techniques of communication. In so doing, we have not attempted to make judgments or cast any aspersions on candidates or their methods. We do not intend to do so now. However, we would be remiss (or at least not very observant) if we failed to acknowledge some of the most important questions or concerns that have been raised regarding the modern campaign.

The first question asked by many students of political communication is simply: Will these trends continue? Will the new techniques of communication continue to play a dominant role in the campaigns of the future? While we do not have the benefit of a political crystal ball, our answer is yes. It seems unlikely that the methods of campaigning will revert to those of an earlier day. People have seldom turned away from technology, and there is no political precedent for doing so. In fact, just the opposite has occurred. As new methods of transportation and communication were developed, they were incorporated into political campaigns, often before they were widely employed in other situations. Thus there seems little prospect that candidates or their staffs will shun current technology or turn their backs on the future. However, the very fact that new tools of communication have changed the nature and methods of campaigning has resulted in more calls to alter campaigns. Every four years political parties, political scientists, candidates, and legislators call for such things as shorter primary seasons, more stringent finance reforms, and requiring public debates between presidential candidates. And while there have already been some alterations in the way campaigns are financed as well as the presidential primary schedule, there may well be additional modifications in the years to come. So in this respect, political campaigns may undergo some changes. But in the largest sense, the trends we have indicated throughout the book, trends that have made communication the preeminent factor, will continue.

A second question that has been raised by many is basic to the thrust of this book. And that is: Does campaigning make a difference? Apparently those who ask the question do so because they see such trends as the steady decline in voter participation and party affiliation and the growth in general citizen apathy and uninterest as clear signs that political campaigns have little or nothing to do with election results. Obviously, we disagree with this point of view. For one thing, as any number of examples illustrate, campaigns have indeed made a difference in winning and losing elections. If we cite only a few contemporary instances, we would have to include the recent campaigns of John Y. Brown of Kentucky, James Rhodes of Ohio, John Warner of Virginia, and Mario Cuomo and Lewis Lehrman of New York in the 1982 primaries. Moreover, without political campaigning in the primary states, such candidates as George McGovern and Jimmy Carter would not have received the nominations of their parties. Indeed, if campaigning makes no difference to election returns, why then are there more and more candidates, even on local and state levels, who spend enormous amounts of time and energy planning and implementing campaigns? Campaigns have become a major industry, and it is difficult to believe this would have happened if the contenders doubted its worth. Finally, and from our point of view, most important, we believe that beyond determining winners and losers, political campaigns serve many useful functions for voters and candidates. While some of these functions are important symbolically, others have instrumental value. Taken together, however, they more than justify the financial, physical, and mental rigor of the contemporary political campaign.

The third question raised by the growing emphasis on political campaigns as communication phenomena is related to the whole area of ethics. This book has touched on several ethical questions that are conspicuous in the new politics including the appropriate use of speechwriters, public opinion polls, media advertising, and computers for fund raising. Throughout the book, we have generally chosen to describe, not evaluate or judge. But anyone interested in political campaign communication cannot fail to be concerned with its ethical dimensions. "Dirty politics" has been around long before the advent of "unfair" or "unethical" television spot advertisements. In fact, it has been a part of political life since the first election campaign. While the Watergate episode of the early 1970s may have elevated smear tactics to dirty tricks, and while campaign principles, practices, and issues may change from election to election, practitioners do not. Office seekers and their advisors are human beings. They remain subject to the foibles and temptations that have always confronted people. We have seen no evidence that contemporary candidates and their advisors are inherently less ethical than those of prior generations. However, the new communication-oriented politics as well as the new trends in investigative reporting have doubtlessly brought questions regarding political ethics into sharper focus.

The fourth question raised by the growing emphasis on communication in political campaigns is that of cost. Many have expressed concern about the high costs of political campaigning. In recent years, the expenses associated with effective campaigning have increased dramatically. As costs escalate, there are those who feel that we have reached, or are fast reaching, the point where access to money will become the chief determinant of a candidate's success.

Similarly, campaigns are becoming more expensive in terms of human resources. Candidates and their associates are spending enormous amounts of time and effort. In recent years, contenders such as Ronald Reagan, George Bush, and Jimmy Carter have made running for president into full-time jobs lasting several years. Candidates such as Senators Howard Baker and Frank Church have found it difficult to campaign while simultaneously employed in responsible positions. Though the demands of presidential campaigning are unusually high, these same demands are often placed on those who seek lesser offices. Members of Congress or members of many of the state legislatures, for example, take extended recesses during the election period. Challengers find it necessary to temporarily abandon their professions, often taking leaves of absence. Because time demands are high, it may make it increasingly difficult for many citizens to seriously consider running for public office.

Moreover, as we have seen, candidates are not the only individuals who face high costs in money and time when they choose to run. Often responsibilities must be borne by their spouses, children, business associates, and close friends. The use of family and friends as surrogates, fund raisers, and in other campaign-related activities, places heavy burdens on all. In sum, the length of current campaigns and the demands they make on the financial and time resources of candidates and associates are costs that have grown so dramatically in recent years that many concerned individuals are calling for reforms.

Many reforms, such as shortening the length of campaigns, mandating television and radio stations to donate time to candidates, and even total government financing of campaigns, have been suggested. Only time will tell whether proposals such as these have merit. But clearly the costs of campaigning have skyrocketed as campaign communication grows in sophistication.

The fifth question raised by the growing emphasis on communication in political campaigns involves the extent to which public expectations are being affected. Many political observers have commented on the growing apathy of voters. Are campaigns fostering an illusion of competency that is at such variance with reality that public disillusionment is an inevitable result? The sophisticated communication principles and practices discussed in this book may be distorting the public's expectations about officeholders. By creating the image of

311

enormously talented heroes, the campaign creates public expectations that officeholders cannot fulfill. When candidates assume office, they prove to be mere mortals. Public disappointment, natural in light of the high expectations set during the campaign, may contribute to apathy.

The final issue raised by the nature of campaigns concerns candidates. The skills of advocacy necessary for election are not necessarily the skills of compromise and deliberation necessary for effective governing. Today, the closest advisors of many elected officials are their pollsters, speechwriters, and other communication specialists, not their issue experts or party liaisons. While this fact clearly evidences the dominance of communication in campaigns, it also gives rise to disturbing questions. Can a nation, or even a county, be adequately governed by officials and advisors whose skills are those necessary for successful political campaigning?

Questioning political campaign principles and practices is not unique to U.S. citizens of our generation. Changes have always and should always prompt debate. We must view current questions about political campaigning in this same manner.

Contemporary political campaigning is by no means perfect. It has never been perfect in the past, and we see no reason to expect perfection in the future. Critics will always question practices, ethics, costs, and effects. And they should. Surely no activity is more central to our way of life than the establishment, maintenance, and transfer of leadership through free elections. Political campaign communication is the apotheosis of the democratic experience. It warrants our constant reexamination and reappraisal. We know of few Americans who would wish it otherwise.

Index

313

and, 96-97; foreign policy and, 102-3; issues and, 95-96; legitimacy and, 87-88; pseudoevents and, 90-91; surrogates and, 99-103; symbolic trappings and, 86-87; task forces and, 92-93; world leaders and, 94-95

Institute for Social Research (University of Michigan), 7

International Harvester Good Government Committee, 12

interpersonal communication: between candidates and voters, 283-91; between the candidate and prospective financial contributors,291-97; between voters,297-300; between voters, mass media, and voting behavior, 300-2; door-to-door-canvass and, 289-91; coffees and, 287-89

Jackson, Andrew, 77, 177
Jackson, Henry (Scoop), 47, 188
Javits, Jacob, 162
Jaworski, Leon, 192
Jefferson, Thomas, 77
Johnson, Andrew, 177
Johnson, Lyndon, 89, 102, 220, 252

Kaid, Lynda Lee, 284
Katz, Elihu, 132, 144, 266
Kefauver, Estes, 53, 241
Kendell, Amos, 177
Kennedy, Edward, 31, 33, 42, 47, 59, 93, 103, 110, 113, 204, 212, 225, 226, 252

Kennedy, John, 13, 14, 60, 77, 97, 109-10, 141, 179, 203-4, 235-38, 241, 243, 247, 247-48, 252-53, 258, 264-67, 268-69
Kennedy, Robert, 247
Kessler, Frank, 95
Kessler, Martha Stout, 192
Khrushchev, Nikita, 241
Kim, Jin Keon, 271
Kimsey, William D., 271-72
King, Coretta, 192
King, Martin Luther, Jr., 59
King, Martin Luther, Sr., 58-59
"king-makers", 6, 7
Kissinger, Henry, 220
Klapper, Joseph, 130
Kraus, Sidney, 142, 271

Landon, Alfred, 239
Larson, Janet K., 269
Lazarsfeld, Paul, 129-35, 149
Lehrman, Lewis, 309
Leuthold, David, 266-67
Lincoln, Abraham, 48, 177, 233-38, 244
Linkugel, Wil, 226-27
Lodge, Henry Cabot, 240-41

Maddox, Lester, 249
mass media: candidate relationships with, 34-35; contemporary studies of, 137-39; diffusion of information and, 139-42, 146, 148; early studies of, 126-37; gatekeeping and, 135-36; hypodermic effect and, 127-29, 143, 147;

influence of, 32-33, 123-55; "limited effects" or social influence model and, 129-36, 138-39, 143; "multistep flow" and, 134; reconceptualization of the classics and, 148-51; role in 1976 Presidential campaign, 43; selective exposure and, 132; "two-step flow of communication" and, 133-34, 139; uses and gratifications and, 142-45, 148

McAdoo, William, 79

McCarthy, Eugene, 33, 44, 249

McCombs, Maxwell, 146

McGovern, George 12, 14, 33, 51, 58, 100, 109, 111-12, 174, 184, 286, 290-91, 309

McGovern-Fraser Commission, 53

McKinley,William,101

McLeod, Jack, 146, 266

McPhee, William, 132

McQuail, Dennis, 139, 144

Metzenbaum, Howard, 33

Michel, Robert, 12

Mondale, Walter, 25, 33, 270

Moody, Blair, 240

"mosaic model of communication", 42

Moynihan, Patrick, 52

Mussolini, Roberto, 128

national action committee, 25

National Confectioners Association, 12

National Congressional Club, 11

National Conservative Political Action Committee ("Nick-Pack"), 11

national nominating conventions, 36, 48-60

National Research Council, 62

National Rifle Association Political Victory Fund, 12

new right groups, 11-12

news conferences, 213-23; events leading to, 213-15; purposes of, 215-18; strategies of, 218-23

Nimmo, Dan, 259

Nixon, Richard, 56, 60, 77, 80-81, 95-97, 100, 108, 111, 146, 177, 184, 225, 234, 241, 243, 244, 247-48, 253, 258, 264-66, 268

Nunn, Sam, 182

O'Donnell, Kenneth, 247-48

Orr, C. Jack, 218

overt political action, 42-43

parasocial interaction, 43

party unity, 58-59

Patterson, Thomas, 42, 43, 46, 148-51

Pepper, Robert, 271

Pfau, Michael, 268

Pierce, Franklin, 49

Plumb, J. H., 4

political action committees (PAC's), 9-12

political campaign communication: debates in, 233-73; in the future, 308-9; interpersonal communication and, 281-303; public speaking in, 161-93; mass channels of, 123-55; recurring forms of, 197-228

political campaigns: changes in, 5-15, 307-12; communicative functions of, 23-65; communicative styles and strategies of, 69-118; consummatory functions of, 29; importance of, 3-5; "instrumental" functions of, 29-35; ritualistic activities of, 27-28, 57

political parties: decline in influence of, 6-7, 9, 14-5

Populists, 53

Prentice, Diana B., 269

presidential primary: history of, 52-54

pressure groups (*see* political action committees)

primaries, 35-47, 52-54; determination of "front-runner" in, 46-47; development of public images in,41-42 direct feedback in, 39-41; involvement in political process and, 42-46; promises made in, 46

Progressives, 53

public opinion polls, 61-63, 168-70

public speaking: audiences and, 162-68; competency and format in, 170; decision to speak and, 162-70; need and

justification of "stock speeches" and, 171-72; political speechwriting and, 177-88; speech modules and, 172-76; surrogate speakers and, 188-92; use of polls and, 168-70; use of stock speeches and, 171-77

Reagan, Ronald, 8, 11, 28, 32, 33, 38-41, 54, 59, 96, 109, 124, 173-76, 184, 208, 210, 211, 225, 227, 244, 248-56, 258-61, 262, 265, 269-70

Record, Jeffrey, 182

Reston, James, 136

"rhetoric of despair", 110

"rhetoric of optimism", 110

Rhodes, James, 33, 309

Rieselbach, Leroy N., 266, 270

Ritter, Kurt, 210-11

Robbin, Jonathan, 13

Robinson, John P., 300

Rockefeller, Nelson, 58, 179, 184, 188

Rogers, Everett, 140-41

Roosevelt, Franklin Delano, 60, 77, 79, 93, 102, 108, 110, 131, 178, 184, 188, 206, 224, 239-40, 252

Roper, Elmo, 123-24, 266

"Rose Garden Strategy", 84, 100

Sanders, Keith R., 298

Savage, Robert L., 141

Scott, Winfield, 99

Sears, David O., 265-66, 270

Sears, John, 40-41

Seward, William, 177

About the Authors

JUDITH S. TRENT is professor of communication arts and faculty coordinator for sponsored research in the humanities and social sciences at the University of Dayton. She has written and spoken widely on the subject of political campaign communication.

ROBERT V. FRIEDENBERG is professor of communication and theatre at Miami (Ohio) University. He has published widely in speech communication journals and served as a campaign communications specialist for the Republican National Committee and as a manager, speechwriter, and media consultant in over 70 political campaigns.